CONSTITUTIONAL INTERPRETATION

THE BASIC QUESTIONS

CONSTITUTIONAL INTERPRETATION

THE BASIC QUESTIONS

SOTIRIOS A. BARBER

AND

JAMES E. FLEMING

OXFORD
UNIVERSITY PRESS

OXFORD
UNIVERSITY PRESS

Oxford University Press, Inc., publishes works that further Oxford University's objective of excellence in research, scholarship, and education.

Copyright © 2007 by Oxford University Press, Inc.
Published by Oxford University Press, Inc.
198 Madison Avenue, New York, New York 10016

Oxford is a registered trademark of Oxford University Press
Oxford University Press is a registered trademark of
Oxford University Press, Inc.

Library of Congress Control Number: 2006938845

ISBN: 978-0-19-532857-8 (Cloth) 978-0-19-532858-5 (Pbk.)

Printed in the United States of America on acid-free paper.

Note to Readers:

This publication is designed to provide accurate and authoritative information in regard to
the subject matter covered. It is based upon sources believed to be accurate and reliable and is
intended to be current as of the time it was written. It is sold with the understanding that the
publisher is not engaged in rendering legal, accounting, or other professional services. If legal
advice or other expert assistance is required, the services of a competent professional person
should be sought. Also, to confirm that the information has not been affected or changed by
recent developments, traditional legal research techniques should be used, including checking
primary sources where appropriate.

*(Based on the Declaration of Principles jointly adopted by a Committee of the
American Bar Association and a Committee of Publishers and Associations.)*

You may order this or any other Oxford University Press publication
by visiting the Oxford University Press website at www.oup.com

Sotirios A. Barber is Professor of Political Science at the University of Notre Dame. He is the author of *On What the Constitution Means* (1984), *The Constitution of Judicial Power* (1993), and *Welfare and the Constitution* (2003), and coauthor of *American Constitutional Interpretation*, 3d ed. (2003, with Walter F. Murphy, James E. Fleming, and Stephen Macedo).

James E. Fleming is the Leonard F. Manning Distinguished Professor of Law at Fordham University School of Law. He is the author of *Securing Constitutional Democracy: The Case of Autonomy* (2006) and coauthor of *American Constitutional Interpretation*, 3d ed. (2003, with Walter F. Murphy, Sotirios A. Barber, and Stephen Macedo).

FOR OUR FAMILIES

"Just what our forefathers did envision, or would have envisioned had they foreseen modern conditions, must be divined from materials almost as enigmatic as the dreams Joseph was called upon to interpret for Pharaoh."

—Justice Robert H. Jackson,
Youngstown Sheet & Tube Co. v. Sawyer
(1952) (concurring opinion)

"Constitutional law can make no genuine advance [without] a fusion of constitutional law and moral theory."

—Ronald Dworkin, *Taking Rights Seriously* (1977)

CONTENTS

PREFACE

Constitutional debate in the United States over more than two centuries has concerned several broad and connected questions: how and for what ends to arrange governmental institutions and powers; what the Constitution means in general and for concrete controversies; how to decide what it means; and who decides what it means. This book is concerned chiefly with the penultimate question: how to decide constitutional meaning, or which approach to the meaning of the Constitution is best. We canvass a number of answers to this question and conclude that the "philosophic approach" is the best or most defensible approach.

What we're calling the philosophic approach is close to what Ronald Dworkin calls the "moral reading" of the Constitution.[1] We adopt and support with further arguments Dworkin's proposal in the early 1970s that fidelity to the American Constitution *as written* requires that judges and other interpreters make up their own minds about constitutional meaning in a spirit of self-critical striving to realize our constitutional commitments and to interpret the Constitution to make it the best it can be. Though we take the terms as roughly equivalent, we prefer the broader "philosophic approach" to "moral reading" largely because we believe that fidelity to the Constitution requires a reliance on the social sciences in addition to the "fusion of constitutional law and moral theory" for which Dworkin famously called,[2] and because we think fidelity in constitutional interpretation demands an emphasis on the powers and ends of government

---

[1] Ronald Dworkin, *Freedom's Law: The Moral Reading of the American Constitution* (Cambridge, MA: Harvard University Press, 1996).
[2] Ronald Dworkin, *Taking Rights Seriously* (Cambridge, MA: Harvard University Press, 1977): 149.

that Dworkin neglects out of greater concern for rights as limitations on government.

Americans have debated how to interpret the Constitution for a long time. Shortly after the Constitution's adoption in 1789, the nation saw a division between "strict" and "liberal" constructionism that persisted until the 1970s, when the distinction was folded into other dichotomies, such as "interpretivism versus non-interpretivism" and "originalism versus non-originalism." Broader developments in jurisprudence and philosophy have influenced and continue to influence these debates. Shaped by such far-flung influences, the debate over approaches to constitutional meaning has evolved into an abstruse and multifaceted affair. Our aim in this book is to focus on the controlling practical issues of this complex debate in a manner that will engage both the specialist in constitutional theory and the informed general reader.

By "the informed general reader" we mean one with some knowledge of the milestones of American constitutional history, including landmark decisions of the United States Supreme Court. Though our focal point is the constitutional document, not its judicial gloss, we regularly refer to the latter to illustrate our points about the former. We try to engage the reader's participation by presenting our position as an extended argument that appeals at all points to his or her everyday moral and non-moral intu-itions. We try to avoid appeals to authority of any other kind, academic or political. As befits this ambition, we do our best either to avoid technical language or—when avoiding technical terms costs more in readability than it gains—to clarify technical terms.

Our biggest challenge has been to maintain a focus on the one question of how best to approach constitutional meaning. This single focus is hard to maintain for a reason that we, together with Walter Murphy and Stephen Macedo, discuss at length in our casebook, *American Constitutional Interpretation*: the question of *how* to interpret the Constitution is inter-twined with the questions of *what* the Constitution is and *who* may interpret it.[3] The question of *who* may interpret the Constitution has had a heavy influence on constitutional commentary over the centuries. For reasons we needn't discuss here, history has settled that question for most Americans. With few exceptions, most Americans take the Supreme Court's near-monopoly on constitutional interpretation for granted. Politicians

---

[3.] Walter F. Murphy, James E. Fleming, Sotirios A. Barber, and Stephen Macedo, *American Constitutional Interpretation*, 3rd ed. (New York: Foundation Press, 2003): 14–21.

who have opposed this monopoly have included some of the nation's best and some of its worst. The names of the former include Thomas Jefferson, Abraham Lincoln, and Franklin Roosevelt. Alexander Bickel, a Yale law professor who ranks among the most influential constitutional theorists of the twentieth century, labeled the difficulty that these statesmen had with the Court's monopoly on constitutional interpretation as "the counter-majoritarian difficulty."[4] Put simply, the alleged difficulty is that judicial review invalidating legislative and executive actions as unconstitutional is contrary to majority will and in this sense undemocratic. A determination to avoid or minimize this alleged difficulty (along with opposition to the substance of the Court's decisions) has motivated most of the approaches to constitutional interpretation that we consider in this book. Yet no necessary connection is evident between *what* the Constitution means and *who* may say what it means. There would be a connection only if you assumed that the Constitution means nothing—nothing, that is, other than what the Supreme Court says it means, to paraphrase an oft-quoted remark by Charles Evans Hughes (before he became Chief Justice): "We are under a Constitution, but the Constitution is what the judges say it is."[5] But no one does or seriously can hold such a view, for, as Hughes's critics have long observed, one must have some independent knowledge of who and what the Supreme Court is before one can say the Constitution means what the Supreme Court says, and that independent knowledge can originate in no other place than the Constitution itself.

Given the aim of this book, we bracket the problem of *who* may engage in constitutional interpretation. Our prescriptions here are not tailored to meet the so-called counter-majoritarian difficulty. We talk mostly about the Court when illustrating our arguments and findings, but these arguments and findings apply to any interpreter, including legislatures, executives, and ordinary citizens trying to decide for themselves what the Constitution means. Though we have argued separately in previous writings against any judicial monopoly,[6] we relegate the *who* question

---

4. Alexander M. Bickel, *The Least Dangerous Branch* (Indianapolis, IN: Bobbs-Merrill, 1962): 16–18.

5. Charles Evans Hughes, *Addresses* (New York: G. P. Putnam & Sons, 1908): 139.

6. *See, e.g.*, Sotirios A. Barber, *On What the Constitution Means* (Baltimore: Johns Hopkins University Press, 1984): 157–58, 196–99; Sotirios A. Barber and James E. Fleming, "The Canon and the Constitution Outside the Courts," *Constitutional Commentary* 17 (2000): 267; James E. Fleming, "The Constitution Outside the Courts," *Cornell Law Review* 86 (2000): 215; James E. Fleming, "Judicial Review Without Judicial Supremacy: Taking the Constitution Seriously Outside the Courts," *Fordham Law Review* 73 (2005): 1377.

here to a matter of institutional design, substantive democratic theory, and ultimately, political anthropology (in recognition of its dramatic implications for political culture).

The *what* question—the question of what the Constitution as a whole is—enjoys a different status here. As we show in Chapter 2, the question of whether the Constitution is a code of detailed historical conceptions or a charter of abstract moral concepts is central to the question of *how* to interpret the Constitution. Furthermore, as we show in Chapter 3, interpreters who assume that the Constitution is designed chiefly to *limit* government—negative constitutionalists—will interpret the Constitution differently from positive constitutionalists—those who hold that the Constitution's chief aim is to *empower* government (while still respecting certain fundamental rights). These issues regarding the normative properties of the Constitution are crucial to the question of which approach (or approaches) to constitutional meaning is (or are) best, and we do address them.

We acknowledge with gratitude the generous help of our friends and colleagues, Walter Murphy and Stephen Macedo. They read and commented extensively on drafts of the manuscript, as did Mark Brandon, Ronald Kahn, Sanford Levinson, Linda McClain, and Lawrence Solum, as well as Fordham University School of Law J.D. candidates Stacey Daniel and Lauren Cowan. We also benefited from presenting portions of the book in the Fordham University School of Law Faculty Workshop Series, especially from the comments of Martin Flaherty, Abner Greene, Robert Kaczorowski, Charles Kelbley, and Benjamin Zipursky, and we appreciate the support of Dean William Michael Treanor and Associate Dean Matthew Diller. No doubt this would be a better book had we followed the advice of all of these individuals.

SAB, Notre Dame, IN
JEF, New York, NY

PART I

CHAPTER 1

THE PRESUPPOSITIONS OF
CONSTITUTIONAL INTERPRETATION

When American lawyers, judges, politicians, and ordinary citizens talk about "constitutional law," they usually refer to a large body of legal propositions that form part of what the United States Supreme Court has said about the American Constitution. According to one of these propositions, for example, the Equal Protection Clause of the Fourteenth Amendment prohibits state governments from segregating the races in public schools.[1] Another such proposition is that the Commerce Clause of Article I, § 8 authorizes Congress to regulate the hours and wages of the nation's work force, including employees of state and local governments.[2] Each of these propositions is currently valid in the sense that the Court currently holds each to be true. But it was not always so, for in each case the Court departed from what it had previously said about the Constitution.[3] Whether in law schools or liberal arts programs, courses in "constitutional law" are mainly courses not about what *the Constitution* itself might mean or might say directly to the American people; they are courses about the different and competing things that *the Supreme Court* has said about the Constitution over more than two centuries of adjudication. Most courses in "constitutional law" are thus history courses of a sort—courses about the history of what the Supreme

---

[1] Brown v. Board of Education, 347 U.S. 483 (1954). The Equal Protection Clause of the Fourteenth Amendment provides: "nor shall any State . . . deny to any person within its jurisdiction the equal protection of the laws."

[2] Garcia v. San Antonio Metropolitan Transit Authority, 469 U.S. 528 (1985). Article I, § 8 authorizes Congress "to regulate Commerce with foreign Nations, and among the several States, and with the Indian Tribes."

[3] Plessy v. Ferguson, 163 U.S. 537 (1896) (overruled in *Brown*); National League of Cities v. Usery, 426 U.S. 833 (1976) (overruled in *Garcia*).

Court has said about the Constitution. Concern with the Court and its history needs little justification, of course, because the Court has an obvious impact on American life (witness *Brown v. Board of Education* (1954),[4] holding that racially segregated public schools deny equal protection; *Roe v. Wade* (1973),[5] recognizing the right of a woman to decide whether to terminate a pregnancy; and *Bush v. Gore* (2000),[6] resolving the outcome of a contested presidential election). And a sense of how the Court has arrived at where it is now is more often than not a fairly good indicator of where the Court is likely to go next. This practice of relying on the Court for constitutional meaning is too firmly established in America to change any time soon, though some critics of the judiciary's supremacy in constitutional interpretation have argued for "taking the Constitution away from the courts" or for locating authority to interpret the Constitution in "the people themselves."[7]

Yet, there must be more to what the Constitution means than what the Supreme Court has said or is likely to say it means. Even Charles Evans Hughes's famous remark, "We are under a Constitution, but the Constitution is what the judges say it is,"[8] presupposes meaning that is independent of the Court's interpretations; for we have to have some independent knowledge of the Constitution to identify the judges to whom Hughes was referring. That there is "something more" is indicated by the stubborn sense or intuition that the history of what the Court has said is a progression of *different interpretations of a constitutional document that changes only through formal amendment.* That Americans generally have this sense or intuition is indicated by two familiar and related facts of our national experience: the justices of the Supreme Court commonly claim (1) that, however controversial their interpretations might be, those interpretations are *faithful* to the Constitution itself and (2) that those who disagree with them are *wrong*—wrong, that is, about the Constitution. These related claims presuppose that the meaning of the Constitution does not depend on anyone's special interpretation of the Constitution. Put differently, the claims of fidelity and

---

4. 347 U.S. 483 (1954).
5. 410 U.S. 113 (1973).
6. 531 U.S. 98 (2000).
7. *See* Mark Tushnet, *Taking the Constitution Away from the Courts* (Princeton, NJ: Princeton University Press, 1999); Larry D. Kramer, *The People Themselves: Popular Constitutionalism and Judicial Review* (New York: Oxford University Press, 2004).
8. Charles Evans Hughes, *Addresses* (New York: G. P. Putnam & Sons, 1908): 139.

fallibility presuppose that the Constitution means something in and of itself. Those who reject these presuppositions cannot sensibly say that anyone, including the Court, is ever, or can ever be, right or wrong about what the Constitution means.

Whether the Constitution can mean anything in and of itself is a matter of considerable disagreement among philosophers, political scientists, legal scholars, and jurists. Neither author of this book has answered the question for himself to an intellectual certainty, and each of us is presently inclined toward a different answer. Our aim here is chiefly descriptive and analytic. Descriptively, we note, as related facts, what no one can successfully deny: American lawyers, judges, politicians, and ordinary citizens generally talk about the Constitution and the Court as if the Court can get the Constitution wrong, and in doing so they presuppose that the Constitution has meaning independently of what the Court or any other interpreter might say it means. We believe that this particular presupposition, whether ultimately defensible or not, is an ineluctable part of the political consciousness of Americans who hold political opinions. In this book, we explore basic questions raised by the presupposition that the Constitution means something in and of itself. These questions concern:

1. the kinds of things to which the Constitution's words and phrases (like "equal protection" and "commerce") refer;
2. the kind of thing (a contract? a code of concrete historical rules? a charter of abstract moral principles?) the Constitution as a whole is (or *What* is the Constitution?);[9]
3. the most defensible approach (or approaches) to constitutional meaning (or *How* should the Constitution be interpreted?);
4. who (if anyone) might have the final say about constitutional meaning (or *Who* may authoritatively interpret the Constitution?); and
5. the limits to constitutional interpretation as distinguished from lawmaking or amendment.

We call these questions *interpretive questions* to distinguish them from the *substantive questions* of constitutional law. Answers to the substantive

---

9. For a work that conceives the enterprise of constitutional interpretation on the basis of these three fundamental interrogatives—*What?*, *How?*, and *Who?*—see Walter F. Murphy, James E. Fleming, Sotirios A. Barber, and Stephen Macedo, *American Constitutional Interpretation*, 3rd ed. (New York: Foundation Press, 2003).

questions purport to tell us, for example, whether capital punishment is sometimes or always cruel in violation of the Eighth Amendment's prohibition of cruel and unusual punishments,[10] whether the right to decide to have an abortion or to enter into a homosexual relationship is protected by the liberty guarantee of the Due Process Clauses of the Fifth and Fourteenth Amendments,[11] or whether the Boy Scouts of America (a "private" organization) has a constitutional right to exclude homosexuals and atheists.[12] Answers to what we're calling the interpretive questions purport to tell us *what* kind of thing the Constitution is, the kinds of things to which its words refer; *how* best to approach the meaning of the Constitution; and *who* if anyone has the last word about that meaning. The substantive issues of constitutional meaning are the bottom-line questions of constitutional law; they are what interest lawyers and ordinary citizens first. The interpretive issues, though interesting in their own right, become compelling for most of us typically only after we become aware of their implications for the bottom-line legal questions.

To see the implications of the interpretive questions, one need only read any of the difficult cases in the Supreme Court over the past two centuries. A legal question in the famous case of *McCulloch v. Maryland* (1819) was whether Congress could override a state's opposition and establish a national bank with branches in the states.[13] The answer turned on what kind of thing the Constitution is (a general charter or a detailed code) and whether to interpret the powers delegated to Congress in Article I, § 8 broadly or narrowly. The legal question in the infamous case of *Dred Scott v. Sandford* (1857)[14] was whether an African-American could ask a federal court to determine whether he was being lawfully held as a slave. The answer turned on the role of framers' intentions in constitutional interpretation, how to find out what the framers intended, and whether to conceive the relevant intentions concretely or abstractly. For the Court in *Dred Scott*, Chief Justice Roger B. Taney sought the meaning

---

[10.] Roper v. Simmons, 543 U.S. 551 (2005).
[11.] *Roe*; Lawrence v. Texas, 539 U.S. 558 (2003). The Due Process Clause of the Fourteenth Amendment provides: "nor shall any State deprive any person of life, liberty, or property, without due process of law." Likewise, the Due Process Clause of the Fifth Amendment, which applies to the federal government, provides: "nor shall any person . . . be deprived of life, liberty, or property, without due process of law."
[12.] Boy Scouts of America v. Dale, 530 U.S. 640 (2000).
[13.] 17 U.S. 316 (1819).
[14.] 60 U.S. 393 (1857).

of the nation's principles (here "all men are created equal" as proclaimed in the Declaration of Independence) in concrete historical practices and prejudices at the time of the founding, while some of Taney's critics, like Abraham Lincoln, insisted that the "all men" spoken of in the Declaration referred to *all men* as a matter of abstract moral principle.

To mention more recent cases, the legal question in *Lawrence v. Texas* (2003)[15] was whether a state could make it a crime for consenting adults of the same sex to engage in intimate sexual acts. The answer involved interpretive questions like whether the meaning of "liberty" in the Fourteenth Amendment is to be determined by well-reasoned judgments regarding the nature of liberty or, rather, by what state laws had "traditionally" or historically conceived liberty to be as of 1868, when that amendment was ratified. One side (the dissenters) wanted to exclude from its conception of "tradition" recent trends in American and European law favoring homosexual rights, while the other side (the majority) argued for including that "recent tradition," leaving readers to ask whether the nature and the normative force of "tradition" lies in concrete historical practices or abstract moral principles. The legal question in *DeShaney v. Winnebago County Department of Social Services* (1989)[16] was whether a state agency established to protect children from child abuse had a judicially enforceable constitutional duty to protect a child from the perfectly predictable harm of a violent parent. This question involved different views of the nature of the Constitution as a whole: one side (the majority) held that the Constitution was designed to protect people from the government, not private actors from each other, while the other side (the dissenters) argued that the state had a duty to protect the child because the child could not protect himself and because the existence of a state child welfare system had lulled Wisconsinites into complacency about the extent to which the state was in fact looking out for abused children. Again, the legal question in *Brown* was whether the Equal Protection Clause of the Fourteenth Amendment permitted the states to segregate the races in the public schools. This case turned largely on whether constitutional meaning could be settled by past interpretations of the Constitution formed under markedly different social circumstances.

When we say that in controversial cases like these the legal answer *turns on* the interpretive answer, some readers might interpret us to say

---

15. 539 U.S. 558 (2003).
16. 489 U.S. 189 (1989).

that the interpretive theories of the justices *caused* them to decide the legal questions as they did. Some readers might take us to say, in other words, that the Court in *DeShaney* or *Brown* would have reached a different decision had the justices held different theories of what kind of thing the Constitution is or whether constitutional meaning should be settled by past cases decided under different circumstances. If we are saying this, some would say that we are wrong, because justices decide cases as they do on the strength of their personal political preferences, not their answers to such abstract philosophic questions as the nature of the Constitution and the best approach to constitutional meaning. These observers would say that while judges routinely rationalize their decisions in terms of broad "judicial philosophies" and "constitutional principles," rationalization is mere rationalization, after-the-fact window dressing for decisions reached on personal political grounds.

We readily concede that this cynical view of how most judges proceed may in fact be true. Indeed, each of us, pointing to his own list of cases, is convinced that it often is true. What we jointly deny is that, everywhere and always, it must be true. For if it must be true of judges— if they just cannot rise above their self-validating partisan preferences— something analogous must be true of those academic writers who hold a cynical view of judges. If judges, for some reason, cannot honestly be concerned with what the balance of argument and evidence shows about the nature of the Constitution (what kind of thing it is) and constitutional meaning (how to interpret it and what its words and phrases mean), then it is hard to see how scholars can honestly be concerned with what the balance of argument and evidence shows about the nature of judicial decision. If judges must decide controversial legal questions in self-serving ways, can scientists and scholars answer controversial scientific questions in other than self-serving ways?

That judicial decision is inevitably self-serving is a controversial proposition because judges typically deny it. Typically, they claim fidelity to the law, no matter how controversial their decisions might be. To say, therefore, that "judicial decision is inevitably self-serving" is to say, implicitly, that "*it is true* that judicial decision is inevitably self-serving even though the judges deny it."[17] It is thus to answer a controversial

---

[17.] As we observe in Chapter 2, philosophers have pointed out for thousands of years that skeptics contradict themselves when they say "there is no truth," for that is elliptical for "*it is true that* there is no truth."

scientific question from what implicitly purports to be a concern for the truth of the matter, as distinguished from some self-serving account of the matter. If scientists can tackle controversial issues about judicial conduct from a concern for the truth or best account, why can't judges answer controversial constitutional questions from a concern for the truth or best interpretation? Is there something especially defective about the kinds of persons who are attracted to careers in law and legal academia, as compared to the kinds of persons who are attracted to the natural and social sciences? We are aware of no scientific evidence to this effect—no evidence that there's something inherently dishonest about the people who concern themselves professionally with constitutional questions. Could it be, then, that there's something special about the questions of constitutional meaning? As distinguished from scientific questions concerning what motivates judicial and academic judgments about constitutional meaning, do the questions of constitutional meaning themselves have some special property that compels otherwise honest people to claim that they are trying to do what's right under the law when they are really manipulating the law to give constitutional legitimacy to their self-serving views or partisan preferences?

Perhaps there is something unique about the questions of constitutional meaning: unlike scientific questions, you might say, answers to constitutional questions (what the Constitution is and what it means) have immediate political implications that attract or repel us emotionally. Take the Court's action in *DeShaney*. Six of the justices may have concluded that the Constitution does not obligate the government to help a helpless child because they had reservations about "the welfare state" and because they feared that they could find no principled line between imposing an obligation upon government to shelter children from predictable violence and imposing an obligation upon government to shelter children from hunger, ignorance, and lack of meaningful economic, social, and political opportunities. Because constitutional questions typically have political implications like this, they involve our emotions, and one might submit that our emotions prevent a detached and self-critical effort to pursue the truth, even where there might be an objective truth or best interpretation to pursue.

Our response to this last point is that scientific questions can have implications no less immediately political and emotional than constitutional questions. Leaving aside the difficulties of distinguishing scientific from moral or political questions (a difficulty manifest in such questions as when human life and personhood begin), consider such widely acknowledged scientific questions as the origin of the cosmos, the origin of the species, whether some people are born homosexual, the causes of global warming, *and* the extent, if any, to which a sincere and self-critical concern for constitutional principle can influence decisions in constitutional cases. No observer of American politics today can deny the immediate political implications of any answer we might give to any of these scientific questions. If you believe the weight of the scientific evidence supports Darwin's view of the origin of species, you're likely to believe it's wrong to force "intelligent-design theory" on public school children; you may even believe it's wrong to license private schools that forbid the teaching of evolution. (If not, you may believe it's wrong not to offer children the opportunity to learn such alternative theories.) If you believe the scientific evidence indicates that sexual orientation is heavily influenced by genetic inheritance, you're likely to believe that discrimination against homosexuals is wrong. (Again, if not, you may believe the contrary.) If the science of psychology could show that judges cannot avoid imposing their personal values on the rest of us, many of us would conclude that the American institution of judicial review is indefensible.

There is nothing unique about the scientific questions in these particular examples. Whether an acknowledged scientific question in fact does have an immediate political implication is entirely a matter of circumstance. At one point, after all, it was a matter of political consequence whether what we now call the solar system was heliocentric or geocentric. In the 1940s and 50s, Mendelian genetics was officially out of favor in Stalinist Russia. And, at this writing, many Americans see immediate political implications to admittedly factual questions, like whether there's a correlation between abortions and breast cancer or whether Iraq had a hand in the destruction of the World Trade Center on September 11, 2001. If no one can confirm the truth (or falsity) of any proposition that has political implications, then no one can say "(it's true that) answers to constitutional questions do no more than rationalize personal preferences," for that proposition has a clear political implication of its own: the illegitimacy of judicial power in America.

Whether judges can honestly seek the Constitution's true meaning, or whether the Constitution has a true meaning to be sought, no one doubts that judges typically *claim* to be concerned with the Constitution's true meaning and that judicial rhetoric therefore *presupposes* the possibility of true constitutional meaning or best interpretation. That possibility should be kept open for at least two reasons. First, we have just seen that it is difficult to close, for there is no reason to deny the possibility of constitutional truth or its honest pursuit that would not also apply to the possibility of scientific truth and its honest pursuit—something we cannot deny while asserting (as scientific truths of semantics and psychology) the impossibility of constitutional meaning and its honest pursuit. Second, even if constitutional principles were used merely to rationalize decisions reached on other grounds, such principles would constrain constitutional decisions to some extent, for we can imagine many actions of government that would be difficult to rationalize in constitutional terms. Consider, for example, an open and forthright use of tax dollars to cultivate a Christian world view among the nation's school-age population. Or a serious attempt to enforce laws criminalizing fornication or birth control. What would we say about an open and forthright attempt to limit the franchise (or not count the votes) of minority populations? What would we say about a declaration that the state governments may not tax private property to pay for public schools? These examples are hypothetical, of course, but that doesn't make them unrealistic. They are consistent with the political ambitions, principles, or conduct of influential groups in America today. And the fact that they are clearly unconstitutional indicates something of the Constitution's power to constrain political choice.

In speaking of interpreters seeking the Constitution's true meaning or best interpretation, we may seem to be presupposing that there is a moral reality without providing a persuasive method for discovering what it consists of. We need to make two important points. First, we do not argue that there *is* a moral reality; instead, we argue that the enterprise of constitutional interpretation *presupposes* that conscientious, responsible interpreters are seeking the true meaning or best interpretation of the Constitution. This presupposition does not entail a claim that there *is* a true meaning in the constitutional materials themselves, much less guarantee that there is one. In short, we are making a claim about the *presuppositions* of constitutional interpretation, not what some readers might interpret as an "ontological" claim about moral reality.

Second, we ourselves are divided concerning the "ontological" debate between moral realism and constructivism (or deep conventionalism)— to simplify, between the view that constitutional interpretation seeks the true meaning of real concepts embodied in the Constitution and the view that it seeks the best interpretation of *our* constitutional practice, tradition, and commitments.[18] For that reason as well as others, we have written this book to be agnostic between moral realism and constructivism (or deep conventionalism).

In Chapter 2, we further explore some of the principal questions of constitutional interpretation previewed here: *What* is the Constitution? *How* should it be interpreted? *Who* may authoritatively interpret it? In particular, we consider whether any theory of constitutional interpretation can avoid the need to make moral judgments about the meaning of the Constitution and whether our constitutional scheme commits the primary responsibility for making such judgments to legislatures rather than to courts.

[18.] *Contrast* Sotirios A. Barber, *The Constitution of Judicial Power* (Baltimore: Johns Hopkins University Press, 1993): 202–36 (defending a moral realist constitutional theory) *with* James E. Fleming, *Securing Constitutional Democracy: The Case of Autonomy* (Chicago: University of Chicago Press, 2006): 61–85 (developing a constitutional constructivism by analogy to John Rawls's political constructivism in John Rawls, *Political Liberalism* [New York: Columbia University Press, 1993]).

CHAPTER 2

THE PRINCIPAL QUESTIONS OF CONSTITUTIONAL INTERPRETATION

Interpreting the American Constitution is a cognitive activity that takes place in a specific kind of context and proceeds from specific assumptions. The context is one of disagreement (often, but not necessarily, in connection with judicial cases and controversies) about whether an act of government is either permitted or required by some provision or associated principle of the Constitution. The assumptions at work in this context are: (1) that the Constitution, faithfully followed, would limit what the government may do; (2) that those limits can be known with reasonable confidence; and (3) that reasonable persons would regard those limits in general as serving a paramount good.[1]

The principal questions of constitutional interpretation emerge from conflicts concerning the different forms that these assumptions take. Some observers say, for example, that constitutional limits are chiefly concerned with how governmental decisions are made (matters of "process"), not fundamentally with what government may decide to do (questions of "substance"). Some say these limits are to be found and declared by courts of law; others see this power to determine limits as shared by the other branches of the national government, by the states, and even by the people themselves. Some say constitutional meaning should be sought in the intentions or original meanings of the framers and ratifiers, not, as others would have it, by consulting contemporary social needs or by

---

[1] To say that reasonable persons would regard those limits in general as serving a paramount good is not to deny that reasonable persons might criticize certain limits—or certain understandings of those limits—as imperfect, undemocratic, or otherwise flawed. *See* James E. Fleming, *Securing Constitutional Democracy: The Case of Autonomy* (Chicago: University of Chicago Press, 2006): 220–26; Sanford Levinson, *Our Undemocratic Constitution* (New York: Oxford University Press, 2006).

elaborating abstract moral concepts embodied in the constitutional text. Some say the Constitution seeks no more than the minimal preconditions for social cooperation and individual initiative; others say the Constitution is designed to foster a way of life dedicated to personal freedom, security, and economic prosperity as earthly goods (as distinguished from, for example, the salvation of souls in an afterlife); still others might say the Constitution aspires to be a shining city on a hill, committed not only to earthly goods but also to religious goods. All of these issues are aspects of the basic questions distinguished in Chapter 1: *What* is the Constitution? and *How* should it be interpreted? Some implicate the further question *Who* may authoritatively interpret it?

To show these assumptions at work and the questions they point to, we shall consider two classics of the literature of American constitutional thought, an article by William Rehnquist and an article by Ronald Dworkin. Rehnquist wrote his article when he was an associate justice of the Supreme Court; it was published in the *Texas Law Review.*[2] Dworkin's article was originally published in the *New York Review of Books* and subsequently republished (with slight changes) in his book *Taking Rights Seriously.*[3] These two articles represent quite different reactions to the Supreme Court's actions under the leadership of Chief Justice Earl Warren. Appointed by President Dwight Eisenhower in 1953, Warren actively worked for a unanimous decision in *Brown v. Board of Education* (1954).[4] By the time Warren retired in 1969, the Court had gone on to forbid religious observances in public schools, trim Congress's power to investigate alleged Communist subversion, strengthen the rights of defendants in criminal proceedings, broaden rights of political protest in time of war, and enhance the rights to vote and to have one's vote counted equally. These actions provoked a reaction on the part of southern whites, religious fundamentalists, and other elements of the ideological right that has yet fully to run its political course. The Warren Court's "reforms" or "excesses" (depending on one's point of view) also inspired waves of academic commentary, some supportive, some critical. The modern debate over approaches to constitutional interpretation is one of these waves, and publication of the Rehnquist and Dworkin articles were major

---

[2] William H. Rehnquist, "The Notion of a Living Constitution," *Texas Law Review* 54 (1976): 693.

[3] Ronald Dworkin, *Taking Rights Seriously* (Cambridge, MA: Harvard University Press, 1977): 131.

[4] 347 U.S. 483 (1954).

events in this debate. These articles preview what we will call in subsequent chapters the "narrow originalist approach" and the "philosophic approach," respectively.

The Warren Court, in the manner typical of courts, claimed constitutional authority for the dramatic changes that it produced in American law: it claimed fidelity to the Constitution. A reading of the Dworkin and Rehnquist articles reveals three basic reactions to this claim. First, Dworkin approves of the changes; he also agrees that they flow from the Constitution itself or from an honest attempt to apply its terms. Second, Rehnquist disapproves of the changes; he feels that they represent the values of liberal social reformers driven by a "living Constitution" that changes with the times, not an honest attempt to apply the Constitution's terms. Both Rehnquist and Dworkin recognize a third position, which Rehnquist identifies as that of an unnamed lawyer who argued in an appellate brief that the Supreme Court should act as the "'conscience of contemporary society.'"[5] We shall call Rehnquist's "brief writer" the "living-constitution liberal." This liberal generally agrees with Rehnquist that the Warren Court's leading decisions flow not from the Constitution but from what the justices of that court felt were the needs of contemporary society. Unlike Rehnquist, however, the living-constitution liberal approves of the actions of the Warren Court. Dworkin rejects the living-constitution liberal's conception of constitutional interpretation but shares her approval of the decisions of the Warren Court. This leaves us with the following arrangement of positions concerning the Warren Court:

	Actions of the Warren Court	Warren Court's claim to constitutional fidelity
Rehnquist	disapprove	disagree
Dworkin	approve	agree
Living-Constitution Liberal	approve	disagree

As this table indicates, an observer's interpretive stance (indicated by the second column) needn't demonstrate much about his or her politics (the first column). People as different politically as living-constitution liberals like the "brief writer" and conservatives like Rehnquist can agree

---

5. Rehnquist, *supra* note 2, at 695.

on important interpretive questions. Indeed, we are confident that many readers of this book who think of themselves as liberals will agree with many of Rehnquist's views about constitutional meaning, at least initially. As we shall see, Rehnquist's theory of constitutional interpretation holds surprises for those who associate ideological conservatism with old-fashioned beliefs about values and morality.

I. Rehnquist's Criticism of the Notion of a "Living Constitution"

In his article, "The Notion of a Living Constitution," Rehnquist attacks the idea that the Constitution's "vague" and general words and phrases give judges opportunities to keep the Constitution responsive to changing social conditions.[6] This has been a very popular idea among constitutional scholars, judges, politicians, and editorial writers since the decade after World War II because it seems to rescue constitutional government from "the dead hand of the past," making it serviceable to modern needs, while keeping judicial power in reserve for use against patent injustices like the old Jim Crow regimes of America's White South. Probably for this reason, Rehnquist tries to assure his readers that he doesn't oppose all senses of the phrase "living constitution." He agrees that provisions of the Constitution (like "equal protection of the laws," "commerce among the several states," and "unreasonable searches and seizures") are general enough to cover problems unforeseen by the Constitution's framers. He cites with seeming approval views of renowned figures like Justice Oliver Wendell Holmes, Jr., and Chief Justice John Marshall often invoked by proponents of a "living Constitution" and says that "courts are of course warranted in giving [general constitutional provisions] an application coextensive with their language."[7] He even acknowledges that the political values of individual judges will influence their interpretations of general words and phrases. He insists, however, that any legitimate application of general constitutional provisions to modern problems must be "tied to the language of the Constitution"—they must reflect "values . . . derived

---

6. *Id.* at 693.
7. *Id.* at 694, 696–97, 699 (citing classic statements by Holmes and Marshall in Missouri v. Holland, 252 U.S. 416 (1920), and Marbury v. Madison, 5 U.S. (1 Cranch) 137 (1803)).

from the language and intent of the framers."[8] And while he falls short of clarity about the acceptable sense of "living constitution," he is clear about the unacceptable sense of it. Under this unacceptable version, he says, "nonelected members of the federal judiciary may address themselves to a social problem simply because other branches of government have failed or refused to do so."[9] The pivotal question for the reader of Rehnquist's article is whether there in fact are any constitutional cases where judges (1) fail to link their decisions to constitutional text and/or intent of the framers and (2) act "simply because other branches of government have failed or refused to do so."

Rehnquist cites two widely discredited cases from the past as examples of judicial "forays into problem solving": *Dred Scott v. Sandford* (1857) and *Lochner v. New York* (1905).[10] But readers of these cases will see immediately that they are poor examples of what Rehnquist says he's talking about: decisions that are (1) cut loose from constitutional language and framers' intent and (2) motivated solely by a desire to solve social problems that other parts of government won't address. The *Dred Scott* Court acted not because Congress wouldn't address the slavery controversy but because Congress had addressed the problem in a manner that the Court disapproved. So the Court acted to disable Congress from further attempts to prohibit slavery in the territories.[11] Moreover, the *Dred Scott* decision was disconnected from neither the language of the Constitution nor the intent of the framers. The Court cited several constitutional provisions that affirmed the "right of property in a slave."[12] It also claimed grounding in a plausible account of the founding generation's racist attitudes and intentions concerning Americans of African descent.[13]

---

8. *Id.* at 698, 695.
9. *Id.* at 695.
10. *Id.* at 700, 700–04; Dred Scott v. Sandford, 60 U.S. 393 (1857); Lochner v. New York, 198 U.S. 45 (1905).
11. We acknowledge that Congress in 1854 had repealed the 1820 Missouri Compromise in the Kansas-Nebraska Act, so the current Congress had itself indicated its rejection of the 1820 act. This was a rejection on policy grounds, however, not constitutional grounds. Moreover, we are not suggesting that the Court's decision in *Dred Scott* was rooted simply in political disapproval as opposed to a sincerely believed view about what fidelity to the Constitution required. For insightful analysis, *see* Mark A. Graber, Dred Scott *and the Problem of Constitutional Evil* (New York: Cambridge University Press, 2006).
12. 60 U.S. at 411, 451–52.
13. *Id.* at 407–11.

The *Lochner* decision also fails to meet Rehnquist's test for judicial overreach. There the Court acted to overrule a policy of the New York legislature limiting the number of hours bakers could work to sixty per week; it didn't act to fill a vacuum caused by legislative inaction. The Court also acted pursuant to a not unreasonable (if arguably erroneous) interpretation of constitutional language, the "liberty" protected by the Due Process Clause of the Fourteenth Amendment. And it acted to protect an economic liberty or property right (management's lawfully-earned bargaining power over labor) that is not clearly inconsistent with the pro-business commitments of at least some leading framers, like Alexander Hamilton, a co-author of *The Federalist*.

Rehnquist could have mentioned decisions of the Warren Court that might meet at least one of his criteria for judicial overreach, like *Brown v. Board of Education* (1954), *Reynolds v. Sims* (1964),[14] and *Gideon v. Wainwright* (1963).[15] One can say of each of these cases that the Court acted at least partly because the political branches of state or national governments had failed adequately to address problems like substandard education for black youth, unfairly apportioned state legislatures, and unfair trials for criminal defendants who couldn't afford a lawyer. None of these decisions meets both parts of Rehnquist's test, however, for in each the Court invokes an arguably sound reading of a specific constitutional provision like the Equal Protection Clause, the Due Process Clause, or the Sixth Amendment's guarantee of the right to counsel. But these cases do meet part of his test, while *Lochner* and *Dred Scott* meet no part of it. Why, then, does Rehnquist choose *Lochner* and *Dred Scott* to illustrate the unacceptable version of "living constitution"? Why not choose cases like *Brown*, *Reynolds*, or *Gideon*? One possibility is that *Brown*, *Reynolds*, and *Gideon* are widely approved at least on moral grounds by both professional and lay opinion in America, while *Lochner* and *Dred Scott* are widely held in infamy. Rehnquist presumably would want to associate the position of his critics with infamous cases. He would hardly want to associate his own position with the morally dubious practices that *Brown*, *Reynolds*, and *Gideon* sought to correct. So, we can speculate, Rehnquist chooses his examples in a way that puts his interpretive position in a favorable moral light—he wants to be on the side of what his readers are likely to regard as justice and decency. The reader should

14. 377 U.S. 533 (1964).
15. 373 U.S. 335 (1963).

keep this strategy in mind when assessing the heart of Rehnquist's position, to be considered below.

In the meantime, let us point out that Rehnquist's examples don't work. He cites no case in which the Court fails to connect its answer to a provision of the constitutional text. Nor can he do so, for such a decision would not answer a constitutional question—it would be unrecognizable as a constitutional decision, a decision about what the Constitution means. Rehnquist all but acknowledges this when he says:

> The brief writer's version of the living Constitution is seldom presented in its most naked form, but is instead usually dressed in more attractive garb. The argument in favor of this approach generally begins with a sophisticated wink [which represents the following argument]—why pretend that there is any ascertainable content to the general phrases of the Constitution as they are written since, after all, judges constantly disagree about their meaning? . . . Any sophisticated student of the subject knows that judges need not limit themselves to the intent of the framers, which is very difficult to determine in any event. Because of the general language used in the Constitution, judges should not hesitate to use their authority to make the Constitution relevant and useful in solving the problems of modern society.[16]

With this attribution to the brief writer, Rehnquist executes an unannounced shift. He shifts the recommended ground of constitutional decision from the *actual language of the constitutional text* to the *intentions of the Constitution's framers.* He is forced to do this because he can show no historical example of judges failing to justify answers to constitutional questions in terms of arguably plausible interpretations of constitutional language (this despite common objections in recent years to the Court's protection of "unenumerated" rights).[17] Failure to tie a decision to constitutional language, therefore, cannot be part of a meaningful test of when courts exceed their authority. Rehnquist's real test is (if anything)

---

16. Rehnquist, *supra* note 2, at 698–99.
17. *See, e.g.,* Griswold v. Connecticut, 381 U.S. 479, 507–27 (1965) (Black, J., dissenting) (discussed in Chapter 5); Roe v. Wade, 410 U.S. 113, 173–77 (1973) (Rehnquist, J., dissenting); Bowers v. Hardwick, 478 U.S. 186, 194 (1986); Planned Parenthood v. Casey, 505 U.S. 833, 979–81 (1992) (Scalia, J., concurring in the judgment in part and dissenting in part); Robert H. Bork, *The Tempting of America* (New York: Free Press, 1990): 110–26.

lack of fidelity to framers' intent. Framers' intent is the ultimate authority and source of meaning for Rehnquist in constitutional cases. For him as a judge sworn to uphold the Constitution, terms like "due process" and "equal protection" mean no more than what the framers expected them to mean. Rehnquist thus holds in his article (contrary, incidentally, to his view twenty-one years later in *City of Boerne v. Flores*)[18] that while the language of the Fourteenth Amendment is broad enough to cover problems that the framers didn't anticipate, section 5 of the Amendment leaves these unanticipated problems to be addressed by Congress, not the courts.[19] (Here, evidently, a conception of *Who* may interpret the Constitution follows from a conception of *How* to interpret it.) The courts are responsible for section 1 of the Amendment, the section that guarantees due process and equal protection. Of these provisions and the Civil War Amendments (the Thirteenth, Fourteenth, and Fifteenth Amendments) generally, Rehnquist says: "I think they [the framers] would have said those amendments were designed to prevent from ever recurring abuses in which the states had engaged prior to that time."[20] This last statement seems inconsistent with his earlier statement that judges may legitimately apply constitutional provisions coextensively with their language (which may be broader than abuses extant prior to their adoption). If Rehnquist believes judges are not supposed to look beyond the abuses that the framers concretely had in mind when they adopted a constitutional provision like the Equal Protection Clause of the Fourteenth Amendment, we are entitled to wonder whether, despite his assurances, he can honestly distinguish a right from a wrong sense of "living constitution." For here he seems opposed to any sense of it.

In any case, Rehnquist apparently thinks the problems of modern life are increasingly matters left open to political choice, not constrained by constitutional principle. He thinks the Constitution "was designed to enable the popularly elected branches of government, not the judicial branch, to keep the country abreast of the times."[21] For a "living

---

[18.] 521 U.S. 507 (1997) (narrowly construing Congress's power under section 5 of the Fourteenth Amendment).

[19.] Rehnquist, *supra* note 2, at 700. Section 5 of the Fourteenth Amendment provides: "The Congress shall have power to enforce, by appropriate legislation, the provisions of this article."

[20.] Rehnquist, *supra* note 2, at 700.

[21.] *Id.* at 699.

constitution" in some forward-looking sense, Rehnquist would substitute a constitution that's dynamic in reverse: it is increasingly irrelevant in the sense that it does not constrain political choice. On his view, the Constitution establishes, empowers, and limits a democratic government; as the passage of time pushes the framers' concrete intentions ever further into the past, the Constitution functions as an increasingly narrow set of negative restraints on policy makers, leaving them an ever wider range of policy options. Rehnquist believes these options include tolerating "conceded social evil[s],"[22] evils that the framers did not see or anticipate and that popular majorities may decide not to address, for reasons of cost or no reason at all. With this understanding of the Constitution's basic functions and the nature of constitutional meaning, Rehnquist implicitly denies the constitutionality of the Warren Court's leading decisions—which presume that constitutional principles are abstract and have a broader reach than the framers' concrete intentions—though he refrains from attacking them directly and by name.

The "living constitution" that Rehnquist rejects would authorize judges to go beyond the well-documented racism of the Civil War era and interpret an idea like "equal protection for all persons" in view of what the judges believe the proper extension of "person" and the true meaning or best understanding of "equal protection" might be. Were interpretation of the Fourteenth Amendment limited to what its framers had concretely in mind, "persons" might cover only "black persons" and thus might not cover "female persons" or "homosexual persons" or "corporate persons" or "unborn persons." Should moral and scientific argument and evidence prove that some or all of these kinds of things were kinds of real persons or entitled to be treated as such by law, the Amendment nonetheless would not protect them from popular hostility or indifference. And the sole reason would be that, whether females or homosexuals or corporations or fetuses are or should count as persons, the framers didn't have them concretely in mind.

Rehnquist's position on constitutional meaning and the role of judges goes against conventional wisdom. He offers three arguments for it. First, he says, the "living constitution" thesis is wrong about the "nature of the Constitution," which was designed to establish a majoritarian representative democracy, not rule by unelected judges.[23] This is a poor

---

22. *Id.* at 700.
23. *Id.* at 699.

argument because it begs important questions; it simply assumes several propositions that have to be argued for. Chief among these is that the Constitution does not mean what it says—that, for example, despite the presence of "persons" in the text of the Fourteenth Amendment, the Amendment protects not persons but only what the framers specifically wanted to count as persons on the occasion of the Amendment's adoption. Rehnquist also assumes that a genuinely democratic community can't appreciate its intellectual and moral limitations and establish a government that can help it realize its aspirations by rising above those limitations. On this assumption, a genuinely democratic community couldn't be interested in genuine fairness to real persons. It could only be interested in its particular understanding of personhood and fairness, whether that understanding proves scientifically and/or morally right or wrong. Rehnquist also assumes, for reasons he doesn't give, that his particular view of representative democracy is the right view. He assumes, again without argument, historical or philosophic, that the framers valued representative democracy (as he conceives it) above other goods (like real fairness to real people) or that they *ought to have* preferred representative democracy (as he conceives it) to other goods. He makes no arguments that the Constitution establishes his conception of representative democracy as opposed to competing understandings of it as embodying, for example, a constitutional democracy that places substantive limitations on what majorities may do to persons.[24]

Second, Rehnquist argues that defenders of a "living constitution" ignore the "disastrous experiences" with judicial lawmaking, like the *Dred Scott* and *Lochner* cases.[25] But this too is a poor argument, as we have seen, because these cases don't exemplify judicial overreach as Rehnquist defines it. In each of these cases, the Court cited constitutional provisions as they might well have been understood by important segments of the founding generation. In fact, scholars have shown that the Court's opinion in *Dred Scott* is an especially clear example of the intentionalist (more commonly, the "originalist") approach to constitutional interpretation

---

[24.] For the distinction between majoritarian representative democracy and constitutional democracy as competing conceptions of the form of government embodied in our Constitution, *see* Walter F. Murphy, James E. Fleming, Sotirios A. Barber, and Stephen Macedo, *American Constitutional Interpretation*, 3rd ed. (New York: Foundation Press, 2003): 43–59.

[25.] Rehnquist, *supra* note 2, at 699, 700–04.

that Rehnquist says he favors.[26] We don't suggest that *Dred Scott* and *Lochner* are sufficient to condemn Rehnquist's approach, for some intentionalists or originalists have argued that *Dred Scott* and *Lochner* were wrong about their reading of both the Constitution and the founding.[27] We're saying that because the *Dred Scott* and *Lochner* opinions do attend to constitutional text and framers' intent, they demonstrate nothing about what happens when courts ignore constitutional text and framers' intent. Rehnquist may believe, of course, that these cases were so patently wrong about constitutional text and framers' intent that their references to text and intent were mere pretexts for decisions reached on other grounds. But he doesn't argue in this way, and it would be hard for him to do so. He acknowledges that constitutional provisions are often open to conflicting interpretations, framers' intent is often difficult to ascertain, and judges are influenced by their personal philosophies. If disagreement—even strong disagreement—were sufficient to condemn an opinion as pretextual, and if mistakes—even "disastrous" ones—were always sufficient to condemn the processes and institutions that produced them, then some might think that we might as well give up on government by humans and pray for government by divine or other superhuman authority.

Rehnquist's remaining, third argument against the "living constitution" is the most problematic and revealing one. Here he would say that no constitution makers should be interested in real fairness for real persons—as opposed to their own view of fairness for what (or whom) they want to count as persons—because there is no "real fairness" to be interested in and no compelling reason for counting as persons those persons or things that a community's majority doesn't want to count as persons. Propositions about what fairness requires and about who or what ought to count as persons are what Rehnquist calls "value judgments" or "moral judgments." Moral judgments are mere matters of personal conscience, he says, and "[t]here is no conceivable way in which I can logically demonstrate to you that the judgments of my conscience are superior to the judgments of your conscience, and vice versa." Individual moral judgments can "take on a generalized moral rightness or goodness" when enough people get behind

---

26. Christopher L. Eisgruber, "*Dred* Again: Originalism's Forgotten Past," *Constitutional Commentary* 10 (1993): 37.

27. For criticisms of *Dred Scott* and *Lochner* by originalists, *see, e.g.*, Bork, *supra* note 17, at 28–34, 44–46; Christopher Wolfe, *The Rise of Modern Judicial Review: From Constitutional Interpretation to Judge-Made Law*, rev. ed. (Lanham, MD: Rowman & Littlefield, 1994): 68–70, 144–63.

them and incorporate them in the Constitution and the laws. But it is the mere "fact of their enactment that gives them whatever moral claim they have upon us as a society," not "any intrinsic worth" or "someone's idea of natural justice."[28] (Rehnquist's moral skepticism may be surprising to his supporters who hold old-fashioned conservative views about values and morality being objective.) Arguments for a "living constitution" erroneously assume some source of value other than mere enactment by popular majorities, like equal protection itself, as opposed to the particular view of equal protection that attracted a constitutional majority in 1868, when the Equal Protection Clause was ratified. By licensing judges to invoke this allegedly independent good, defenders of a "living constitution" license "an end run around popular government."[29]

Rehnquist's position faces two sets of difficulties: one centers on his view of popular government or democracy, the other involves his evident theory of meaning. Though Rehnquist doesn't acknowledge it, democracy competes with other forms of government and there are different versions of democracy. We shall see in Chapter 3 that the authors of *The Federalist* reject simple majoritarian representative democracy and hold all forms of government answerable to justice and other goods deemed prior to government. *The Federalist* thus disagrees with Rehnquist on the obligations of democracy. Thomas Jefferson's understanding of democracy differs from Rehnquist's, as does Abraham Lincoln's, for both Jefferson and Lincoln derive democracy from, and obligate democracy to, "self-evident truths" of political morality (proclaimed in the Declaration of Independence) whose existence Rehnquist denies. Rehnquist himself assumes both that democracy is the best form of government and that his understanding of democracy is the best or the only understanding.

But what, on Rehnquist's account, could possibly make democracy a political good? What argument could prove democracy better than its competitors, especially at a time when global environmental and economic problems challenge the world's scientists, not to mention the competence of ordinary citizens and the capacity for coordinated response of the planet's culturally divided peoples? Even if democracy is able to meet the world's problems, why assume that Rehnquist's version of democracy is the best? If Rehnquist thinks his view of democracy is closest to the truth about democracy, then he has to admit that there are moral and scientific

---

[28.] Rehnquist, *supra* note 2, at 704.
[29.] *Id.* at 706.

truths favoring democracy, truths that don't depend on mere enactment by popular majorities. Democracy itself, in other words, would be the best form of government even if all of the world's peoples should decide to abandon democracy for, say, an aristocracy of scientific experts and international bankers who knew how to escape looming environmental and economic calamity. And Rehnquist's version of democracy would either coincide with democracy itself or approximate it as closely as circumstances permitted. Despite his ostensible subjectivism about values and skepticism about moral truth, therefore, Rehnquist assumes that his version of democracy is both correct and a thing of "generalized moral goodness."

A related problem is Rehnquist's apparent theory of meaning. By assuming that democracy is good and that his theory of democracy is best despite different conceptions of democracy, Rehnquist assumes that "democracy" (the word) refers to *democracy* (the thing) and that people can misapply "democracy." An example of misapplying "democracy" would be to label "democracy" (at its intellectual and moral best) a system that empowered unelected judges to second-guess the value judgments of the people's immediate representatives. Such a theory, Rehnquist would say, misapplies the term "democracy" because it errs about the nature of democracy.

To say this, however, Rehnquist would have to abandon his view that political morality is a mere matter of political enactment. If he continues to deny the existence of moral truths independent of enactment, he has to cite the law that enacts his view of democracy. Is the meaning of goods like due process and equal protection found in framers' intent, while the meaning of goods like democracy and constitutionalism is found elsewhere? Rehnquist does not claim that the nation knowingly enacted his conception of democracy into law. He can't say that the Constitution enacts it, for he believes the Constitution is a product of it. In the end, it's not clear that he can answer the question: What's wrong with what he calls "an end run around popular government"? If the nation as a whole accepted the practice of end runs around popular government, would that cause Rehnquist to abandon his position that it is a generalized wrong? Do two centuries of judicial review under a "living constitution" indicate that the nation has accepted what Rehnquist calls "courts making end runs around popular government"? These questions show that Rehnquist has problems, not that he is wrong, and we shall have to return to his position in the pages that follow (in particular, in Chapter 6, where we criticize narrow or concrete originalism).

II. Dworkin's Call for a Fusion of Constitutional Law and Moral Philosophy

We turn now to Ronald Dworkin's essay, published originally as "The Jurisprudence of Richard Nixon" in the *New York Review of Books* and subsequently, with slight revisions, as "Constitutional Cases" in his book *Taking Rights Seriously*.[30] Dworkin, as we have noted, generally approves of the innovations in constitutional law made by the Warren Court. More importantly for us, Dworkin accepts the claim of the Warren Court, typical of courts in constitutional cases, that its decisions represent good-faith efforts to apply the provisions of the constitutional text. Dworkin seems to claim that one can be *faithful to an unchanging text* while supporting *changes in interpretations of that text*. And what justifies this claim is perhaps the best-known distinction of his legal philosophy: the distinction between constitutional *concepts* and competing *conceptions* of those concepts.[31] To understand this distinction and its implications, we must reflect on the context in which Dworkin introduces it.

Dworkin's article is an attempt to discover if critics of the Warren Court—chiefly President Richard Nixon (who appointed William Rehnquist as associate justice)—have a publicly defensible reason for their opposition to what they call the "judicial activism" of the Warren era. Going through their possible reasons one-by-one, Dworkin contends that the "Nixons" of this world do not have a publicly defensible reason for their position on the *activism* of the Warren Court.[32] (He is too polite to suggest that their opposition flows from disapproval of the *content* of decisions like *Brown*, *Reynolds*, and *Gideon*.) Dworkin argues, for example, that the Constitution's so-called "plain words" can't constitute a reason for opposing the decisions of the Warren era because the meaning of constitutional words and phrases is simply not plain in the sense of being uncontroversial when applied to questions like whether segregated public schools deny equal protection, whether legislative apportionments must accord "one person, one vote," and what constitutes a fair criminal trial. Nor, says Dworkin, can Nixon's real reason lie in some general rule to uphold the decisions in prior cases of the Supreme Court, for Nixon and

---

[30.] Dworkin, *supra* note 3, at 131.
[31.] *Id.* at 134.
[32.] *Id.* at 132.

his allies and successors call for overturning *some* prior judicial decisions, like those involving school prayer and abortion.[33]

Perhaps, says Dworkin, the Nixons of this world favor a *strict constructionist* approach to constitutional meaning. In that case, their reason for opposing the Warren Court is to be found in arguments for strict constructionism in constitutional interpretation. In analyzing the meaning of strict constructionism, Dworkin introduces his famous distinction between *concepts* and *conceptions*. His analysis starts by identifying two senses of "strict constructionism," the first being fidelity to the constitutional text, and the second being a narrow view of individual rights against the government.[34] Dworkin contends that these senses of "strict constructionism" are separate and distinct—that, in other words, *fidelity to the constitutional text* neither means nor amounts to *a narrow view of constitutional rights*. To show this, he observes that the First Amendment declares that "Congress shall make no law . . . abridging the freedom of speech" and, accordingly, fidelity to the text as written would invalidate *any law* that restricts speech, certainly any law deliberately designed to restrict speech. Yet "a narrow view of individual rights would permit many such laws, ranging from libel and obscenity laws to the Smith Act," the McCarthy-era law that made it a federal crime to join the Communist Party and to advocate violent overthrow of the government.[35] Dworkin goes on to say that observers who confound these two senses of strict construction do so from a "theory of meaning" that is "too crude."[36]

According to this "crude" theory, the meaning of general constitutional terms like "due process" and "equal protection of the laws" is limited to what the framers of these provisions had concretely in mind at the time they wrote the provisions (recall our analysis of Rehnquist's views). Beyond that, according to the "crude" theory, the most to which a constitutional provision could refer would be things the framers themselves *would have included if they had thought about them*. By this theory, *Brown* was correctly decided only if the framers of the Fourteenth Amendment actually believed that the Amendment outlawed racially segregated public schools or (a fatal concession, as we shall see in Chapter 6)

---

[33]. *Id.*; Engel v. Vitale, 370 U.S. 421 (1962); Abington School District v. Schempp, 374 U.S. 203 (1963); Roe v. Wade, 410 U.S. 113 (1973).

[34]. Dworkin, *supra* note 3, at 133.

[35]. *Id.*

[36]. *Id.* at 134.

if they professed principles that *would have* outlawed racially segregated schools.[37] Dworkin tries to demonstrate the fallacy of this theory of meaning through the following thought experiment:

> Suppose I tell my children simply that I expect them not to treat others unfairly. I no doubt have in mind examples of the conduct I mean to discourage, but I would not accept that my "meaning" was limited to these examples, for two reasons. First I would expect my children to apply my instructions to situations I had not and could not have thought about. Second, I stand ready to admit that some particular act I had thought was fair when I spoke was in fact unfair, or vice versa, if one of my children is able to convince me of that later; in that case I should want to say that my instructions covered the case he cited, not that I had changed my instructions. I might say that I meant the family to be guided by the *concept* of fairness, not by any specific *conception* of fairness I might have had in mind.[38]

On the strength of this thought experiment, Dworkin is able to conclude that judges who would be faithful to the constitutional text would be sensitive to the fact that the grand normative provisions of the Constitution, like "equal protection" and "due process," are written as general *concepts*, not particular *conceptions*. For that reason, judges who seek to be faithful to the *text as written* have no choice but to decide for themselves what these provisions mean for the cases they have to decide.[39] These judges will follow a policy of *judicial activism* (i.e., a policy of deciding for

---

[37] *Id.*

[38] *Id.* (emphasis in original). In developing the distinction between *concepts* and *conceptions*, *id.* at 103, Dworkin cites a well-known article by W. B. Gallie, "Essentially Contested Concepts," *Proceedings of the Aristotelian Society* 56 (1965): 167. Gallie argued that the relevant concepts are "essentially contested": one might interpret him as meaning that we can only choose among conceptions, and that there is no such thing as going for the concept itself. Our version of the concept/conceptions distinction, like that of Dworkin, is very different from such an understanding. Far from saying that concepts are *essentially contested*, we say that concepts are *essentially meaningful*, and that it is a presupposition of ordinary discourse that they are. On our version, as well as on Dworkin's, there are better and worse conceptions of equality, for example, and the different conceptions of equality compete to be the best conception of the concept of equality. The distinction between concepts and conceptions is nobody's property: it belongs to ordinary discourse and it is immediately intelligible to anyone. We, like Dworkin, develop the distinction in a way we regard as useful and intelligible. We thank Larry Solum for pushing us to clarify this point.

[39] Dworkin, *supra* note 3, at 136.

themselves) as opposed to policies of *deferring* either to legislative opinion (statutes) or to the opinions of past judges (precedents). For deferring to others is fidelity to them (albeit perhaps for good reasons), not fidelity to the constitutional text.

Like the father in Dworkin's thought experiment, the framers of general constitutional concepts (along with everyone else, legislators and judges included) have to admit that their conceptions of these concepts can be no more than *mere* conceptions—i.e., conceptions that can be wrong. Fidelity to the general concepts that are actually written in the text therefore requires that, like the children in Dworkin's thought experiment, future interpreters decide constitutional meaning for themselves in a spirit of continuing self-criticism and willingness to change for the better, the better to realize our constitutional commitments.[40] Dworkin points out that had the children's thinking for themselves not been consistent with their father's instructions, he would have meant something quite different from what he said. He would have meant not "treat others fairly," but "do as *I* say fairness demands." In the latter case, what's uppermost in the father's mind isn't fairness or his children's being fair or their reputations for fairness; it's *his authority* over his children.[41]

Dworkin argues that advances in our understanding of the Constitution and of constitutional interpretation require "a fusion" of constitutional law and moral philosophy or political philosophy.[42] We offer our interpretation of this statement in Chapters 5 and 10 (it does not mean recruiting

---

[40.] *Id.* at 136–37.

[41.] *Id.* at 135.

[42.] *Id.* at 149. Dworkin himself spoke of a fusion of constitutional law and "moral theory," but we will use the formulation "moral philosophy." Though "moral theory" or "moral philosophy" might connote the subject of individual ethics, or how an individual ought to live, we employ a more capacious sense of the term. For our purposes here, "moral philosophy" will refer to any systematic and self-critical inquiry into the true meaning or best understanding and application of normative terms in any normative context, including constitutional discourse. "Moral philosophy" will refer also to systematic and self-critical inquiry into the knowability of normative terms, together with the existence of what they are taken to refer to. "Moral philosophy" thus includes questions that can be classified as questions of political philosophy. These questions include inquiry into the relationship between individual persons or citizens and government, the rights and responsibilities of citizens, the obligations of government, the meaning of political and constitutional commitments to equality, liberty, fairness, and the like. We acknowledge overlap between what we're calling moral philosophy and what some call political philosophy. Indeed, Dworkin himself occasionally blurs this distinction by speaking of normative questions of justification in constitutional interpretation as matters of "political morality." *See, e.g.,* Ronald Dworkin, *A Matter of Principle* (Cambridge, MA: Harvard University Press, 1985): 143–45, 165.

philosophers to the bench or applying the teachings of philosophers in doctrinaire ways). But for now we can say that what justifies Dworkin's call for such a fusion is what he has shown to be the Constitution's own require-ment that its interpreters think self-critically for themselves about the meaning of controversial constitutional provisions embodying general concepts. Thinking for yourself indicates philosophy because philosophy is the most refined form of thinking for yourself, and moral and political philosophy are the most refined forms of thinking for yourself about such questions as what makes a father a good father, a trial a fair trial, treatment of persons treatment as equals, and a constitution a good constitution.

But can philosophy answer such questions? Some philosophers say no; they see answers to these questions as essentially arbitrary—that is, as matters of conventional agreement, subjective commitment, or even raw power. The fact that Dworkin first wrote this argument for publication in the *New York Review of Books* is a matter of some significance to this ques-tion. The *Review* is not a specialized scholarly journal. While written mostly by specialists in different fields, the *Review*'s articles are addressed to educated general readers in their capacities as citizens or to lay readers concerning developments in the arts and sciences. Significant also is the openly political aim of Dworkin's article: he wrote to influence the judg-ment of his fellow citizens about matters relating to the practice of judi-cial review. As one citizen speaking to others, Dworkin assumes—and must assume—a background philosophy in which giving and exchanging reasons about political matters makes sense—giving and exchanging reasons as opposed to programming people with propaganda or shout-ing them down. This background philosophy is one that presupposes the possibility of moral truth together with the human capacity to approxi-mate moral truth. By moral truth in the present context we mean propo-sitions about what's right and wrong politically, propositions that can be objectively true or false, objectively closer or further from what's simply right or the best understanding. Dworkin, in this article, thus allows for the possibility of moral facts and moral objectivity. He can imagine admitting that some act he once thought fair could later prove "in fact unfair."[43] He recognizes that "[t]he policy of judicial activism" practiced by the Warren Court "presupposes a certain objectivity of moral principle."[44] And Dworkin takes direct issue with the kind of moral

---

[43]. Dworkin, *supra* note 3, at 134.
[44]. *Id*. at 138.

skepticism in Rehnquist's article when he remarks that "[v]ery few American politicians" would be able publicly to deny the existence of rights against the state—to deny, that is, that popular majorities and their governmental agents are answerable to objective standards of right and wrong.[45]

We would make a slightly stronger statement of this last point. We propose that it's impossible not just for politicians, but for anyone, coherently to deny moral objectivity in any debate over what people ought to believe or how they ought to conduct their affairs. Philosophers have pointed out for thousands of years that skeptics contradict themselves when they say "there is no truth," for that is elliptical for "*it is true that there is no truth.*" The same applies to people who say or assume that (it is true that) we ought to conform our beliefs or our conduct to the truth that no "ought" statement can be true or false. Those who deny moral objectivity in any political debate invariably contradict themselves. We have seen this contradiction in Rehnquist's argument. Try as he might to assert that there is no demonstrable moral truth, he ends up assuming not only that democracy is (truly) a real good but that his controversial conception of democracy is objectively superior to its competitors. We are not claiming, the reader should note, that there categorically *is* a moral reality or, for that matter, any reality about which anyone can be objectively better or worse informed. We're divided on this ancient and complex philosophic question. What we are saying is that *no one can successfully deny the possibility* of moral objectivity in any conversation about how we ought to conduct our affairs, including conversations about how judges or other interpreters of the Constitution ought to perform their duties. What is more, the very enterprise of constitutional interpretation presupposes that responsible, conscientious interpreters are seeking the true meaning or best interpretation of the Constitution.[46] And if one can't deny the possibility of moral truth or the moral character of constitutional terms like "equal protection" and "due process"—or that constitutional interpretation presupposes that interpreters are seeking the true

---

45. *Id.* at 138–39.
46. As stated in Chapter 1, in speaking of interpreters seeking the Constitution's true meaning or best interpretation, we are making a claim about the *presuppositions* of constitutional interpretation, not what some readers might interpret as an "ontological" claim that there *is* a moral reality. Moreover, we have written this book to be agnostic between moral realism and constructivism (or deep conventionalism).

meaning or best interpretation of the Constitution—then there's reason to consider Dworkin's call for a fusion of constitutional law and moral philosophy. We shall revisit this subject.

Returning now to Dworkin's thought experiment, we ask why he can be so confident that the experiment is a success. How can he be sure his readers will agree that any father would want to be understood as interested, not in his authority over his children, but in his children's welfare, elements of which would be their fairness and their reputations for fairness? (Remember Dworkin's point: if the father intends the *concept* of fairness, he's interested in fairness and wants to cultivate this virtue in his children; if, however, he intends no more than *his conception* of fairness, he's interested in his authority over his children.) Dworkin assumes we would all agree that the difference between these two possibilities is the difference between a good father and, at least in one respect, a bad father. In this way, Dworkin indicates something about the process of interpreting authority generally: persons faithful to some authority will try to interpret its pronouncements in ways that preserve its goodness. So we would interpret the words of a father in a manner informed by a background idea of what makes for a good father—and, presumably, we would interpret a constitution in an analogous way, by an idea of what makes for a good constitution. As Dworkin came to put it in subsequent work, the commitment to fidelity to the Constitution entails that we should interpret it so as to make it the best it can be.[47]

Dworkin was far from being the first philosopher to notice this principle of interpretation. In Plato's *Apology of Socrates*, we find Socrates trying to make sense of the statement of the Oracle at Delphi that "no man is wiser than Socrates."[48] Socrates is puzzled by the statement because he knows that he knows nothing. Yet he wants to believe that no god, being a god, can lie, so he seeks an interpretation of the god's statement that would reconcile his sense that he knows nothing with what he wants to believe about the god's truthfulness. After a lengthy and fruitless search for someone wiser than himself, Socrates finds the reconciliation he seeks in the fact that whereas he knows that he is ignorant, others think they know something when they actually don't. Socrates thus

---

[47.] Ronald Dworkin, *Law's Empire* (Cambridge, MA: Harvard University Press, 1986): 176–275; Dworkin, *supra* note 42, at 146–66.

[48.] Plato, *Apology of Socrates*, 20e–23b.

proves to be the wisest after all, just as the god said. Socrates knows that he does not know, whereas others think they know but don't, and that must be what the god meant.

The father in Dworkin's thought experiment stands to his children as the Constitution's framers ("the founding fathers") stand to us—we being what the Preamble of the Constitution refers to as the "Posterity" of the founding generation. Like the father in Dworkin's thought experiment, the founding generation expresses an interest not in its authority over its posterity, but in the latter's well-being, that is, in our well-being. Thus, the Constitution refers to itself as ordained and established for the sake of ends like "the common defence" and "the general Welfare." True, Article VI does refer to the Constitution as "the supreme law of the land," but what is declared law is an instrument of such goods as the common defense and the general welfare. And, again like the father in Dworkin's thought experiment, the Constitution acknowledges its fallibility by allowing (in Article V) for amendments and by promising (in the First Amendment's protection of freedom of speech) that constitutional government won't silence its critics. To the extent that the relationship of our generation to the Constitution parallels the child-parent relationship in Dworkin's thought experiment, a practice of judicial independence and "activism" may be both a precondition and a mandate of the Constitution—essential to our ability to make sense of the Constitution as a good constitution, dedicated to what it expressly says it's dedicated to (as opposed to being dedicated to following the authority of the founding fathers as such).

To this point, we have been focusing on one aspect of the basic question *What* is the Constitution: whether it is a code of concrete historical conceptions (Rehnquist's view) or a charter of abstract moral concepts (as Dworkin argues). One's answer to this question has important implications for one's answer to the question *How* should we interpret the Constitution. In the next chapter, we take up another aspect of the *What* question: Does the Constitution embody a positive constitutionalism— empowering government to pursue certain ends or positive benefits—or a negative constitutionalism—primarily limiting government to protect people from government? In considering this question, we'll offer an account of the principal features of the American constitutional order.

CHAPTER 3

THE PRINCIPAL FEATURES OF THE AMERICAN CONSTITUTIONAL ORDER: THE POSITIVE CONSTITUTIONALISM OF *THE FEDERALIST*

Comment on *The Federalist* is appropriate in any book on constitutional interpretation. Those who don't know that work may assume it is largely irrelevant to modern questions of constitutional law because most of these questions concern the meaning and strength of constitutional rights that were adopted as amendments to the Constitution after *The Federalist* was written. But *The Federalist* contains an account of the larger whole of the Constitution and the constitutional order of which the amendments are parts. What is more, *The Federalist*, now in its third century as the most influential interpretation of the Constitution, warrants some discussion by virtue of this status alone. Our reading of Ronald Dworkin has already exposed one aim of constitutional interpretation—to cast the Constitution in its most favorable light, to make it the best it can be.[1] We can test whether this is a genuine aim of constitutional interpretation by seeing if it is manifest in our most famous example of constitutional interpretation.

The Federalist is a collection of newspaper essays authored in 1787–88 by Alexander Hamilton, James Madison, and John Jay in support of ratification of the Constitution.[2] In this book we'll refer to these authors by the collective pen name they chose for themselves, "Publius." We do so not just for convenience, but because we want to focus the reader's attention on the authors' arguments and away from their personalities and political biographies. Our interest in their arguments is shaped by the

---

[1] *See* Chapter 2.
[2] *The Federalist*, ed. Jacob E. Cooke (Middletown, CT: Wesleyan University Press, 1961).

enterprise at hand. The ultimate aim of constitutional interpretation is to make sense of what the Constitution says, and by "making sense" we mean seeing for ourselves why anyone would voluntarily adopt the Constitution as supreme law. *The Federalist* tries to answer this question not only for the founding generation but also for subsequent generations, and the soundness of that answer has nothing to do with the personalities advancing it. We focus on the broad substantive themes of *The Federalist*, what it can teach about the nature of constitutional interpretation, and what it says about the principal features of the American constitutional order.

I. The Instrumental Nature of the Constitution

Publius opens in a way that confirms the principle that interpretation should cast its object in a favorable light. Instead of describing the Constitution as the result of its political origins—the bargains and compromises of the Constitutional Convention in Philadelphia during the summer of 1787—*Federalist* 1 presents the Constitution as a means to the preservation of the Union and the enhancement of the nation's "liberty, . . . dignity, . . . and happiness."[3] Publius emphasizes the need for strong government on the theory that "the vigour of government is essential to the security of liberty; that, in the contemplation of a sound and well informed judgment, their interests can never be separated."[4] Fully cognizant of the "powerful . . . causes, which serve to give a false bias to the judgment" on either side of virtually any political issue, Publius nevertheless appeals to the "patriotism" and "philanthropy" of his readers when calling on them to demonstrate "by their conduct and example" the feasibility of what he takes to be a universal human aspiration: rising above "accident and force" and "establishing good government from reflection and choice."[5]

What's most remarkable about this opening of *The Federalist* is its contrast with what is today conventional wisdom about the Constitution's basic normative character. Both Dworkin and Rehnquist (whose positions we examined in Chapter 2), despite their profound differences, seem to assume that the Constitution's basic point is to *limit* government in

---

3. *The Federalist* No. 1, at 6.
4. *Id.* at 5–6.
5. *Id.* at 3.

behalf of protecting liberty and other rights *against* government.[6] In this sense, they presuppose a *negative constitutionalism*. Perhaps their view is explained by their careers as lawyers, judges, or teachers of lawyers and judges, for the legal class is interested mostly in litigation, and the typical question in constitutional litigation is whether some part of government has exceeded its authority. Yet Publius is not asking this question. He is a constitution maker, not a litigator, and he wants to *establish* a government. His focus therefore is on why one would want a government in the first place: and no rational person would want a government chiefly for the sake of limiting that government.[7] Like the language of the Constitution's Preamble, Publius's emphasis is on strong government and the *good things* or positive benefits to be secured or facilitated through strong government.[8] By numbering liberty among these good things, he suggests liberty in a well-ordered society—liberty in what, on the eve of the Civil War, Abraham Lincoln was to call "laudable pursuits"[9]—a category whose terms exclude socially harmful liberties, like (we would say) the liberty to enslave persons, to "secede" from the obligations of citizenship, or (in terms of a landmark case during the New Deal) to subsidize a "labor market" that permits mere subsistence wages or less, in derogation of the obligation that "[t]he bare cost of living must be met," if necessary, by the government.[10] *The Federalist* thus embraces a *positive constitutionalism* that prefigures the constitutionalism of Lincoln and the New Deal.

The next block of papers, up to *Federalist* 9, concentrates on the bad things that would result from failure to ratify the proposed constitution. These evils range from vulnerability to foreign powers and civil war at

---

6. For Dworkin's assumption that the basic point of the Constitution is to limit government by protecting individual rights, see, for example, Ronald Dworkin, *Taking Rights Seriously* (Cambridge, MA: Harvard University Press, 1977): 266–78. Rehnquist articulates a conception of the Constitution as a charter of negative liberties protecting individuals against government in his opinion of the Court in DeShaney v. Winnebago County Department of Social Services, 489 U.S. 189 (1989).

7. This may be why Publius says nothing about limiting government in *Federalist* 1 and comparatively little about it in the rest of the book.

8. *See* Sotirios A. Barber, *Welfare and the Constitution* (Princeton, NJ: Princeton University Press, 2003) (defending a positive benefits conception of the Constitution as distinguished from a negative liberties conception).

9. Abraham Lincoln, "Message to Congress in Special Session, July 4, 1861," in *Abraham Lincoln: His Speeches and Writings*, ed. Roy P. Basler (New York: World Publishing Co., 1946): 594, 607.

10. West Coast Hotel v. Parrish, 300 U.S. 379, 399 (1937).

home to failure to discharge the war debt and open the Mississippi to American shipping. Here Publius discusses problems arising both from sources peculiar to the nation's situation in the 1780s and from causes "which have a general and almost constant operation upon the collective bodies of society." He traces all these problems to the "ambitious, vindictive, and rapacious" nature of man,[11] a view whose truth is for our purposes secondary to what it indicates about his basic understanding of the character of the Constitution. Publius's theme is the Constitution's *instrumental* nature—it aims to avoid bad things and to pursue good things.

Federalist 9 starts a discussion of the problem that "domestic faction" has posed to popular governments since ancient Greece: "perpetual vibration, between the extremes of tyranny and anarchy."[12] Publius sees hope for ending this pattern in "the efficacy of various principles" of a recently improved "science of politics." He lists four of these principles: "distribution of power into distinct departments . . . legislative balances and checks . . . judges holding their offices during good behavior . . . [and] representation of the people in the legislature by deputies of their own election."[13] A remarkable feature of this list is the equal ranking accorded to an independent judiciary, a ranking made sensible by the theory of *responsible government* he sets forth in *Federalist* 63, to be discussed. To the list of four principles he then adds one important enough for him to write in capital letters: "I mean," he says, "the ENLARGEMENT of the ORBIT within which such systems [popular governments] are to revolve." This is Publius's introduction to *Federalist* 10. This most famous number of *The Federalist* argues that the "enlargement of the orbit"—or an extended republic—is more than just another principle of the new science of politics; it is a necessary condition for the success of all the other principles.

II. The 10th *Federalist*

The basic argument of the 10th *Federalist* is well known: The violence of domestic faction must be controlled if popular government is to survive. Of the two possible strategies for controlling faction, the first, the destruction of political liberty, is worse than the disease, and destroying

---

11. *The Federalist* No. 6, at 28–29.
12. *The Federalist* No. 9, at 50.
13. *Id.* at 51.

diversity (by cultivating in every person "the same opinions, passions, and interests") is "impracticable" because the causes of diverse opinions, passions, and interests are "sown in the nature of man."[14] This leaves the second, more feasible, strategy, controlling the effects of faction, and that, Publius argues, can best be accomplished in a large representative republic where the opinions of popular majorities are refined through elections of smaller bodies of legislative representatives, and where the discipline of coalition building across many interests enhances prospects of legislation in the common good and respect for the rights of minorities. In the course of this argument, Publius defines "faction" in a way that implies standards of human rights and good public policy that (*pace* Rehnquist)[15] do not depend on majority opinion, and he indicates that the defense of popular government depends on reconciling it to those higher standards. Moreover, he contemplates that (*contra* Rehnquist) a majority can constitute a faction if it is acting contrary to the common good. Publius wrote: "By a faction I understand a number of citizens, whether amounting to a majority or minority of the whole, who are united and actuated by some common impulse of passion, or of interest, adverse to the rights of other citizens, or to the permanent and aggregate interests of the community."[16] He also emphasizes the importance of society's economic divisions. Of this he says three things: (1) "[T]he various and unequal distribution of property" is the "most common and durable source of faction," even more common and durable than differences in religion and political ideology, as strong and potentially calamitous as they are; (2) regulating "these various and interfering [economic] interests forms the principal task of modern Legislation"; and (3) "the protection of different and unequal faculties of acquiring property" is the "first object of Government."[17]

The problems of Publius's argument in *Federalist* 10 are well known. "Value-free" social scientists have complained about Publius's definition of faction, arguing, in morally skeptical fashion, that there can be no standards of good public policy and minority rights beyond what popular majorities decide.[18] This is essentially Rehnquist's position, and it need not detain us long. For if the skeptics are right, there can be no reason for

---

[14.] *The Federalist* No. 10, at 58.
[15.] *See* Chapter 2.
[16.] *The Federalist* No. 10, at 57.
[17.] *Id.* at 57–59.
[18.] *See, e.g.,* Robert A. Dahl, *A Preface to Democratic Theory* (Chicago: University of Chicago Press, 1956): 25–32.

advancing their position, believing it, or acting on it. Democracy can't serve as their reason unless the meaning of "democracy" is something popular majorities can't determine at will and unless the goodness or rightness of democracy is something popular majorities can't deny (as they seem to do when surrendering their affairs to tyrants, an experience of every era). Yet if the meaning and goodness of democracy is beyond the power of majorities to decide, then the skeptics are wrong to deny all meaning and goodness beyond democratic control. And if the meaning and goodness of democracy is beyond popular determination, why can't the same be true of things like liberty, justice, and happiness?

More worthy of our attention is criticism advanced more than a generation ago by Martin Diamond, who (like Socrates confronting the Oracle, discussed in Chapter 2) at once criticized and looked up to Publius. Diamond made a crucial observation: largeness does not guarantee pluralism—Publius can't just assume that movement from a small republic to a large one will automatically produce the political pluralism on which his solution to the problem of majority faction depends.[19] A large territory with a large population could be the setting for political polarization along any number of lines, like race, wealth, and religion. Whether a nation's interest groups are pluralist or polarized depends on how people see themselves politically. What makes Publius so sure Americans will see themselves chiefly in terms of economic interests and not as Catholics against Protestants, blacks against whites, rich against poor? A related problem is Publius's view of modern government's "principal task," which he says is regulating economic conflict. This kind of conflict arises from "the various and unequal distribution of property," which he calls "the most common and durable source of faction." But he also recognizes other sources of social division, like "a zeal for different opinions concerning religion, concerning government, and many other points."[20] Why doesn't he recognize the need to regulate these other kinds of conflict? Will it be enough to leave them to the state governments when the whole point of *Federalist* 10 is that the state governments can't do as well as the national government in controlling the effects of majority factions? If the states could handle the problem of majority religious and ideological factions, what would disable them from dealing with majority economic

---

[19.] Martin Diamond, "*The Federalist*," in *History of Political Philosophy*, ed. Leo Strauss and Joseph Cropsey, 2nd ed (Chicago: Rand McNally, 1972): 631, 648.

[20.] *The Federalist* No. 10, at 58.

factions? Does Publius contradict himself by implicitly relying on the states to address major problems of social division while claiming that they can't handle the problem of majority factions? Is his theory adequate to the full range of problems that he identifies?

We could either give up on Publius at this point or try to find a way to extricate him from his difficulties. To do the latter we might ask an interpretive question of the kind Socrates asked regarding the puzzling words of the Oracle: What are the conditions under which Publius can assume (1) that the large republic will be pluralist and not polarized and (2) that regulating economic conflict at the national level will ameliorate non-economic divisions nationwide? If we find answers to these questions, we must also ask (3) how can the nation achieve and maintain those conditions? In explicating those conditions, we draw upon and expand Diamond's classic analysis.

III. The Large Commercial Republic

The conditions, in short, are those of a large commercial republic.[21] The system outlined in *Federalist* 10 is one in which political interest groups form and reform different social and legislative coalitions that exclude no stable minority for long. Diamond showed that the people who belong in this picture must (1) live in an *urban-industrial society,* for our picture is one of many political interest groups, and an urban-industrial society features many ways to make a living and pursue economic advancement. Where there are few paths to security and wealth, as in an agrarian society, there can't be many economic groups and therefore there can't be many political interest groups that define themselves chiefly in economic terms. A people who see their political interests in terms of their economic interests are more-or-less (2) *a materialistic people.* They want coercive government to secure their physical security and to promote their material well-being. If they care for the salvation of their souls as individuals, they won't insist that the government actively promote or compel the salvation of their neighbors' souls. This makes them appear (3) *religiously and ideologically tolerant.* These people will be (4) *a democratic people* in several ways.

[21.] For a recent reconstruction of Publius's theory of the large commercial republic, *see* Stephen L. Elkin, *Reconstructing the Commercial Republic: Constitutional Design after Madison* (Chicago: University of Chicago Press, 2006).

They will support the idea of (a) *equal economic opportunity* regardless of race, class, religion, and gender, lest the society polarize along these lines. They will value (b) *equal political opportunity* for the same reason.

To avoid polarization and the politics of resentment, the typical citizen of this large commercial republic must have evidence that his or her achievements reflect more or less what he or she has been willing to work for. This evidence can only take the form of (5) *upward (or downward) mobility, for people who start poor (or rich), and a fair distribution of wealth and status* across lines of race, religion, and gender. A poor man who is black must know (or know of) many blacks who are not poor in order to believe that racism isn't a cause of his poverty. He must see poor people become rich and rich people become poor in order to feel that people generally have what they deserve. Such a society would also have to be (6) *a wealthy society*, for much wealth would be needed to feed the economic ambitions of everyone willing to work and to convince people that the system is basically fair in practice, not just in theory. To this Diamond added with caution that perhaps the wealth of this society would have to increase more or less indefinitely—that the society would have to be committed to (7) *ever-expanding personal and national wealth*.[22]

Diamond seemed less comfortable than some of his associates about this last condition of the large commercial republic. Like Tocqueville, he was concerned with whether the individualistic or self-regarding outlook fostered by democracy and commercialism was compatible with self-government and public-spirited citizenship.[23] Indeed, one might well worry that a commitment to unending economic growth eventually leads to a global market whose institutions are beyond the control of any government, economic polarization at home (a growing "income gap") exacerbated if not caused by capital flight to cheaper labor markets first at home and then abroad, and the violent resentment of anti-Western cultures targeted as markets for Western goods and the ideas that come with them. This last prospect has become especially dangerous as technological innovation and interdependence have created the profoundly vulnerable homeland revealed to Americans on September 11, 2001.

---

22. For Diamond's original account of "the large commercial republic," *see* Diamond, *supra* note 19, at 648–50.
23. Martin Diamond, *As Far as Republican Principles Will Admit: Essays by Martin Diamond,* ed. William Schambra (Washington, DC: AEI Press, 1992): 159–61 (commenting on Alexis de Tocqueville, *Democracy in America* (1840): Vol. II, Part II, Chapter 4).

We mention doubts about the seventh condition to underscore the provisional nature of any theory of the Constitution's substantive ends. We're not contending that the features of the large commercial republic define the ends to which the Preamble to the Constitution is dedicated. Those features do seem necessary if the system outlined in the 10th *Federalist* is to work, and for that reason they can serve as conceptions of preambulary ends like justice and the general welfare. But these conceptions—and here we adopt Dworkin's sense of that term (discussed in Chapter 2)—are mere conceptions; better conceptions may be available. It's hardly beyond contention, for example, that well-being is adequately conceived in terms of wealth and the faculties and opportunities for acquiring it. Wealth, after all, is no more than a good that is extrinsic to the intrinsic goods that it buys or enables, like pleasure or health or mobility or wisdom. Would billions in the bank rescue Midas or Scrooge from his misery? Have people been better off, and may they again be better off, in settings that define well-being largely in terms of spiritual achievement? Would people be happier, as some current research suggests, with less economic mobility and more stable families, friendships, and communities?[24]

Assume that the Constitution is what it says it is—an instrument of ends like the peoples' welfare—and acknowledge the gap between any conception of well-being and the real thing, and you may conclude that people who are really well off are people with the capacity to do what the founding generation did: assess their problems and fashion new institutions accordingly. A constitution adequate to real ends (and to pursuing the best understanding of its ends) will preserve the capacity for constructive social and governmental change—including constitutional change. Whether Americans still have this capacity is something we can doubt.[25]

---

24. *See* Robert E. Lane, *The Loss of Happiness in Market Democracies* (New Haven, CT: Yale University Press, 2000): 3–10, 19–31, 60–76, 88–98, 102–19.

25. Many have criticized Article V of the Constitution for its stringent requirements for formal amendments to the Constitution. *See, e.g.*, Sanford Levinson, *Our Undemocratic Constitution* (New York: Oxford University Press, 2006): 20–24. Lawrence Sager argues that the obduracy of Article V to ready and easy amendment of the Constitution has encouraged and fostered "wide-bodied" interpretation of the Constitution's rights-protecting and power-conferring provisions. Lawrence G. Sager, *Justice in Plainclothes: A Theory of American Constitutional Practice* (New Haven, CT: Yale University Press, 2004): 76–77, 214–19. Such obduracy has underscored the character of the Constitution as a charter of generalities and abstract principles as opposed to a code of specific original intentions, meanings, or applications. Thus, Article V has underwritten approaches to constitutional interpretation like Sager's justice-seeking constitutionalism and what we will call the philosophic approach.

But this element of national well-being—the capacity for constructive change—entails that the ends of government include some freedoms of speech, press, political association, religious association, academic inquiry, and all that accompanies them, like political and social diversity and commitments to toleration and a politics of public reasonableness. Seen in this light, freedoms of speech, religion, and the rest are not mere limitations on our collective power as a people: they are elements of that power, for without them we can't pursue real as opposed to merely apparent goods. Like the admirable father in Dworkin's thought experiment,[26] our attitudes and actions confirm that we're really interested in what we say we're interested in: fairness itself, not our conceptions of it. When we tell our children to be fair to others, we would never admit that what we are really doing is trying to assert our authority over them. This is why we wouldn't want to be understood as insisting on our mere conceptions of fairness. Our instructions would thus be those of a good parent: an educational effort motivated by a desire that our children be the best they can be, not an authoritarian or narcissistic effort to make them chips off the old block.

The American Constitution reflects this general view of the world and humanity's place in it. An artifact of the Western tradition, the Constitution preserves an appreciation of human fallibility and the normativity of higher authority (either "nature" or "nature's God") which is common to both the humanist and biblical branches of that tradition. An element of that tradition at least since Homer's time has been pride in a people's ability to acknowledge and provide for the fact that its beliefs and practices may be wrong. The larger community typically becomes aware of that fact through the agency of some individual like Socrates or unpopular minority like the Abolitionists of the nineteenth century and the civil rights leaders of the twentieth century. When individuals or minorities brave "the perils of the community's displeasure" and change the public's mind about the meaning of its commitments and aspirations, the community ultimately honors them as benefactors or even heroes.[27] Indeed, Publius alludes to Socrates in several places.[28] Because the West from the beginning has valued truth over convention and associated the dissenting individual with truth, the individual has had a potential for dignity.

[26.] *See* Chapter 2.
[27.] *The Federalist* No. 71, at 483.
[28.] *The Federalist* Nos. 63, 71.

Recognition of this potential is reflected in American law, especially in the Bill of Rights and the Civil War Amendments.

In sum: we might provisionally conceive the ends of government listed in the Preamble as aspects of the large commercial republic (e.g., growth, equal opportunity, prosperity, fair distribution of wealth and opportunity, upward mobility, and the like). They include security for rights associated with truth-seeking in political decision (like freedom of speech) and the administration of criminal and civil justice (like procedural due process). They involve respect for potential agents of the truth: individuals and minorities who can stand apart from conventional wisdom and teach the community something better or challenge it to respect its best judgment and honor its own commitments and aspirations.

IV. Energy and Responsible Government

From the 10th *Federalist*, our brief account of *The Federalist* turns to No. 15 and Publius's central criticism of the Articles of Confederation. We know in a general way that the Articles were inadequate to the country's needs. If we could learn more of the specifics, we could better appreciate the structure of the government proposed under the Constitution, for we can assume that the new government is designed to avoid the defects of the old.

Federalist 15 discusses "the great and radical vice in the construction" or "structure" of the Articles, which is that the Continental Congress passes laws that apply not directly to individual citizens, but to the several states.[29] Under the Articles, Congress's laws take the form of requests or "requisitions" to the state legislatures, requisitions for things like their individual share of the money Congress needs to pay down the war debt, support ambassadors and embassies abroad, protect settlers on the western borders, and pay the salaries and expenses of legislative and administrative officials at home. Because these requisitions are not backed by credible threats of force against noncompliance, the states don't respond fully and in a timely fashion, and Congress's aims are frustrated. Behind this structural vice, Publius identifies a philosophic mistake: faith that

---

[29.] *The Federalist* No. 15, at 93.

voluntary compliance to law is sufficiently attractive to dispense with effective and credible threats of force against the noncompliant. This pair of structural-philosophic mistakes has deprived the Confederation of what Publius calls "the energy and efficiency of government."[30]

The need for strong government is Publius's leading concern precisely because he is a positive constitutionalist. That is, Publius conceives the Constitution as an instrument imposing positive obligations upon government to pursue certain ends; it is not a charter of negative liberties whose primary aim is to limit government in order to protect the people from government.[31] The very first sentence of the 1st *Federalist* calls for a new constitution to correct "the inefficacy of the subsisting Foederal Government."[32] We have seen that Publius accompanies this call with an important claim that "the vigour of government is essential to the security of liberty; that, in the contemplation of a sound and well informed judgment, their interests can never be separated; and that a dangerous ambition more often lurks behind the specious mask of zeal for the rights of the people, than under the forbidden appearance of zeal for the firmness and efficiency of government."[33] The 15th *Federalist* reminds us of this opening theme and prompts two questions: (1) What or who will supply energy in government? and (2) To what ends will this energy be directed?

Diamond answered the second of these questions with his theory of the large commercial republic and its associated ends: government in America will aim at the social conditions for the successful working of constitutional institutions; these social conditions include a growing economy, a people that values equal economic and political opportunity, and a sense in the community that people have more or less what they've been willing to work for. Diamond's friend and colleague, Herbert Storing, answered the first question: Publius puts the President in the best position to exercise the initiatives of government; the Constitution is a plan for *presidential* government.[34]

---

30. *Id.*
31. Publius's vision is contrary to Rehnquist's "negative liberties" vision in *DeShaney. See supra* note 6.
32. *The Federalist* No. 1, at 3.
33. *Id.* at 5–6.
34. Herbert J. Storing, "The Problem of Big Government," in *A Nation of States: Essays on the American Federal System,* ed. Robert A. Goldwin (Chicago: Rand McNally, 1974): 67.

The kind of energy discussed in *Federalist* 15 and elaborated in the next several papers is a *negative energy*, energy to enforce the law against people who disobey. Energy of a different kind emerges as Publius turns to the specific powers granted to the new government, powers in the sense of authorizations to enact specific kinds of laws (like regulations of commerce) or to take certain kinds of actions (like declaring war). In the beginning of *Federalist* 22, Publius defends the power to regulate commerce in Article I, § 8 in terms of the benefits to the nation of stable trade and financial dealings with foreign nations and among the states of the Union. He goes on to justify "the power of raising armies" in terms of "a vigorous and . . . oeconomical system of [national] defence."[35] The logic of these references is made explicit in *Federalist* 23: *powers are granted for the sake of pursuing ends.* In this number Publius can barely restrain his impatience with critics who say the new government will have too much power. He responds that critics must first decide what they want from the new government. If they want that government to provide national defense, a stable national market, and favorable economic and political relations with other nations, then it follows "that that government ought to be cloathed with all the powers requisite to the complete execution of its trust."[36] This conclusion, he says, "rests upon axioms as simple as they are universal: The *means* ought to be proportional to the *end*. The persons, from whose agency the attainment of any *end* is expected, ought to possess the *means* by which it is to be attained." He goes on to say that how much power may be needed is "*impossible to foresee*" because of "*the extent and variety of national exigencies, or the corresponding extent & variety of the means which may be necessary to satisfy them*" (his emphasis). He applies this proposition not only to national defense, where it would be more acceptable to more people, but also "to commerce, and to every other matter to which its [the new government's] jurisdiction is permitted to extend."[37] So here we find a *positive energy*: energy for passing laws and taking actions in pursuit of the desiderata for which the government was instituted.

Publius recognizes that power in government, while essential, is also risky, for power can be abused. His answer for this difficulty is not to withhold power from the new government, but to arrange the "internal

---

[35] *The Federalist* No. 22, at 137.
[36] *The Federalist* No. 23, at 147.
[37] *Id.* at 147, 149.

structure" of the government in ways that make abuses of power less likely and more easily detected and remedied.[38] When Publius completes his lengthy discussion of "the general mass of power allotted" to the new government, he turns to the government's "internal structure" and the Constitution's "distribution of this mass of power among its [the government's] constituent parts."[39]

Federalist 47 begins this inquiry by acknowledging that the "accumulation of all powers, legislative, executive, and judiciary, in the same hands, whether of one, a few, or many, and whether hereditary, self appointed, or elective, may justly be pronounced the very definition of tyranny."[40] How to keep the several parts of the government in their prescribed places is now Publius's question. He goes on to reject several answers that depend on some form of citizen or official virtue. He will rely neither on the law-abidingness of elected officials (*Federalist* 48) nor on the public's devotion to constitutional boundaries (*Federalist* 49, 50). "[P]ower is of an encroaching nature," he says in No. 48, too strong to be restrained by mere "parchment barriers."[41] And though, says *Federalist* 49, "it seems strictly consonant to the republican theory to recur to the same original authority [i.e., the people] not only . . . to . . . new-model the powers of government; but also whenever any one of the departments [of government] may commit encroachments on the chartered authorities of the others," in the end the people's judgment "could never be expected to turn on the true merits" of a constitutional conflict among the branches of government.[42] Appeal to the people insures that "the *passions* . . . not *the reason*, of the public would sit in judgment," for the people's judgment "would inevitably be connected with the spirit of pre-existing parties . . . springing out of the question itself."[43]

Publius's solution to the problem of "maintaining in practice the separation [of powers] delineated on paper"[44] is announced in *Federalist* 51: "to divide and arrange the several offices [of government] in such a manner as that each may be a check on the other." This system of mutual checks is not one in which virtue checks ambition; it is one in which

---

38. *The Federalist* No. 51, at 347–49.
39. *The Federalist* No. 47, at 323.
40. *Id.* at 324.
41. *The Federalist* No. 48, at 332, 333.
42. *The Federalist* No. 49, at 339, 342.
43. *Id.* at 342–43.
44. *The Federalist* No. 47, at 331.

"[a]mbition must be made to counteract ambition." It "consists in giving to those who administer each department, the necessary constitutional means, and personal motives, to resist encroachments of the others." In this way "the private interests of every individual, may be a centinel over the public rights."[45]

This famous theory of checks and balances is widely assumed to express a negative view of government. Its focus is not on the good things facilitated by government, like national security and a stable national economy; its concern is with the abuse of governmental power and how to prevent it. Checks and balances are thus often linked with other forms of restraints on national power, like the articles of the Bill of Rights and what many see as the Tenth Amendment's guarantee of "states' rights" against federal encroachment. But Publius's theory of checks and balances is (1) part of a larger constitutional theory whose general thrust is clearly positive and, as Storing observed, a closer look at the theory reveals (2) a connection to the positive theme of *energy in government for the sake of good things*.[46] Regarding the first point, recall that Publius sees checks and balances as an alternative to withholding power from the new government. In his scheme the system of checks and balances presupposes the strong government needed to enact and enforce the laws pursuant to constitutional ends. Because it presupposes strong government, the system of checks and balances is not antithetical to strong government; it restrains government in the sense of directing it to its proper ends.

Regarding the second point, Publius has more in mind than "giv[ing] to each department an equal power of self defence."[47] Looking back on the nation's experience with the state governments under the Articles of Confederation, Publius's great fear is the overbearing power of legislatures that harm the public's long-term good by being too responsive to the public's immediate demands. "The legislative power," he says in *Federalist* 48, "is every where extending the sphere of its activity, and drawing all power into its impetuous vortex."[48] In the same number, Publius cites Thomas Jefferson's observation to similar effect and quotes

---

45. *The Federalist* No. 51, at 349. Some have argued that Publius's political theory of separation of powers and checks and balances is anachronistic in light of the development of political parties. *See, e.g.,* Daryl J. Levinson & Richard H. Pildes, "Separation of Parties, Not Powers," *Harvard Law Review* 119 (2006): 2311.

46. *See* Storing, *supra* note 34, at 83.

47. *The Federalist* No. 51, at 350.

48. *The Federalist* No. 48, at 333.

Jefferson's famous remark that "'An *elective despotism*, was not the government we fought for.'"[49] So when Publius turns to the question of how to divide power among the branches, he says in *Federalist* 51 that it will not be sufficient "to give to each department an equal power of self defence . . . [for] [i]n republican government the legislative authority, necessarily, predominates."[50] His "remedy for this inconvenience" is essentially to divide and weaken Congress vis-à-vis the President and to strengthen the President vis-à-vis Congress. An element of this strategy is a President whose tenure and power are largely independent of Congress. And this independent executive power will prove to be the chief source of energy in the new government.

This is not to deprecate the importance either of Congress or of the legislative process, for the President has a major part in the legislative process, and the President can't achieve lasting aims unless they are embodied in or supported by laws that only Congress can enact (leaving aside executive orders). But the Constitution designs a bicameral federal legislature that moves slowly to its conclusions by virtue of the different institutional cultures of its two bodies and the compromises normally needed to unite groups with different interests into shifting majorities. The slowness of this process is functional because it enhances prospects of legislation that is sound and fair and for the common good. But the slowness of the legislative process is not good when the nation needs to move forward in a hurry or in times of legislative gridlock—the times when government is needed most. So after Publius discusses the defects of the Articles, the powers of the new government, and the structure of Congress, he returns to the subject of energy in *Federalist* 70, one of eleven papers devoted to the executive power of the new government.

The beginning of No. 70 is one of the most dramatic and telling parts of *The Federalist*, and it deserves special attention. Here Publius says in effect that if a strong executive is incompatible with democracy, then democracy is indefensible. "Energy in the executive," he says, "is a leading character in the definition of good government," essential to a range of objects, foreign and domestic, from national defense to the security of property and liberty at home.[51] How strong an executive might be needed for these objects Publius doesn't say, but in a most remarkable

---

49. *Id.* at 335 (Publius's emphasis).
50. *The Federalist* No. 51, at 350.
51. *The Federalist* No. 70, at 471.

comment for a republican statesman, Publius notes with apparent approval how often Rome "was obliged to take refuge in the absolute power of a single man, under the formidable title of dictator."[52] Without "multiply[ing] arguments or examples on this head," says Publius, "[a] feeble executive implies a feeble execution of the government. A feeble execution is but another phrase for a bad execution. And a government ill executed, whatever it may be in theory, must be in practice a bad government." He then lists the several "ingredients which constitute energy in the executive" (unity, duration, adequate support, competent powers)[53] and proceeds to discuss each of them over the next several papers.

It is clear by this point in Publius's argument that he regards *energy in the executive* as essential to *energy in government*. But that the former is the leading source of the latter may not be clear, for an energetic executive may mean a vigorous and faithful execution of policies made by some superior authority. Publius dispels this notion in *Federalist 71*. Here he observes that some people "regard the servile pliancy of the executive to a prevailing current, either in the community, or in the Legislature, as its best recommendation." "But such men," he says, "entertain very crude notions, as well of the purposes for which government was instituted, as of the true means by which the public happiness may be promoted." He then argues that while "[t]he republican principle" may require that public opinion shall ultimately control the government, it does not require "an unqualified complaisance" on the part of government "to every sudden breese of [popular] passion . . . or . . . impulse."[54] On those occasions "when the interests [i.e., the true interests] of the people are at variance with their inclinations, it is the duty of the persons whom they have appointed to be the guardians of those interests, to withstand the temporary delusion, in order to give time and opportunity for more cool and sedate reflection."[55] And Publius speaks here not only for himself, but also for the people, or at least for a people sufficiently worthy to establish a government for themselves and future generations. "[T]he people," Publius says, "commonly *intend* the PUBLIC GOOD," but they also "know from experience, that they sometimes err," and on occasions when political leadership "has saved [the people] from very fatal consequences of

---

52. *Id.*
53. *Id.* at 471–72.
54. *The Federalist* No. 71, at 482.
55. *Id.* at 482–83.

their own mistakes," the people have erected "lasting monuments of their gratitude to the men, who had the courage, and magnanimity enough to serve them at the peril of their displeasure."[56]

In looking to the President to supply the energy that government needs to pursue its ends, Publius looks to the most *responsible* member of the government, in the full sense of the term "responsible." Publius sets forth his thoughts on political responsibility in *Federalist* 63, a paper on the advantages to the country of the new Senate.[57] There Publius argues that the Senate is a more responsible part of the legislature than the House of Representatives. This seems paradoxical due to the greater *responsiveness* of the House—a responsiveness to public opinion secured by requiring its members to run for reelection every two years, as opposed to every six years for senators, and by its members having smaller constituencies (a single district rather than an entire state, as for senators). Paradoxical though it seems, however, the longer term and state-wide constituency for senators, the smaller size of the Senate (100 members today as compared to 435 members of the House), and the Senate's added responsibilities, such as ratifying treaties and approving presidential appointments, combine to make the Senate a more responsible body than the House.

Publius explains by analyzing the concept of responsibility. To paraphrase his analysis, responsibility is normally responsibility *to* someone *for* some result. Under the Constitution as written, the national government is responsible *to* the American public *for* pursuing constitutional ends as *real goods*—goods, that is, about which the public may at any given moment be wrong. On those occasions, a fully responsible government would have to reconcile the two legs of responsibility, the *to* and the *for* of responsibility. To accomplish this, government would have to stand up against public opinion and attempt to change the public's mind in the direction of the public's true interests. So the function of a fully responsible government is essentially educative; a fully responsible government makes the public sensible of its true interests or (in this imperfect world) what the best arguments and evidence show to be the best current conception of those interests.

The Senate is more responsible than the House owing to the conditions under which an agent is fairly held to be responsible. Publius argues in *Federalist* 63 that an agent can't fairly be responsible *to* some principal

---

56. *Id.*
57. *The Federalist* No. 63, at 423–24.

unless the agent is *visible* to the principal. (Ask four plumbers to repair one leaky faucet and it's not clear exactly who did the job.) Nor can a principal fairly hold the agent responsible for the work unless the agent has the tools for the job. (One doesn't expect an electrician to repair a leaky faucet.) To be fairly held responsible for a job, an agent must have *power* and *visibility*. And the Senate has both in fuller measure than the House. Senators are more powerful because they have longer terms of office and added responsibilities. Each of them is also a member of a smaller legislative body, which makes each more visible.[58]

The President is more responsible than the Congress for the same reason that the Senate is more responsible than the House. No functionary in this system has more visibility than the President, and none has as much power. True, the Congress may have more *formal* power, but the President is the most important single actor in the legislative process, and the President enjoys more *strategic* power than any other official. The nation learned the great importance of the President's strategic power in the presidencies of Abraham Lincoln and Franklin D. Roosevelt. The power exerted by these presidents would not have surprised the author of *Federalist* 70 and 71. The nation learned the same lesson in the first term of the presidency of George W. Bush.

We conclude with two points on Publius's theory of responsible government. Some will surely say that it is incompatible with democracy. Publius could respond that those who say this aren't real friends of democracy. For they either (1) deny that there are objectively better conceptions of goods like justice and the public interest or (2) insult democracy by implicitly denying that democrats can aspire to those better conceptions and arrange their institutions accordingly. The insult to democracy can be removed by denying that justice is better than injustice or denying that there are better or worse conceptions of justice and other goods. But if justice is no better than injustice or if there are no better or worse conceptions of these things, then democracy is no better than tyranny and democracy can mean whatever some power wants it to mean.

---

58. Under the original Constitution, members of the Senate were elected by the state legislatures. Under the Seventeenth Amendment, we now have direct election of Senators by the people of each state. The fact that Senators are now more responsive to popular opinion than they might have been under the original Constitution does not affect our argument that the Senate remains a more responsible body, in Publius's sense, than the House of Representatives.

It's hard to see how a friend of democracy could accept any of these skeptical positions, for they leave us no reason to befriend democracy.

Finally, we should note what Publius's theory of responsible government means for judicial power in America. Alexander Bickel was one of the most influential constitutional theorists of the last half of the twentieth century. Bickel was a moral skeptic.[59] He denied that goods like justice and the general welfare are real and that we can have objectively better or worse conceptions of them. This caused Bickel to be deeply troubled by the power of the Supreme Court to substitute its view of constitutional principles like equal protection and due process for the views of elected officials at the state and national levels.[60] For, as Dworkin correctly noted, judicial assertiveness on behalf of constitutional principles presupposes "a certain objectivity" of moral principle.[61] If one view of liberty is as good as another, then the Court has no warrant to substitute its view for that of some legislature, whatever the latter may be. Yet Bickel at one point in his career wanted to support the Warren Court, largely because of its heroic decision in *Brown v. Board of Education* (1954).[62] So the problem for Bickel was how to support the Court's power to stand up to public opinion in the name of justice even though he thought there really were no objectively better conceptions of justice. His famous term for this problem was "the counter-majoritarian difficulty"[63] (said to be posed by judicial review in a democracy). And he proposed a resolution to it that was as wrong as it was successful in legal academe (which was and remains as skeptical about the philosophic status of constitutional principles as Bickel was).[64]

Unlike Bickel, Publius was not hobbled by a conception of judicial review as posing a "counter-majoritarian difficulty." In *Federalist* 78, Publius famously rebutted the argument that judicial review was undemocratic

59. *See* Alexander M. Bickel, *The Least Dangerous Branch* (Indianapolis, IN: Bobbs-Merrill, 1962) [hereinafter Bickel, *The Least Dangerous Branch*]: 42, 199, 226; Alexander M. Bickel, *The Morality of Consent* (New Haven, CT: Yale University Press, 1975): 23–25, 123.
60. Alexander M. Bickel, *The Supreme Court and the Idea of Progress* (New York: Harper & Row, 1970): 45–100.
61. Dworkin, *supra* note 6, at 138, discussed in Chapter 2.
62. *See* Edward A. Purcell, Jr., "Alexander M. Bickel and the Post-Realist Constitution," *Harvard Civil Rights-Civil Liberties Law Review* 11 (1976): 521, 524; Alexander M. Bickel, "The Original Understanding and the Segregation Decision," *Harvard Law Review* 69 (1955): 1.
63. Bickel, *The Least Dangerous Branch, supra* note 59, at 16–18.
64. *See* Sotirios A. Barber, *The Constitution of Judicial Power* (Baltimore: Johns Hopkins University Press, 1993): 147–78.

by arguing that judicial review implies, not judicial supremacy, but constitutional supremacy: the supremacy of the higher law of "We the People" embodied in the Constitution over the ordinary law of the agents of the people represented in legislation.[65] Furthermore, Publius saw the task of constitutional government as one of leading public opinion, not following it—a task of improving public opinion by reconciling it to objective standards of right and wrong. Unlike Bickel, Publius felt that if democracy could not be reconciled to higher standards of political morality, democracy was indefensible. Publius's theory of judicial power was part of his theory of responsible government.[66] He saw the federal judiciary as one of the instruments for making the public sensible of its true interests. Though Publius may well have disapproved of specific decisions of the Supreme Court over the years—for the Court can be wrong about justice and the general welfare—he would not have complained that the Court is an undemocratic institution. He would have seen judicial review as one of the ways American democracy redeems the image of rectitude it projects to the world or, as Dworkin put it, as one of the institutions for making the Constitution the best it can be.[67]

Thus far, we have been focusing on aspects of the basic question *What* is the Constitution? and incidentally *How* should we interpret the Constitution? For the remainder of the book, we'll focus on the *How* question and, therewith, on competing approaches to constitutional interpretation.

---

[65] *The Federalist* No. 78, at 524–25.

[66] For detailed argument, see Sotirios A. Barber, "Judicial Review and *The Federalist,*" *University of Chicago Law Review* 55 (1985): 836.

[67] *See* Chapter 2.

PART II

CHAPTER 4

APPROACHES TO CONSTITUTIONAL INTERPRETATION

We turn now to the approaches to constitutional interpretation. We'll ask whether a "plain words textualist" approach or a "structuralist" approach or some other "approach" can help interpreters decide such difficult questions as whether the liberty provision of the Due Process Clause protects the right of a woman to decide whether to terminate a pregnancy[1] or the right of a person to enter into a homosexual relationship without fear of criminal prosecution.[2]

We've actually been talking about approaches to interpretation for some time now. When we discussed Rehnquist, Dworkin, and Publius, we saw that Dworkin favors a "philosophic" approach to difficult constitutional questions, while Rehnquist claims to favor a historical or "originalist" approach. We saw that Publius's approach is more like Dworkin's approach than Rehnquist's. But lest we get carried away with "approaches," we should attend to some cautionary considerations.

I. Some Reservations about Approaches

Talk of approaches risks a conclusion that is embarrassing in constitutional discussion. This problem emerges from two facts: the term "approach" is a spatial metaphor whose logic may not be perfectly transferable to nonspatial contexts, and approaches are always approaches to things other than themselves. It is true that one can't get to Rome before approaching it and that this usually means deciding how to get there.

---

[1] Roe v. Wade, 410 U.S. 113 (1973).
[2] Lawrence v. Texas, 539 U.S. 558 (2003).

But traversing a space is not integral to understanding something, and we have reason to resist concluding that we can have no understanding of the Constitution before deciding how to approach it. Approaches to constitutional meaning are now connected with partisan differences, either politically partisan or philosophically partisan or both. Rehnquist's historical or originalist approach is thus connected (rightly in all respects or not) to a moral skepticism and a conservative political vision or agenda. Dworkin's philosophic approach is associated (again, rightly or not) with a moral objectivism and a liberal political vision. Preoccupation with approaches thus may tempt us to conclude that our access to the Constitution is unavoidably limited to what some partisan view will reveal. This proposition may of course be true, but it is hardly one we should concede without resistance, for we shouldn't concede that our view of the Constitution *must* in all respects be partisan.

If all of our ideas, thoughts, or intuitions about the Constitution were constrained by some partisan perspective or approach—call this the "approach hypothesis"—we couldn't hope to say "the Constitution itself" indicated a particular approach. Though Rehnquist might favor one approach and Dworkin another, neither could claim to have the Constitution on his side. But if the Constitution itself indicated no particular approach, how could we decide which approach is best? We might approach the choice of approaches by asking which conforms best to some other standard, like justice. But if our view of the Constitution had to depend on some antecedent choice of approach, how could our view of justice or any other normative standard be different? The approach hypothesis thus points to the conclusion that, whether we realize it or not, any and all of our views of the Constitution—certainly any of our controversial views—ultimately are arbitrary. This corollary of the approach hypothesis is contrary to what we presuppose in debating constitutional questions, including questions of which approach is best, for good-faith debate could not occur between parties who believed their positions to be fundamentally arbitrary. So a normative theorist who takes approaches too seriously swallows her own tongue. Though she participates in a debate that presupposes a truth or best understanding of the matter under debate and the normative force of that truth or best understanding on her beliefs and conduct, she implicitly denies all of these possibilities.

Writers on normative questions who take approaches too seriously also tend to misdescribe the apparent facts of our ordinary behavior, facts that constitute evidence of a *pre-approach awareness* of the Constitution.

Academic constitutional theorists aside, ordinary lawyers, judges, politicians, and citizens spend far more time debating first-order or substantive constitutional questions—like what the Constitution requires regarding free speech, searches and seizures, the waging of war, and the like—than second-order or interpretive questions involving originalist, structuralist, philosophic, and other approaches to the first-order issues. And when ordinary lawyers, judges, politicians, and citizens do debate the second-order issues, as they increasingly have done in recent years, they still assume *some* pre-approach grasp of the Constitution itself. For their debate is (thought by all sides to be) about approaches *to* some specific thing, and they couldn't debate about approaches to something of which they had utterly no prior awareness.

Is this pre-approach awareness of the Constitution by the debaters an awareness of one and the same thing—one thing that is shared by all sides of the debate? It seems so to the typical debater, for she believes she debates approaches to the Constitution, not what she sees as the Constitution. The evidence lies in what debaters typically say. Our debater doesn't say "x is the best approach to what I personally see as the Constitution." She says "x is the best approach to the Constitution." Were she to say the former she would leave nothing to debate politically.

This pre-approach awareness of the Constitution is connected to another possibility likely to be missed by those who entertain the approach hypothesis: more than one approach or a fusion of approaches to constitutional meaning may be defensible. In our ordinary lives as lawyers, judges, politicians, and citizens, we begin with what seems an unself-conscious, unproblematic impression of the Constitution. We then run into problems of what the Constitution means for this or that political issue. These problems of meaning come in different varieties. Sometimes we have doubts about constitutional meaning while agreeing on where and how to look for meaning. At other times we disagree on where and how to look. Under current circumstances, for example, we tend to agree that the meaning of "Letters of Marque and Reprisal" referred to in Article I, § 8 is a question for some form of historical research, and so, with no sense that we are doing something controversial, we consult works like law dictionaries and legal digests that record historical usage. We act differently when we have questions about the meaning of provisions promising "due process of law" and "equal protection of the laws."

Some writers believe that "equal protection" and "due process" refer to objective qualities of relationships and processes, or that some versions of these relationships and processes can be true or objectively better or more defensible than others—they believe, for example, that Hitler's version of equal protection and due process would be wrong (for everyone, everywhere) even if Hitler's brand of fascism should arrive at a complete and irreversible domination of world opinion. These writers would engage in moral philosophy in quest of the true or objective meanings or best understandings of these constitutional concepts. Other writers deny that "equal protection" and "due process" refer to anything more than arbitrary conventions or the arbitrary preferences of particular persons or groups. These writers would choose nonphilosophic methods like historical research, introspection, or even speculation about what will appeal to the prejudices of their readers.[3]

We're far from treating philosophic and nonphilosophic methods as approaches to be separated and selected as one might wish, for we don't think responsible analysts can ignore Dworkin's call for a fusion of constitutional law and moral philosophy.[4] We say this because no matter what one's approach, a philosophic choice seems unavoidable at some level, and we believe such choices, to be responsible, must be explicated and defended, which means submission to philosophic processes. But the fact of unavoidable philosophic assumptions doesn't mean we can separate something called "the philosophic approach" from the insights, concerns, and objects of other approaches. We can't look for the meaning of the Equal Protection Clause as applied to affirmative action, for example, without consulting historical and present-day opinion on the subject, along with judicial precedent, the likely consequences of different policies, the experience of other nations, and so forth. And one reason we can't do this is that the Equal Protection Clause is part of the Constitution and the Constitution promises more than equal protection. It promises equal protection in a context that demands attention to other goods that would be defeated if we ignored things like precedent and consequences.[5] So we accept a version of Dworkin's point: fidelity to the Constitution requires not just a philosophic approach to constitutional meaning, but a fusion of philosophic and other approaches.

We'll say more later about this fusion of approaches. For now we'll point out how the Constitution's Preamble might support the case for

---

[3.] *See* Chapter 11 (analyzing arguments of pragmatists like Stanley Fish).
[4.] *See* Chapter 2.
[5.] Michael S. Moore, "A Natural Law Theory of Interpretation," *Southern California Law Review* 58 (1985): 277, 313–18 (analyzing rule of law virtues in interpretation).

a fusion of approaches. The Preamble says, in part: (1) We the People . . . (2) in Order to . . . (3) establish Justice . . . and secure the Blessings of Liberty (4) to ourselves and our Posterity, do ordain and establish (5) this Constitution. Propositions (1) and (4) direct us to the Constitution's authorship, or rather problems connected to the Constitution's authorship: Who is this people? What separates it from others, and what does it stand for? Was it ever sufficiently unified with itself and with its past to justify imputing one set of identifying ends to all its generations (its posterity)? What reason is there to believe it will be so unified with its future? Proposition (2) implicates the Constitution's instrumental aspect. It invites us to reflect on the interpretation of instrumental norms generally and to ask whether there's a case for an ends-oriented interpretation of this particular constitution.[6] Proposition (3) justifies asking what Justice and the Preamble's other ends really are or what is our best understanding of them. We say "really are" because while each of these ends is modified by the other ends, none is in quotation marks. Though the Preamble issues from a specific people and is addressed to a specific people—a fact that legitimates inquiries, historical and social-scientific, into the meanings and commitments of that people—the Preamble purports to refer to Justice itself, the Blessings of Liberty themselves, and so forth. And because this last fact argues for seeking that to which the words purport to refer, it argues for moral philosophy and sometimes even scientific judgment, depending on the provision in question. Proposition (5) pulls us back to a historically local text, namely, this particular constitution of 1789 and its amendments, even though the text purports to refer to transhistorical ends and to address an infinite future and a potentially global community (consider Article IV's provision for admitting new states and the explicitly global appeal of the 1st *Federalist*).[7]

In sum, while we hold the subject of competing approaches to be important, we caution against a preoccupation with approaches that precludes the possibility of a constitutionally best or most defensible approach or fusion of approaches.

---

6. Even traditionalists like Martin Diamond have suggested this. *See* Sotirios A. Barber, *Welfare and the Constitution* (Princeton, NJ: Princeton University Press, 2003): 38–41 (analyzing arguments of Martin Diamond, "*The Federalist*," in *History of Political Philosophy*, ed. Leo Strauss and Joseph Cropsey, 2nd ed. (Chicago: Rand McNally, 1972): 631).

7. *See The Federalist*, ed. Jacob E. Cooke (Middletown, CT: Wesleyan University Press, 1961): No. 1, at 3.

II. Some Approaches

Debate over approaches to constitutional interpretation is far from confined to the legal academy. This is evidenced by the fact that battles surrounding the nomination and confirmation of federal judges have rarely been more intense than at this writing. The public debate reflects divisions not just about the meaning of specific constitutional provisions, but, increasingly, about the nature of the Constitution itself, what form of democratic self-government it embodies, and what approach (or approaches) to constitutional interpretation is (or are) most defensible—to wit, the basic questions that we are exploring in this book. We believe that some of the participants in both the public and the academic debate are wrong in their interpretive conclusions, notwithstanding the validity of some of their first-order substantive concerns about actual decisions of the Supreme Court.

We begin our discussion by pairing the principal approaches with their specific sources of constitutional meaning. Our typology of approaches isn't the only one,[8] but we think it covers the controlling issues.

Source of constitutional meaning	Name of approach
Plain words of the constitutional document	textualism
Current social consensus on what the words mean	consensualism
Nature of things the words refer to/best understanding of concepts embodied in the words	philosophic approach
Intentions or original meanings of framers/ratifiers/founding generation	originalism
Document's arrangement of offices, powers, and relationships	structuralism
Doctrines of courts and judicial precedents	doctrinalism
Preferences of dominant political forces	pragmatism

[8.] Our typology here is similar to, though not the same as, the typology put forward in the casebook we co-authored. Walter F. Murphy, James E. Fleming, Sotirios A. Barber, and Stephen Macedo, *American Constitutional Interpretation*, 3rd ed. (New York: Foundation Press, 2003): 389–439. Probably the best known typology of approaches or "modalities" in constitutional interpretation to be formulated in recent years is that of Philip Bobbitt. He distinguishes historical, textual, doctrinal, prudential, structural, and ethical argument. Philip Bobbitt, *Constitutional Fate: Theory of the Constitution* (New York: Oxford University Press, 1982): 3–8.

With the exception of the philosophic approach, all of these approaches claim to avoid the need for a fusion of constitutional law and moral philosophy. We will systematically show that, contrary to their aims and pretensions, they cannot avoid philosophic choices. We will try to persuade you that there is one constitutionally best or most defensible approach or fusion of approaches that is complex enough to accommodate the valid concerns and genuine insights of several (though not all) approaches. Our argument will fall short of final and dogmatic conclusions, however; for indeed the approach for which we argue requires us to concede that it may be wrong and thus to welcome arguments on the other side.

CHAPTER 5

TEXTUALISM AND CONSENSUALISM

The *textualist* says we can find what the Constitution means by consulting the *plain words* of the constitutional document. The *consensualist* consults a *current social consensus* on what the words of the document mean. We treat these two approaches together because both claim to consult conventional understandings of the meanings of the words. There is a short and a long answer to each of these claims.

The short answer begins by recalling the occasion for interpretation: we are self-consciously concerned with interpreting a text when the meaning of the text is puzzling or controversial. In constitutional interpretation, in particular with cases that reach the Supreme Court, we are concerned with interpretation in "hard cases." Hard cases are generally conceived as cases in which we don't agree on what the Constitution means or how to find what the Constitution means. By the very definition of hard cases, therefore, plain words textualism and conventionalism can't be useful approaches to constitutional meaning. For, if (1) the text were plain or (2) we shared a consensus on what it meant, the case wouldn't be a hard case. That's the short answer to the claims of plain words textualists and consensualists.

The long answer concludes that the textualist and the consensualist reason, not from plain words or social consensus, but from a conception of democracy that is controversial enough to require a philosophic defense—a defense they seek to avoid, but can't responsibly avoid. In critiquing plain words textualism and consensualism, we'll focus on Justice Hugo Black and Professor Michael Perry, who are exemplars of these respective approaches. Our criticisms of their theories of constitutional interpretation apply as well to other proponents and versions of consensualism and (the "plain words" variety of) textualism.[1] (In this chapter, we criticize the plain words version of textualism. In Chapter 6, we support Ronald Dworkin's view that the constitutional text as written embodies moral concepts and abstract intentions and therefore that textualism, properly understood, is equivalent to the philosophic approach.)

I. Justice Black and Plain Words Textualism

Justice Black is our best known plain words textualist. The long answer to the plain words textualist starts by considering his view of the Ninth Amendment in *Griswold v. Connecticut*.[2] The Ninth Amendment provides: "The enumeration in the Constitution, of certain rights, shall not be construed to deny or disparage others retained by the people." As most readers read the Amendment, it says (in plain words?) that constitutional rights are not exhausted by the enumeration of rights in the constitutional text—that the rights of Americans include rights in addition to those enumerated. Yet Justice Black's plain words textualism holds precisely

---

[1.] Justice Antonin Scalia also claims to be a textualist, but careful analysis of his writings on constitutional interpretation and of his controversial, supposedly textualist, opinions shows him to be a concrete intentionalist or narrow originalist of the sort we criticize in Chapter 6. *See* Antonin Scalia, *A Matter of Interpretation* (Princeton, NJ: Princeton University Press, 1997); Antonin Scalia, "Originalism: The Lesser Evil," *University of Cincinnati Law Review* 57 (1989): 849; Planned Parenthood v. Casey, 505 U.S. 833, 998 (1992) (Scalia, J., concurring in the judgment in part and dissenting in part). For example, Scalia would say that the word "liberty" in the Due Process Clause of the Fourteenth Amendment doesn't apply to abortion (or doesn't "say anything about" abortion), not because the best understanding of the word "liberty" doesn't include procreative liberty, but because the persons who wrote and ratified the word "liberty" didn't concretely have a right to abortion in mind or would not have applied the word "liberty" to protect such a right (or he might say simply that the original meaning of "liberty" did not include a right to abortion). Or, to take another example, he would say that the Equal Protection Clause of the Fourteenth Amendment doesn't apply to homosexuals qua homosexuals, not because the best understanding of the word "person" doesn't include homosexuals, but because the persons who wrote and ratified the word "person" didn't concretely have homosexuals in mind or would not have applied the word "person" to include homosexuals qua homosexuals (or he might say simply that the original meaning of "persons" did not include homosexuals qua homosexuals). Scalia believes that the meanings of words in the text are exhausted by their original meanings, by which he means the concrete historical conceptions of those words (as definitions or as applications). We discuss these issues in the next chapter.

[2.] 381 U.S. 479 (1965). *See also* Hugo LaFayette Black, *A Constitutional Faith* (New York: Alfred A. Knopf, 1969): 3 (developing his "constitutional philosophy" and "constitutional faith" in a plain words variety of textualism and a conception of the role of the courts in our constitutional system of "governments controlled by the people themselves").

that the only constitutional rights are those enumerated in the text. The Ninth Amendment is thus widely taken to be a refutation, on the face of the Constitution itself, of Justice Black's approach to interpreting the Constitution. The Amendment seems to show that plain words textualism suffers from a contradiction: by implying rights beyond those enumerated in the constitutional text, the Ninth Amendment plainly indicates that one may not limit oneself to the plain words of the constitutional text![3]

In *Griswold*, the majority opinion of Justice William O. Douglas recognizes a right to privacy—at least the right of married couples to use contraceptives—that is not specified in the plain words of the constitutional text but is implicit in the letter and spirit, penumbras, or emanations of the First, Third, Fourth, and Fifth Amendments. Douglas also invokes the Ninth Amendment to justify the majority's approach to interpreting the Constitution: as not limiting constitutional rights to those specifically enumerated in the text.[4] In concurrence, Justice Arthur Goldberg emphasizes the role of the Ninth Amendment in justifying the protection of such rights.[5] Justice Black vigorously dissents on the ground that the right of privacy is not enumerated in the constitutional text.[6] He offers a theory of the Ninth Amendment (essentially, a federalism account that conceives it as replicating the Tenth Amendment's principle that powers not delegated to the national government are reserved to the state governments or to the people) that enables him to disregard the Ninth Amendment's apparent promise of "unenumerated" rights. His justification for denying rights not enumerated flows from a background theory of democracy. Justice Black believes that it's undemocratic for unelected judges to invent rights against majoritarian government beyond those rights specified in the text. He can reconcile democracy with judges' applying *written* constitutional rights against the democratically elected branches of government because, in theory, *written* constitutional rights express the will of the sovereign people. But, according to Justice Black, *unwritten* constitutional rights are the mere inventions of judges, and because the Ninth Amendment seems to authorize unwritten rights, we must either disregard the Amendment or construe it into insignificance, as he does.

---

3. For a similar critique of "clause-bound interpretivism" (a term that embraces what we are calling Justice Black's "plain words textualism"), *see* John Hart Ely, *Democracy and Distrust* (Cambridge, MA: Harvard University Press, 1980): 12–14.

4. *Griswold*, 381 U.S. at 483–85.

5. *Id.* at 486–96 (Goldberg, J., concurring).

6. *Id.* at 507–27 (Black, J., dissenting).

Justice Black's treatment of the Ninth Amendment shows that he takes his bearings not simply from what seems to most people as the plain words of the constitutional text, but from a controversial reading of the constitutional text—a reading that reflects a background theory of democracy. Democracy is surely an important value, but the word, "democracy," does not appear in the constitutional text. And neither constitutional text nor constitutional history compels us to accept Justice Black's particular conception of democracy. That conception is something that one must argue for. And the kind of argument needed is political-philosophic in essence, for one would be contending that Black's conception is better in some way (as more conducive to the people's happiness, more in keeping with justice, or better accounting for and justifying the principal features and commitments of the constitutional order) than competing conceptions. Responsibly conducted, therefore, Black's approach would be a philosophic approach to the text. Black's claim to be governed by plain words turns out to be a way to escape responsibility for controversial choices.

II. Professor Perry and Consensualism

Professor Michael Perry is a good representative of the consensualist approach, and a good example of that approach is his view of the right to abortion. Perry contends that the Supreme Court went too far in *Roe v. Wade* (1973) because the American public is divided on the abortion question except in cases of rape, incest, and serious fetal deformity.[7] The public generally does agree that a woman should have a right to decide to have an abortion under those narrow circumstances, says Perry, but there's no current consensus on a right to choose under different circumstances. Therefore, he concludes, the constitutional right should be

---

[7.] Michael J. Perry, *Morality, Politics, and Law* (New York: Oxford University Press, 1988): 174–78 [hereinafter Perry, *Morality, Politics, and Law*]. In earlier work, Perry had argued instead that consensus supported Justice Blackmun's opinion of the Court in *Roe* recognizing a broader right of a woman to decide whether to terminate a pregnancy. Michael J. Perry, "Abortion, the Public Morals, and the Police Power: The Ethical Function of Substantive Due Process," *UCLA Law Review* 23 (1976): 689, 733; Michael J. Perry, *The Constitution, the Courts, and Human Rights* (New Haven, CT: Yale University Press, 1982): 145. Perry's later work may be less skeptical about values than his earlier work. *See, e.g.*, Michael J. Perry, *Toward a Theory of Human Rights: Religion, Law, Courts* (New York: Cambridge University Press, 2006): 3–13.

limited to those circumstances, and state legislatures should be constitutionally free either to permit or to outlaw abortions in other circumstances.

Perry's position on the right to abortion can be represented as the following syllogism:

- Major premise: Liberty (as guaranteed by the Due Process Clause of the Fourteenth Amendment) includes only what a current social consensus says it includes.
- Minor premise: A current social consensus supports no more than a liberty to decide to have an abortion in cases of rape, incest, or serious fetal deformity.
- Conclusion: Therefore, liberty (at present) includes a liberty to have an abortion only in those three circumstances.

Despite Perry's turn to social consensus for deciding what liberties we presently have (here regarding abortion), he turns to other things for (1) the kind of thing liberty is (his major premise) and (2) what people believe about abortion (his minor premise). His minor premise is true, he believes, because it corresponds to a state of affairs in the real world: as a matter of sociological fact (he claims) people actually do believe what he says they believe about abortion. A parallel reason supports his assumption that his major premise is true. His major premise is also a statement about how the world actually is. He assumes that the world is populated by different kinds of things, and that liberty (like chess and baseball but unlike trees, frogs, and stars) is whatever society says it is. He assumes, moreover, that liberty *ought* to mean what it *does* mean—i.e., that we ought to conform our conduct to what liberty does mean. That Perry harbors this last assumption is evident in his conclusion that the Supreme Court ought not to have recognized a right to abortion beyond the alleged social consensus about liberty.

Note well that Perry is far from suggesting that his major premise (that consensus properly determines what liberties we have) is true because a social consensus holds it to be true. Why he doesn't say this and couldn't plausibly say this is a matter of some importance. He can't say a consensus supports his major premise, for many people would deny the truth of that premise. They would deny that premise because they would deny its implications. Let's see what some of those implications are. If, as Perry claims, the meaning of constitutional guarantees like liberty were determined by a social consensus, then it would be impossible for a government that faithfully represented a stable social consensus to violate a constitutionally protected liberty. A general formulation of Perry's major premise would make it impossible for a socially entrenched Nazi regime convinced of its rectitude to act "unfairly" against the last remaining Jew. If, as Perry suggests, a word like "liberty" referred to nothing beyond the beliefs of some community, then evidence for the meaning of "liberty" would lie solely in how people used the word. Under that theory, liberty itself wouldn't exist, only liberty talk (or fairness talk, or equal-protection talk, and the like). People might think they were talking "about liberty" (or fairness or equal protection), but they wouldn't really be talking "about" anything—they would just be talking. Implications like this are either offensive or strange to ordinary beliefs about morality and the world, and it is for this reason that, even if (somehow) true, Perry's major premise could hardly attract a social consensus.[8]

If a consensus doesn't tell Perry that his major premise is true, what does? What tells him that the meaning of a constitutional guarantee like liberty is determined not by liberty itself but by a social consensus? The answer for Perry is democracy. He holds that the meaning of words like "liberty" is determined by a social consensus because he thinks that's the only way to legitimize the power of unelected judges who invoke those words to invalidate the actions of elected bodies. By saying that elected officials violate constitutional rights only when they act against a social consensus—only, in other words, when some well-organized minority (like the Catholic Church in the Connecticut birth control controversy in *Griswold*) pressures the government to act against the preferences of the

---

[8.] Parties debating the abortion question ordinarily assume that the idea of "liberty" (conjoined in this case with the idea of "equality") already either does or does not embrace a right to abortion, with one side contending that (in fairness) it does and the other side contending that (in fairness) it doesn't. Perry departs from this commonsense view of what the debate is about—that is, the scope of liberty/equality. He holds, in effect, that the debate can't really be about the scope of liberty/equality (a philosophic question), because liberty/equality neither embraces nor excludes a right to abortion (or a right to life), and that it will neither embrace nor exclude either right *until the parties reach a consensus on the question*. See Perry, *Morality, Politics, and Law, supra* note 7, at 155–56. Perry holds, in other words, that the relevant Fourteenth Amendment provisions (regarding liberty and equality) are *meaningless* in contexts other than rape, incest, or serious fetal deformity, and will remain meaningless until a social consensus on abortion in other contexts emerges. That's why he thinks the Supreme Court cannot truthfully say that the Fourteenth Amendment says anything about abortion in cases other than rape, incest, or serious fetal deformity. "But if the Constitution says nothing about the issue either way," an obvious rejoinder would go, "what's wrong with the Court's trying to resolve the question?" Perry's answer, reminiscent of Rehnquist's (discussed in Chapter 2), is that to do so would be assuming "an imperial judicial role," *id.* at 178, which is another way of declaring it offensive to democracy.

majority—Perry finds a way to reconcile judicially enforced constitutional liberty with democracy. So, democracy tells Perry that he's right about what determines the meaning of liberty.

But how does Perry know he's right about democracy? What tells him what "democracy" properly refers to? He doesn't say social consensus tells him what democracy means. He can't plausibly claim this for the same reason he can't plausibly claim a social consensus for the meaning of liberty in his major premise. By holding that democracy (not a social consensus) requires that consensus determines the meaning of liberty, he implies that elected officials who remain faithful to what the people want cannot violate anyone's liberty. That in turn would imply no real individual rights against the community because the community would be the very source of rights. Many Americans would disagree; they would side with the Declaration of Independence and a lengthy constitutional tradition (remember our discussions of *The Federalist* in Chapter 3) that holds that fundamental constitutional rights flow not from the community but from higher authority, like "self-evident truths" or "nature" or "nature's God." The least we can say, therefore, is that there's no evidence of a social consensus behind Perry's conception of democracy.

Unless Perry is willing to admit that his conception of democracy is arbitrary, he's left with one option: his conception of democracy, if true, must conform to or best approximate democracy itself or the best understanding of our form of government. He must refer his conception of democracy to a reality—a presumed moral reality or the best understanding of our form of government—beyond what people might happen to believe about democracy. Without reference to such a moral reality, he'd have no basis other than his arbitrary personal preferences for rejecting other conceptions of democracy, like that of *The Federalist*.[9]

In the end, Perry seems to believe:

1. "Democracy" refers to democracy itself, and moral reality determines the proper use of "democracy," no matter what people say or believe about democracy.
2. "Liberty," however, is different; it refers not to something real—something not determined by people's beliefs—but only to what a social consensus holds to be acceptable liberties.

---

9. As stated in Chapter 1, we ourselves are divided concerning the "ontological" debate between moral realism and constructivism (or deep conventionalism). For that reason as well as others, we have written this book to be agnostic between moral realism and constructivism (or deep conventionalism).

This leaves Perry to explain the relevant difference between democracy and liberty, why "democracy" refers to something real, while "liberty" is determined by social consensus or convention. Until he explains this, we can doubt the coherence of his position. Perry is not unaware of these problems. He states at one point that although democracy enjoys "axiomatic status" in American political culture, democracy is not axiomatically prior to "all other fundamental values." He recognizes also that no particular conception of democracy is axiomatic, and that any given conception "must be defended" in terms of how it serves the Constitution's "central aspirations." He sees the contest among theories of interpretation as part of a broader debate over which view of democracy best serves these aspirations. He identifies these aspirations as, most generally, "liberty and justice for all" and, more specifically, such textually enumerated human rights as the freedoms of speech and religion and "racial and other sorts of equality."[10]

One would think that a writer who held these views would favor interpreters, judicial and otherwise, thinking for themselves in a self-critical spirit about the best the Constitution can mean in hard cases. And, in fact, Perry does support broad public "conversations" about constitutional "aspirations" and whether they embrace such rights as a woman's right to decide whether to terminate a pregnancy or the right of the unborn to life. But Perry has a conventionalist theory of meaning that combines with a conventionalist view of values to defeat any aspiration to truth or best understanding not only about values like liberty and justice but even about democracy. Sacrificed to Perry's moral conventionalism is any hope of defending any particular view of democracy in terms of its service to aspirations like liberty and justice. If notions like liberty and justice are meaningless beyond their consensual applications, why wouldn't the same be true of democracy?

Since the controlling idea of Perry's theory is democracy, and since, when conceiving of democracy, he appears to consult a moral reality, not a social convention, his approach, at bottom, is no more consensualist than Justice Black's is textualist. Both rely on controversial conceptions of democracy that they leave undefended—but which need to be defended—and both thus unwittingly support the case for a fusion of

---

10. Perry, *Morality, Politics, and Law, supra* note 7, at 164–67.

constitutional law and moral philosophy. (The same holds true for other "plain words" textualists and consensualists of whom Black and Perry are exemplars.)[11]

III. Consensualism and the Philosophic Approach

Two recent Supreme Court decisions and a classic dissent show that consensualism embodies rather than avoids a philosophic approach to constitutional interpretation. Justice John Marshall Harlan, in dissent in *Poe v. Ullman* (1961),[12] articulated a famous understanding of the "liberty" protected by the Due Process Clause in terms of a "living" tradition or an evolving consensus. Harlan conceived that liberty as a "rational continuum" of ordered liberty, not merely as a code or "series of isolated points pricked out" in the constitutional document (a view he attributed to Justice Black). Furthermore, Harlan understood judgment in constitutional interpretation to be a "rational process" that conceives of tradition as a "living thing"—"[w]hat history teaches are the traditions from which [this country] developed as well as the traditions from which it broke"— not as a mechanical process of formulas or bright-line rules (again, a view he attributed to Justice Black).[13] He reiterated the main arguments of his dissent in *Poe* in his concurrence in *Griswold*.[14]

In *Planned Parenthood v. Casey* (1992)[15]—which reaffirmed the central holding of *Roe v. Wade* (1973)[16] recognizing the right of a woman to decide whether to terminate a pregnancy—the joint opinion of Justices Sandra Day O'Connor, Anthony Kennedy, and David Souter embraced Justice Harlan's approach. It conceived the due process inquiry as requiring "reasoned judgment" in interpreting the Constitution, understood as a

---

11. For a fuller criticism of Perry's consensualism, *see* Sotirios A. Barber, "Michael Perry and the Future of Constitutional Theory," *Tulane Law Review* 63 (1989): 1289. For extensive criticism of Perry's position and those of other consensualists, including Alexander M. Bickel's—which prefigured Perry's position as well as those of other modern consensualists—*see* Sotirios A. Barber, *The Constitution of Judicial Power* (Baltimore: Johns Hopkins University Press, 1993): 147–78.
12. 367 U.S. 497, 542–43 (1961) (Harlan, J., dissenting).
13. *Id.*
14. 381 U.S. at 499–502 (Harlan, J., concurring in the judgment).
15. 505 U.S. 833 (1992).
16. 410 U.S. 113 (1973).

"covenant" or "coherent succession" whose "written terms embody ideas and aspirations that must survive more ages than one" to guarantee "the promise of liberty." The joint opinion stated: "We accept our responsibility not to retreat from interpreting the full meaning of the covenant in light of all of our precedents."[17]

Justice Kennedy's majority opinion in *Lawrence v. Texas* (2003)[18]— which overruled *Bowers v. Hardwick* (1986)[19] and struck down as a violation of liberty a statute that prohibited intimate sexual conduct between persons of the same sex—reflected a similar understanding of liberty and of constitutional interpretation. Kennedy wrote:

> Had those who drew and ratified the Due Process Clauses of the Fifth Amendment or the Fourteenth Amendment known the components of liberty in its manifold possibilities, they might have been more specific. They did not presume to have this insight. They knew times can blind us to certain truths and later generations can see that laws once thought necessary and proper in fact serve only to oppress. As the Constitution endures, persons in every generation can invoke its principles in their own search for greater freedom.[20]

This passage underscores that the Court conceived the Constitution as an abstract scheme of principles to be elaborated over time—in a "search for greater freedom"—not as a concrete code of specific conceptions and enumerated rights or as a deposit of historical practices to be discovered and preserved.

In these decisions, the justices do not shrink from a philosophic approach in deciding what are the traditions from which we have broken, in interpreting the full meaning of our covenant of abstract aspirational ideals, or in elaborating our constitutional principles in search for greater freedom. What is more, the evolving consensus or tradition as a "living thing" elaborated in these decisions is hardly uncontroversial, and the justices don't pretend that it is. Engaging in reasoned judgment about our Constitution's commitment to liberty requires a moral inquiry or philosophic approach.

---

[17] *Casey*, 505 U.S. at 849, 901; *see also id.* at 847–48 (resisting the "temptation" to abdicate the responsibility to engage in "reasoned judgment" in the due process inquiry).

[18] 539 U.S. 558 (2003).

[19] 478 U.S. 186 (1986).

[20] *Lawrence*, 539 U.S. at 578.

IV. The Philosophic Approach: A Preliminary View

While Dworkin's fusion of constitutional law and moral philosophy may be the only responsible approach to hard cases, that cannot be the end of the interpretive debate, for any philosophic approach to interpretation faces formidable objections. Influential constitutional theorists and jurists of all ideological stripes object to any such approach for one or several reasons. These critics claim that a philosophic approach would be (1) undemocratic, (2) un-American, (3) dangerous, and/or (4) fruitless.

Some theorists and jurists regard any fusion of constitutional law and moral philosophy as undemocratic because they associate philosophy with socially detached quests for truths that seem to be beyond the capacities and concerns of ordinary people and everyday life.[21] Some believe public preoccupation with philosophic issues is both un-American and dangerous because (as we saw in Chapter 3) the American founders deliberately planned to steer politics away from grand philosophic and theological questions toward compromisable economic concerns.[22] Some theorists and jurists consider philosophy's quests fruitless because they associate philosophy with the quest for truth beyond convention and they conceive of truth not as correspondence with reality beyond convention but with convention itself—truth, that is, as coherence with or representative of what some relevant community believes, whatever it happens to believe.[23]

Defenders of a philosophic approach have answers to these objections, but let's not rush to those answers. Let's ponder the criticisms and consider additional approaches that claim to avoid philosophic choice. For the criticism of philosophy is far from arbitrary. Socrates is the greatest exemplar of the philosopher in the Western tradition, and his way of life (including his refusal to perform remunerative work) does indicate

---

21. *See, e.g.*, Robert H. Bork, *The Tempting of America* (New York: Free Press, 1990): 16–17, 133–38, 242, 251–59, 353–54; Benjamin R. Barber, *Strong Democracy* (Berkeley and Los Angeles: University of California Press, 1984): 94–96, 142–43.

22. *See, e.g.*, Walter Berns, "Judicial Review and the Rights and Laws of Nature," *Supreme Court Review* 49 (1982): 58–66; Harvey C. Mansfield, Jr., *America's Constitutional Soul* (Baltimore: Johns Hopkins University Press, 1991): 101–14, 209–19.

23. Bork, *supra* note 21, at 49, 61–67, 121–23, 241–59; Robert H. Bork, "Neutral Principles and Some First Amendment Problems," *Indiana Law Journal* 47 (1971): 1, 2–3, 10; Sanford Levinson, *Constitutional Faith* (Princeton, NJ: Princeton University Press, 1988): 9–89, 170–79. *See also* our discussion of the "pragmatism" of Richard Posner and Stanley Fish in Chapter 11.

disagreement between philosophers and us ordinary folks about life's most urgent and most important activities. A glance at later philosophers like Hegel and Heidegger suggests that philosophers often speak a language of their own about concerns well beyond those expressible in everyday discourse. And controversies in America today about abortion, same-sex marriage, and other "social issues" may well suggest that judges who act like philosophers by thinking for themselves without deferring to tradition or consensus or popular opinion are helping to tear the nation apart. These problems summon us to look for nonphilosophic approaches to constitutional meaning—approaches that aim and claim to avoid philosophic disputation about the best the Constitution can mean, in favor of less controversial judgments about constitutional meaning. We accept that summons. Accordingly, we'll devote Chapters 6 and 7 to narrow and broad versions of originalism, which some see as cousins of the "plain words" textualist approach and the consensualist approach, respectively. (It is no surprise that some would include Justice Black in the narrow originalist camp[24] and that Professor Perry identifies himself as being in the broad originalist camp.)[25] Then, we'll turn to structuralism and doctrinalism before returning to the philosophic approach.

[24.] *See* Ely, *supra* note 3, at 2 (identifying Justice Black as the "quintessential [clause-bound] interpretivist"—Ely's term that embraces what we are calling "plain words textualism" as well as "narrow originalism").

[25.] *See* Michael J. Perry, *The Constitution in the Courts* (New York: Oxford University Press, 1994): 8–10, 28–53.

CHAPTER 6

NARROW ORIGINALISM/
INTENTIONALISM

Suppose we knew the intentions (or original meanings or original understandings)[1] of the men who wrote or ratified the Fourteenth Amendment. Would this knowledge help us decide—in a manner that avoids the need for philosophic reflection and choice—whether a woman has a right to terminate a pregnancy or marry someone of a different race or of the same sex—whether, that is, the government needs a compelling reason to deny a woman these choices? Yes, says contemporary intentionalism, most often called "originalism" (we shall use the terms interchangeably), a position whose popularity with the ideological conservatives who now dominate the federal bench has made it the subject of exhaustive scholarly analysis. In this chapter, we'll address a relatively *narrow or concrete originalism*; in the next chapter, we'll turn to a relatively *broad originalism*; we'll distinguish both from an *abstract originalism* that is equivalent to the philosophic approach. We shall see that originalism/intentionalism, narrow or broad, provides no escape from philosophic choice, for it is only through philosophic argumentation that one can

---

[1.] Some originalists in recent years have emphasized the "original meaning" or the "original understanding" of the framers and ratifiers, as distinguished from the intentions of the framers. *See, e.g.,* Antonin Scalia, *A Matter of Interpretation* (Princeton, NJ: Princeton University Press, 1997): 16–18, 37–38; Robert H. Bork, *The Tempting of America* (New York: Free Press, 1990): 143–45. Through this shift in nomenclature, they presumably hope to avoid the problems with framers' intentions as a source of constitutional meaning. The distinction between intention and meaning is a refinement that cuts no ice with us. Everyday speakers of a language confound "meaning" with "intent" because speakers normally pick a word that conveys what the word is generally taken to mean. "What do you intend?" is thus often equivalent to "What do you mean?" Our criticisms of narrow originalism in this chapter and of broad originalism in Chapter 7 apply not only to versions of originalism that stress framers' intentions but also to versions that speak of original meanings and original understandings. For economy of expression, we shall speak mostly of framers' intentions, but we use that term interchangeably with original meanings or original understandings.

answer questions that must be answered before the historical search for intentions can even begin. And, once that search begins, only through the philosophic approach can we decide what those intentions are.

I. Prior Philosophic Questions about Intentions

These prior questions are philosophic questions of different kinds. They include who we ought to count as "framers" for constitutional purposes. (Some or all members of the Philadelphia Convention? Members of the state ratifying conventions? The general public or citizenry?) Our prior questions also include what counts as evidence for original intention or meaning. (Official records and documents—the constitutional text, for example? Private correspondence by members of the Philadelphia Convention and the state ratifying conventions? Public opinion of the 1780s and the 1860s? The social practices of the 1780s and the 1860s, by this or that description of those practices? What historians say about the social practices, statute books, and common law of the relevant time? Philosophic works influential at the relevant time? The aspirations of those eras, by this or that account of those aspirations?) We must also consider the questions of what an intention is, the sense in which a group of people (as distinguished from an individual) can have an intention, and whether to count what Ronald Dworkin has called an intention's *concrete* aspect or its *abstract* aspect.[2] Should we say, on the concrete side, that a framer who referred to "fair trials" or "commerce" or "military forces" intended no more than the specific steps he thought constituted procedural fairness, the specific activities known to him as commercial, or the specific kinds of military force known to him at the time? Can we reasonably avoid saying, on the abstract side, that a framer speaking of fairness or commerce or military force must be understood as referring to things whose meaning is determined by their nature or the best understanding of their nature, not by his concrete expectations or understandings? How else would we explain the universal agreement that Congress needed no constitutional amendment to establish an air force?

We can't find answers to these prior questions in framers' intentions, of course, for we must decide these questions before commencing the

---

[2] Ronald Dworkin, *A Matter of Principle* (Cambridge, MA: Harvard University Press, 1985): 48–50.

quest for framers' intentions.[3] Acknowledging the force of such criticisms, leading conservative thinkers like Charles Fried and Richard Posner have rejected intentionalism for substantive arguments of their own about what the Constitution ought to be read to mean.[4] Robert Bork clings to intentionalism *for judges*, even if not for theorists like himself (in the sense that he acknowledges that theorists must make arguments for intentionalism, not merely make the circular assertion that the framers intended intentionalism). He asserts that intentionalism would be mandatory for judges even if the framers had not intended intentionalism for judges. Bork supports intentionalism for judges, not because anyone intended intentionalism for judges, but because he feels intentionalism best serves an imperative of democracy, namely, restraints on judicial discretion.[5] But because Bork's view of democracy is controversial and lacks a clear source in either constitutional text or judicial tradition, it is either arbitrary or dependent on a philosophic argument, an argument about what democracy ought to mean that neither he nor any other originalist has made.

Assume, however, that some philosopher had successfully shown that democracy demands intentionalist or originalist judges. Bear in mind that a successful theory of democracy would have to contend, not that the theorist's private version of democracy demands intentionalist judges, but that *democracy itself* demands intentionalist judges *and* that the moral weight of democracy overpowers all competing considerations to make intentionalism for judges a constitutional imperative. (To satisfy yourself of the validity of these requirements on our theorist, imagine your reaction to someone who said, "You should adopt my theories of democracy and of what's good and right because my theories are *my* theories.") And if our philosopher had made the requisite case, she would then have to show whether originalist judges should seek what Dworkin calls the framers' *abstract intentions* or their *concrete intentions.*[6]

As we consider these options, keep sight of where we are in this discussion. We seek an approach to constitutional meaning in controversial

---

3. *See id.* at 34–57; Walter F. Murphy, "Constitutional Interpretation: The Art of the Historian, Magician, or Statesman?," *Yale Law Journal* 87 (1978): 1752.

4. Charles Fried, *Order and Law* (New York: Simon & Schuster, 1991): 55–88; Richard A. Posner, "What Am I? A Potted Plant? The Case Against Strict Constructionism," *The New Republic*, Sept. 28, 1987, at 23; Richard A. Posner, "Bork and Beethoven," *Stanford Law Review* 42 (1990): 1365.

5. Bork, *supra* note 1, at 154–55.

6. *See* Chapter 2.

cases, and we've seen that plain words textualism and consensualism can't work in such cases. The problems of these approaches and the discovery that they are based on controversial philosophic assumptions argue for a fusion of constitutional law and moral philosophy. We have acknowledged objections, however, that such a fusion may be undemocratic, un-American, dangerous, and ultimately fruitless. So now we're seeking an approach that avoids these risks. Intentionalism or originalism may be such an approach. But that prospect can't be established by an intentionalist argument. Intentionalism must be defined and defended by a philosophic argument. Intentionalist *theorists* can't escape the burdens and responsibilities of philosophic reflection and choice. Intentionalism's only hope is that *judges* can escape the burdens and responsibilities of philosophic reflection and choice. And so, again, assume the theorists have done their philosophic work successfully—assume they've shown who ought to count as framers, what should count as evidence of their intentions, how to deal with disagreements among leading framers, and so forth. Intentionalist theorists still would face the question—a philosophic question—of what kind of intention their judges should seek: *abstract intentions* or *concrete intentions*?

Should intentionalist judges assume the framers intended to refer to the *concepts* of "due process" and the rest, in which case the framers' intentions would be *abstract intentions*? Or did the framers intend to refer to their *conceptions* of "due process" and the rest, in which case their intentions would be *concrete intentions*? To answer this question, constitutional theorists will have to show whether abstract intentionalism or concrete intentionalism is better or worse in light not of some arbitrary standard like what just happens to be this or that conception of democracy, but in light of what's really good or right or democratic, as best we can tell. In practice, this means offering what one's audience can count as good reasons for concluding that intentionalism for judges is as good, right, or democratic an approach to constitutional interpretation as is presently feasible.

II. Moral Philosophy, Abstract Originalism, and Textualism Revisited

Our philosophic defender of intentionalism or originalism can argue for *abstract* originalist judges without any sense of alienation from what she's arguing for. The reason is that abstract originalist judges, just like their philosophic defenders, would accept Dworkin's call for a fusion of constitutional law and moral philosophy. *Abstract originalism is for all intents and purposes equivalent to the philosophic approach.*[7] And both are equivalent to textualism, properly understood (as distinguished from the plain words version of textualism we have criticized in Chapter 5). Let us explain.

The words and phrases of the constitutional document express a relatively clear set of intentions or meanings *if* by meanings we mean general concepts or ideas and *if* by intentions we mean abstract intentions.[8] We have clear evidence in the constitutional text that, through their representatives or the framers, "We the People of the United States" intended to provide "due process of law," "equal protection of the laws," regulations of "commerce" and other things in a complex institutional scheme for achieving "Justice," "the common defence," "the general Welfare," and the other goods or ends listed in the Preamble. These expressions are as clear as they can be if they are taken to refer not to anyone's version of due process, equal protection, and the rest but to due process itself, equal protection itself, and so on. But if the framers intended the *concept* of due process itself, as distinguished from some *conception* of that concept, they had to intend a role for moral philosophy in constitutional interpretation, for philosophic reflection and debate is the best way to approach the meaning and scope of due process, equal protection, and the Constitution's expressed ends.

Because constitutional provisions like due process are expressed as general concepts, the constitutional text itself is evidence that the framers' intentions were abstract. Thus, the Constitution does not define its terms or give examples of their proper applications. None of its terms comes wrapped in quotation marks. None of its standards is referred to as uniquely "ours." The Constitution doesn't say, for example, that equal protection envisions no more than equality before the law, as distinguished

---

7. We have terminological reservations about the locution abstract "originalism." *See* James E. Fleming, "Are We All Originalists Now? I Hope Not!," unpublished manuscript presented as the Alpheus T. Mason Lecture in the James Madison Program at Princeton University, available at http://web.princeton.edu/sites/jmadison/events/archives/FlemingTalk.pdf. In this book, however, we shall put those reservations aside.

8. Ronald Dworkin, *Freedom's Law: The Moral Reading of the American Constitution* (Cambridge, MA: Harvard University Press, 1996): 7–12; Ronald Dworkin, *Life's Dominion* (New York: Alfred A. Knopf, 1993): 132–44.

from social and economic equality.[9] Nor does it say that the persons promised equal protection are of African descent only.[10] The Constitution's language doesn't exclude white persons from equal protection, or female persons, or unborn persons, or poor persons, or even corporate persons, if these entities are in fact persons or if there are reasons in justice and goodness for treating them as persons. As Dworkin was the first to suggest, the Constitution's use of general, undefined, and unillustrated terms can be judged a failure of draftsmanship only if we assume that the draftsmen didn't want justice, due process, and the blessings of liberty themselves as much as they wanted to impose *their conceptions* of these things on future generations.[11]

III. Concrete Intentionalism

Though there's no support for the concrete view of the framers' intentions in the constitutional text itself—or in the literature of the American founding[12]—a concrete intentionalist judge would have to act as if she believed there were. In one of the paradoxes of her position, the concrete intentionalist judge must insult the motives or deprecate the intelligence of the framers even as she upholds their authority, for she must say, in effect, that their expressed concern for fairness and other goods (as opposed to their mere conceptions of them) was either rhetorical or delusional. She would have to say that they intended *their* conception of justice even if (1) that conception was seen as unjust at the time, or if (2) it should prove unjust later, and if (3) intending injustice is itself unjust.

A second paradox of concrete intentionalism is its separation from its justification, for, as we have seen, only a moral argument can defend concrete intentionalism, yet the concrete intentionalist judge must, if she can, ignore moral considerations in declaring the law and stick to concrete historical intentions, however offensive they may be. And she must

---

[9] *Contra* Plessy v. Ferguson, 163 U.S. 537, 544 (1896).

[10] *Contra* Slaughterhouse Cases, 83 U.S. 36, 81 (1872).

[11] Ronald Dworkin, *Taking Rights Seriously* (Cambridge, MA: Harvard University Press, 1977): 134–37.

[12] *See* H. Jefferson Powell, "The Original Understanding of Original Intent," *Harvard Law Review* 98 (1985): 885; James H. Hutson, "The Creation of the Constitution: The Integrity of the Documentary Record," *Texas Law Review* 65 (1986): 1.

do so despite evidence, in both the constitutional text and in the record we have of the public arguments and the personal correspondence of any figure who might be called a framer, that the constitutional text refers to moral concepts and the framers saw themselves as engaged in something other than an exercise in authoritarian self-assertion.

If our argument to this point is right, the theorist who defends concrete intentionalism contends, in effect, that justice or the people's happiness or some other good demands the kind of democracy in which judges sworn to uphold the Constitution ignore undeniable features of the Constitution's language and tradition together with the people's need to see authority in a favorable moral light. She contends that justice demands that courts uphold admittedly unjust conceptions of constitutional provisions in the teeth of textual and historical evidence supporting a different approach. She contends, in brief, that justice at the wholesale level can demand injustice at the retail level.

Don't assume that no one can defend such a position. Some have argued, for example, that although Jim Crow was admittedly unjust and, at the time of *Brown v. Board of Education* (1954),[13] beyond the political mobilization required to amend the Constitution to overrule *Plessy v. Ferguson* (1896)[14] through the stringent procedures of Article V, *Brown* was bad news for a nation that has much to fear from rule by unelected judges.[15] So it may be possible to argue that a greater good (freedom from judicial imperialism) justifies living with courts that enforce injustice (Jim Crow). And if we've seen why defenders of concrete intentionalism can't themselves be concrete intentionalists, we have yet to see why judges can't be concrete intentionalists.

To prepare for the final round with concrete intentionalism, we must be specific about what a concrete intention might be. Current thinking among intentionalists has settled on two or three answers. One has judges applying the *definitions* or original meanings that the framers attached to particular constitutional terms.[16] A second answer has judges adopting

---

13. 347 U.S. 483 (1954).
14. 163 U.S. 537 (1896).
15. *See* Raoul Berger, *Government by Judiciary: The Transformation of the Fourteenth Amendment* (Cambridge, MA: Harvard University Press, 1977): 407–18.
16. *See* Bork, *supra* note 1, at 143–45; Scalia, *supra* note 1, at 37–38, 44–46; Antonin Scalia, "Originalism: The Lesser Evil," *University of Cincinnati Law Review* 57 (1989): 849, 852, 856–60, 863–64.

the *general outlook or mindset* of the framers.[17] A third version of concrete intentions would have judges looking for the framers' actual *expectations* concerning, or planned *applications* of, specific constitutional provisions to specific situations.[18] Although most intentionalists have all but abandoned this third possibility, we shall have to discuss it.

The *framers' mindset* version of concrete intentionalism (the second version above) can hardly free judges from philosophic choices in hard cases; it can only hope that modern judges view modern problems as *the framers would have done today*. Modern judges, like the framers, would still claim an interest in justice itself—as per the implicit claim in the Constitution's language, the political rhetoric of the ratification period, and the public-spirited rhetoric that is typical of politicians and officials everywhere and at all times. (We are aware of no private correspondence from anyone usually identified as an American founding father or as a framer or ratifier of any constitutional provision that frankly urges the ratification of an admittedly unjust, arbitrary, or purely self-serving provision.) And if modern judges made this claim in good faith, they would remain ready to replace worse conceptions of constitutional provisions with better ones, as long as they thought like the framers when deciding what the better ones would be. Since deciding what's better would involve philosophic responsibilities, modern judges would bear those responsibilities, if only as the framers would have.

But had the framers been interested more in justice than in anyone's particular version of justice—as their rhetoric and the language of the Constitution indicates—then the decisive fact of the framer's mindset would be their interest in justice. So, judges with the framers' mindset would also be interested mostly in justice. This would mean that judges who would think like the framers would forget the framers and concentrate on the morally best interpretations that constitutional language plausibly could bear.[19] Mindset originalism thus turns out to be a variation on

---

17. *See* Michael W. McConnell, "Federalism: Evaluating the Founders' Design," *University of Chicago Law Review* 54 (1987): 1484; Michael W. McConnell, "On Reading the Constitution," *Cornell Law Review* 73 (1988): 359; Michael W. McConnell, "The Role of Democratic Politics in Transforming Moral Convictions into Law," *Yale Law Journal* 98 (1989): 1501; Michael W. McConnell, "Originalism and the Desegregation Decisions," *Virginia Law Review* 81 (1995): 947.
18. *See* Berger, *supra* note 15.
19. *See* Michael S. Moore, "A Natural Law Theory of Interpretation," *Southern California Law Review* 58 (1985): 277, 340–41; Sotirios A. Barber, *The Constitution of Judicial Power* (Baltimore: Johns Hopkins University Press, 1993): 131–35.

abstract originalism, and both are equivalent to the philosophic approach, the bête noire of those who style themselves originalists.

From conceptions as mindsets, concrete intentionalists can move to conceptions as *definitions* or *verbal entities* (our first possibility above): the more or less specific definitions or original meanings allegedly held by the framers. An example of such a definition would be equal protection defined as equality for black Americans in civil rights only, with civil rights defined to include nothing beyond (1) the right to equal benefits (like police and fire protection) under laws designed to protect persons and property, (2) an equal right to contract with other persons for goods and services, (3) and equal access to the civil courts.[20] This intentionalist says, in effect, that in hard cases involving the Equal Protection Clause, judges should ignore the constitutional *definiendum*— equal protection—and concentrate on what research into the historical record reveals as the *definiens*—equal access to the courts, equal right to contract, and so on.

Objections to this approach replay the difficulties of intentionalism generally. How do we decide whose definitions to count and what evidence to derive definitions from? How can we attribute just one definition in the face of apparent disagreements among the founding's leading figures?[21]

[20.] *See* Berger, *supra* note 15, at 166–92.

[21.] Attributing one definition to disagreeing parties would usually mean subsuming their disagreements under terms broader than their clashing conceptions. If one definition of free speech united Hamilton and Madison despite their disagreement about the constitutionality of the Sedition Act, then that definition did not preclude the disagreement. Nor can knowledge of that definition remove the need for reflection and choice between Hamilton's theory and Madison's.

One definition can occupy the same level of generality as the contending conceptions only if one of the contending parties thought he opposed the other but really didn't. Thus an observer might conclude that although Madison thought he opposed Hamilton's definition of "necessary and proper," he really didn't, for the weight of the evidence shows that Hamilton's theory of the Necessary and Proper Clause was essential to what Madison thought more important than preserving states' rights: preserving the Union. Judgments like these force the observer into fresh philosophic and scientific reflections because politicians typically say that things like justice and the people's happiness are the most important things (*see, e.g., The Federalist*, ed. Jacob E. Cooke [Middletown, CT: Wesleyan University Press, 1961], Nos. 45 & 51), and the observer now assumes that the framers' *real* definitions and intentions are what conduce to justice and happiness (which they said were most important), notwithstanding what the framers believed about their definitions and intentions at the time.

Rejecting this quest for real as opposed to apparent definitions and intentions forces an observer back to the strategy of attributing definitions broader than the contending conceptions, which forces the observer to choose one of the contending conceptions.

If we assumed these problems resolved, we would still face the question of what it means to employ someone's definition. Are we faithful to someone's definition of x when we confound the definition with what it is supposed to be a definition of? When intentionalists ignore the *definiendum*, they no longer treat the *definiens as* a definiens. When we define, we define *something*, and a definition can't be known as the definition of something if we ignore the thing to be defined. This seems a feature of our ordinary linguistic practice. Another such feature is our understanding that definitions can be inadequate or wrong, and that when definition is our aim, we should replace worse definitions with better ones when better ones appear. To replace "equal protection" with "equal access to the courts" and the like is therefore not to *define* "equal protection," it is to ignore it. By keeping both the *definiendum* and the proposed *definiens* in mind, we see that the proposed *definiens* is revisable. A concrete intentionalism that confounds *definiendum* and *definiens* thus deviates from a linguistic practice that treats definitions of equal protection and similar terms as no more than revisable theories of their nature.[22] A definitional approach, properly conceived, thus argues for the same result as a mind-set approach, properly conceived: a fusion of constitutional law and moral philosophy.

To avoid this result, our intentionalist might resort to the framers' actual or planned *applications* of constitutional provisions (our third possibility above). He might say, for example, that equal protection would not prohibit segregated schools because the framers of the Fourteenth Amendment allowed segregated schools and discussed no plans to outlaw them.[23] Modern intentionalists shy away from this position for compelling practical reasons. Consistently applied, a framers'-application approach would disable governmental powers as well as individual and minority rights.[24] A framers'-application approach might undermine not only the constitutionality of the nation's labor laws and social welfare programs; it also would undermine the legality of NASA and the Air Force,

---

22. Moore, *supra* note 19, at 296–97, 340–41.

23. Berger, *supra* note 15, at 117–33.

24. *See* McConnell, "The Role of Democratic Politics in Transforming Moral Convictions into Law," *supra* note 17, at 1533; Robert H. Bork, Foreword to Gary M. McDowell, *The Constitution and Contemporary Constitutional Theory* (Cumberland, VA: Center for Judicial Studies, 1985); Christopher Wolfe, *The Rise of Modern Judicial Review: From Constitutional Interpretation to Judge-Made Law*, rev. ed. (Lanham, MD: Rowman & Littlefield, 1994): 57–58.

federal laws against drug abuse, interstate kidnapping, and racketeering, executive agreements with foreign nations, presidential vetoes on grounds unrelated to the preservation of presidential powers, and many other practices of modern government.[25]

Beyond these practical problems lies a theoretical problem with a framers'-application approach: applications of constitutional provisions are *events*, not verbal entities, and only verbal entities can function as norms for guiding conduct or as premises that justify legal decisions. To be useful in constitutional interpretation, therefore, the events in question—the framers' applications of constitutional provisions—would have to be *described*. Because any event can always be described in different ways, because descriptions are contextual, and because different descriptions can justify different legal outcomes, controversial choices among alternative descriptions are unavoidable.

Let us be specific about what descriptions we shall need. Applications of constitutional provisions are events of a kind called *actions*. These actions apply constitutional provisions to concrete acts or practices of government to determine the constitutionality of those acts or practices. The Equal Protection Clause, for example, would be applied to the practice of racially segregating public schools to determine the constitutionality of that practice. The act of applying the Equal Protection Clause would consist of two steps: interpreting the Clause and describing the practice of segregation in terms relevant to one's interpretation of the Clause. These two steps can be represented as the premises of a syllogism—with the major premise stating a rule or principle of law, the minor premise stating a description of the act or practice to which the law applies, and the conclusion representing the decision of the case. How, then, would we represent the framers' application of the Equal Protection Clause to the practice of racially segregating public schools?

The framers of the Fourteenth Amendment (some or all of them) might have described their own action as excluding segregated schools from the prohibitions of the Equal Protection Clause. We shall assume this for present purposes. The actual words of the Clause, however, can hardly be reduced to "permit segregated schools." We can represent the framers' action as a legal syllogism whose major premise is that the Equal Protection Clause prohibits state governmental actions that harm racial

---

[25]. *See* Stephen Macedo, *The New Right v. The Constitution* (Washington, DC: Cato Institute, 1987): 25, 35.

minorities invidiously. The minor premise of the framers' action, on our present assumption, was not a statement about the law of the Constitution; it was a statement about the world. We can formulate their minor premise to say that segregation of the races does no unique harm to racial minorities–that is, if segregation harms anyone, it harms whites as well as blacks. From the major and the minor premises together the holding follows: segregation doesn't deny equal protection.

Because this is a plausible way to represent what the framers did, we can say that the *Brown* Court didn't change the framers' view of the *law* when it rejected the framers' view of the *world* (together with the view of *Plessy* that the regime of "separate but equal" did not harm blacks).[26] Let us assume that the Equal Protection Clause meant the same to both sets of interpreters: states may not harm racial minorities in special ways.[27] But the view of the world had changed between the 1860s, when the Clause was ratified, and the 1950s, when the issue of segregated schools came before the Court. The framers (we are assuming for the sake of argument) thought that forced segregation didn't hurt blacks any more than it hurt whites. The *Brown* Court found otherwise through an argument that used scientific evidence to confirm the testimony of common sense: forced segregation of the races in modern America did indeed harm racial minorities invidiously. In *Brown*, the old major premise combined with the new minor premise to outlaw forced segregation. On the present account of what the framers actually did, the *Brown* Court did not depart from the framers' view of the law, and this description seems as fair as any to the historical record. No less an originalist than Robert Bork has used a similar argument to rationalize his approval of *Brown*.[28] What is more, our account accords with that of the joint opinion in *Planned Parenthood v. Casey* (1992), that *Brown* was justified in overruling *Plessy* because of a change in understanding of the facts about the world.[29]

A heroic (or diehard) strain of originalism might try to prove its originalist bona fides by declaring *Brown* a mistake and by insisting that judges adopt the framers' view of the world in addition to the framers'

[26.] 163 U.S. at 551.

[27.] We put to one side the theoretical debate concerning the best understanding of the Equal Protection Clause—whether it embodies a principle of opposition to caste systems (an anticaste principle) or a principle of racial neutrality—and the possibility that a shift from the latter to the former may have occurred between *Plessy* and *Brown*.

[28.] Bork, *supra* note 1, at 81–84.

[29.] 505 U.S. 833, 862–63 (1992).

view of the law. It might hold that *as a matter of law*, segregation is not harmful—regardless of the scientific or common sense evidence to the contrary—and that segregation will remain harmless *as a matter of law* until the law is changed by formal constitutional amendment. But prudent originalists can't welcome a strategy that serves only to expose the high costs of originalism. It's hard to argue that the framers or anyone else could acquire either the right or the power to establish not only the law but also the facts of life. It's hard to argue that our constitutional system can't operate without resort to descriptions of the world repulsive to science and common sense. Tradition itself is one of the things that makes these arguments hard to advance.[30] The nation's Enlightenment tradition places a heavy burden on any suggestion that the facts of life can be determined by fiat or that the Constitution forces judges to falsify the world. Sometimes we can change the facts of life by altering their causes. But to alter causal relationships successfully, we usually have to understand them first. Laws that force us to falsify reality cripple our hopes for shaping reality, and there's no good reason to view the Constitution as such a law.

IV. What Is the New Originalism? Same as the Old Originalism

Many self-styled originalists are at pains to differentiate themselves from concrete originalists (like Raoul Berger) and to insist that their versions of originalism are not vulnerable to common criticisms of concrete originalism.[31] Keith Whittington is perhaps the leading such

---

[30.] Nature and logic may be others. The perceived nature of nature makes it implausible that we can change the world just by some legal declaration that the world is changed. And it would be self-contradictory to say: "It's a fact of life that the facts of life depend entirely on the judgments of some political authority."

[31.] There is an argument that even Scalia is a new originalist. In "Originalism: The Lesser Evil," *supra* note 16, at 861, Scalia rejects "strong medicine originalism," which he associates with Raoul Berger: roughly, originalism that is prepared to swallow the bitter pill of following whatever historical research shows to be the concrete framers' intention, even if, e.g., it entails that *Brown* was wrongly decided. Instead, Scalia embraces "faint-hearted originalism," *id.* at 863–64: originalism with a dose of evolutionary intent to the Constitution, or a "trace of constitutional perfectionism," e.g., *Brown* was rightly decided. Furthermore, Scalia has supplemented originalism with his understanding that the Constitution includes certain traditions, understood as specific historical practices as distinguished from abstract aspirational principles. Michael H. v. Gerald D., 491 U.S. 110, 127 n.6 (1989) (Scalia, J., plurality opinion). Thus, Bork charges that Scalia is a conservative constitutional revisionist, that is, a new originalist. *See* Bork, *supra* note 1, at 235–40.

"new originalist." He openly professes his new originalism in an article entitled, appropriately, *The New Originalism*.[32] One might think that the new, improved originalists would be scholars and jurists who seek to reconstruct originalism to correct the theoretical flaws of the old originalism, or at least to bolster it against powerful criticisms. But Whittington, with refreshing frankness, provides a rather different account. He says that the new originalists are conservatives in power, whereas the old originalists were conservatives in the minority! His account of the old originalism is that it emerged as a conservative reaction against the Warren Court, and was mostly negative and critical of Warren Court decisions like *Griswold v. Connecticut* (1965), recognizing a right of privacy, and

---

[32.] Keith E. Whittington, "The New Originalism," *Georgetown Journal of Law & Public Policy* 2 (2004): 599. Randy Barnett might also be viewed as a new originalist. *See* Randy E. Barnett, *Restoring the Lost Constitution: The Presumption of Liberty* (Princeton, NJ: Princeton University Press, 2004): 89–130. Barnett accepts a well-known criticism of efforts to find the Constitution's meaning in the *applications* that the framers allegedly had in mind. He agrees with an argument by Paul Brest that it would be impossible to combine into one coherent intention the subjective expectations of numerous drafters and state with any confidence what they jointly would have said about problems beyond their capacity to foresee. *Id.* at 90 (citing Paul Brest, "The Misconceived Quest for the Original Understanding," *Boston University Law Review* 60 (1980): 204). Barnett remains an originalist, however. He believes that (1) word meanings change with the passage of time; (2) constitutions are written to limit the choices of future interpreters; (3) interpreters not bound by "original meanings" will be free to do as they wish; and (4) fidelity to the Constitution as written is fidelity to "original meanings." *Id.* at 94–109. Barnett proposes a new and more "moderate originalism," which he distinguishes from the old or "strict originalism." The old originalism he calls "original intent originalism," and the new originalism is "original meaning originalism." The latter originalism is immune to the criticisms of the old originalism, he contends, because it doesn't have to "aggregate" and apply numerous subjective intentions; it can find constitutional meaning in the ordinary public meanings of words and phrases, as recorded in sources like old dictionaries and documents. *Id.* at 93.

From this alone it should be evident that there's nothing really new about Barnett's originalism. Like Whittington, whom he follows (*see id.* at 119–21), Barnett offers a disguised form of the old originalism. For relying on old dictionaries and documents is relying on the historical definitions and applications of words, rather than the nature of the things they signify (or are ordinarily understood to signify). It is because Barnett assumes that there is no "nature" for a word to signify—because he might assume, for example, that "frogs" and "justice" refer not to frogs and justice (the real things or presumed real things) but to what people believe about frogs and justice—that he can say that separation from original meanings (definitions and applications) leaves interpreters free to do as they wish, thus frustrating the regulatory function of law. One who believed that these words picked out real things about which anyone can err could accept a continuing obligation to strive self-critically for the truth about or best understanding of these things. Such a person would not agree that her choice was between old meanings (definitions/applications) and freedom to decide as she wished, whatever she might wish.

early Burger Court decisions like *Roe v. Wade* (1973), recognizing the right of a woman to terminate a pregnancy.[33] Now that conservatives are in power and have control of the judiciary, Whittington says, originalists need to move from being largely reactive and critical to developing "a governing philosophy appropriate to guide majority opinions, not just to fill dissents."[34] Enter the new originalism.

The new originalism as a governing conservative constitutional theory, Whittington suggests, "is less likely to emphasize a primary commitment to judicial restraint,"[35] the leading aim of the old originalism. Indeed. First, "there seems to be less emphasis on the capacity of originalism to limit the discretion of the judge." Second, "there is also a loosening of the connection between originalism and judicial deference to legislative majorities." Instead, "[t]he primary virtue claimed by the new originalism is one of constitutional fidelity, not of judicial restraint or democratic majoritarianism." In sum, Whittington argues, the new originalism "does not require that judges get out of the way of legislatures. It requires that judges uphold the original Constitution—nothing more, but also nothing less."[36] Critics of originalism have long charged that originalism is not fundamentally a theory of "judicial restraint" or democratic majoritarianism but rather a program for upholding the Constitution as originalists conceive it. The leading theorist of the new originalism now confirms this view of originalism.

How, then, does the new originalism view the Constitution? In his book, *Constitutional Interpretation*, Whittington seeks to reconstruct originalism and rescue it from the flaws of the old originalism (or, he says, its supposed flaws).[37] Immediately below, we will assess his work, but here we preview the punch line of our criticism. Whittington once introduced an article with a quotation from a song by the rock-and-roll band The Who.[38] To encapsulate our criticism of Whittington's originalism,

---

33. Whittington, "The New Originalism," *supra* note 32, at 599–604.

34. *Id.* at 604.

35. *Id.* at 608.

36. *Id.* at 608–09.

37. *Id.* at 605; Keith E. Whittington, *Constitutional Interpretation: Textual Meaning, Original Intent, and Judicial Review* (Lawrence: University Press of Kansas, 1999): 160–61 [hereinafter Whittington, *Constitutional Interpretation*].

38. Keith E. Whittington, "Yet Another Constitutional Crisis?," *William & Mary Law Review* 43 (2002): 2093, 2094 (beginning with an epigraph, "This is no social crisis. Just another tricky day for you," from the song "Another Tricky Day," by Pete Townshend, on The Who, *Face Dances* [1981]).

we too invoke a line from a Who song. The song is "Won't Get Fooled Again"; the lyric is "Meet the new boss. Same as the old boss."[39] This line is apt not only because it suggests that the new originalism suffers from the same flaws as the old, but also because the notion of "boss" calls to mind the authoritarianism of originalism, old and new. (Fittingly, a recent article in the *New York Times* reported that this song by The Who is the top conservative rock song of all time, as chosen by the *National Review*.)[40]

A. Interpretation Does Not Entail Originalism

Originalists sometimes claim or assume that interpretation necessarily entails originalism. This claim ranges from naive or crude versions to sophisticated versions. The claim is most famously illustrated in the old, discredited dichotomy of "interpretivism" versus "noninterpretivism."[41] People who now call themselves originalists used this dichotomy to load the dice in favor of interpretivism, saying that their fidelity to concrete framers' intent or original meaning (which they conflated with constitutional language) made them the only ones who believed in "interpreting" the Constitution, leaving others (whom they called "noninterpretivists") to advocate remaking or changing the Constitution.

Whittington's first move in reconstructing originalism is to concede points to critics of originalism. For example, he more forthrightly grapples with arguments Dworkin has made about interpretation than any other originalist.[42] Unlike Bork and Scalia, he doesn't simply hurl insults about Dworkin being a "noninterpretivist" or even a heretic or expatriate who would subvert the Constitution.[43] For example, Whittington

---

39. "Won't Get Fooled Again," by Pete Townshend, on The Who, *Who's Next* (1971).
40. Ben Sisario, "Listening to Rock and Hearing Sounds of Conservatism," *New York Times*, May 25, 2006 (reporting on a list of the "top 50 conservative rock songs of all time," as chosen by the *National Review*).
41. *See, e.g.*, Thomas C. Grey, "Do We Have an Unwritten Constitution?" *Stanford Law Review* 27 (1975): 703, 703–04; John Hart Ely, *Democracy and Distrust* (Cambridge, MA: Harvard University Press, 1980): 1.
42. *See, e.g.*, Whittington, *Constitutional Interpretation*, *supra* note 37, at 182–87; Keith E. Whittington, "Dworkin's 'Originalism': The Role of Intentions in Constitutional Interpretation," *Review of Politics* 62 (2000): 197 [hereinafter Whittington, "Dworkin's 'Originalism'"].
43. *See* Bork, *supra* note 1, at 136 ("subversion"), 213–14 ("revisionism"), 352 ("heresies"); Scalia, *supra* note 16, at 854 (referring to Dworkin, an American citizen, as "Oxford Professor (and expatriate American)").

appears to concede that Dworkin (and Thomas Grey) are right in saying that "We are all interpretivists" and that the real question is not whether we should interpret or not, but rather *what* the Constitution is and *how* we should interpret it?[44] Thus, Whittington appears to concede that Dworkin has advanced a conception of interpretation that is an alternative to originalism.

What is more, Whittington's project in his companion book, *Constitutional Construction*, is to broaden constitutional discourse to include two ways of elaborating constitutional meaning: not only *interpretation* by courts (the characteristic preoccupation of the old originalists) but also *construction* outside the courts by legislatures and executives.[45] He explains his distinction between interpretation and construction as follows: "Unlike jurisprudential interpretation, construction provides for an element of creativity in construing constitutional meaning. Constructions do not pursue a preexisting if deeply hidden meaning in the founding document; rather, they elucidate the text in the interstices of discoverable, interpretive meaning, where the text is so broad or so underdetermined as to be incapable of faithful but exhaustive reduction to legal rules."[46] But then, just when it begins to look like Whittington is developing a constitutional theory—of interpretation and construction—that might be safe for people who are not concrete originalists, he makes two key moves. First he says that what people like Dworkin (and us) call *interpretation* is really *construction*, and therefore is appropriate for legislatures but not for courts.[47] That is, he tries to deflect the force of Dworkin's criticisms of originalism by saying that Dworkin's conception of interpretation more properly should be understood as a theory of construction, which would be appropriate for legislatures, not courts. This is Whittington's more sophisticated version of Bork's and Scalia's claim that Dworkin is advocating judicial legislation—judges making law, not interpreting it.

---

44. *See* Whittington, "Dworkin's 'Originalism,'" *supra* note 42, at 197–98; Whittington, "The New Originalism," *supra* note 32, at 606–07; Whittington, *Constitutional Interpretation, supra* note 37, at 164–65.

45. Keith E. Whittington, *Constitutional Construction: Divided Powers and Constitutional Meaning* (Cambridge, MA: Harvard University Press, 1999): 1–19 [hereinafter Whittington, *Constitutional Construction*].

46. *Id.* at 5.

47. *See* Whittington, *Constitutional Interpretation, supra* note 37, at 54, 58, 206–12; Whittington, "The New Originalism," *supra* note 32, at 611–13.

Whittington's second move is to say that a commitment to interpretation necessarily entails a commitment to originalism. Indeed, Whittington practically revives a version of the discredited distinction between interpretivism and noninterpretivism. He writes that his "account of originalism largely assumes a prior commitment on the part of constitutional theorists, judges, and the nation to constitutional interpretation." He continues: "If we are to interpret, then I believe we must be originalists."[48] That is, interpretation entails originalism. Whittington adds: "But we may not want to interpret. . . . We may want to engage in a 'text-based social practice,' but that is not the same thing as being committed to interpretive fidelity."[49] In other words, the people who want to do that are not interpreting. Here he echoes the discredited old charge that anyone who is not committed to an originalist conception of interpretive fidelity is a "noninterpretivist" whose real interest is not interpreting the Constitution but changing it.

We want to step back for a moment and offer a hypothesis about what Whittington is doing. Our suggestion is that in responding to criticisms of the old originalism, Whittington tries to *expand* the realm of constitutional discourse to include constitutional construction *outside the courts*; but he does so in order to justify *narrowing* constitutional interpretation *inside the courts* to originalism. All of this is a rhetorically effective way of seeming to agree with arguments that no originalist could answer, while deflecting those arguments and reinstating positions that no originalist can defend. Whittington sketches a notion of constitutional construction by legislatures and executives, and gives such historical examples of it as the impeachment of Justice Samuel Chase in 1804–05, which helped establish subsequent understandings of the purpose and limits of federal impeachment power, and the nullification crisis of 1832–33, which promoted more decentralizing conceptions of federalism.[50] Yet he does not articulate criteria for distinguishing kinds of decisions that are appropriately made by courts through "interpretation" and kinds of decisions that should be left to legislatures and executives through "construction." Nor does he answer the question why courts should limit themselves to what he calls "interpretation" rather than "construction." As stated above, he throws out the old originalist claims about "judicial restraint" and

---

[48.] Whittington, "The New Originalism," *supra* note 32, at 612.
[49.] *Id.* at 612–13.
[50.] Whittington, *Constitutional Construction, supra* note 45, at 17–18.

"democratic majoritarianism." All that is left is his assumption that interpretation necessarily entails originalism.

Whittington's distinction between interpretation and construction is a distraction from the basic questions. The distinction was originally motivated by his early interest in *restraining what was then a liberal federal judiciary—not the discovery of constitutional meaning.* Moreover, as Whittington treats the distinction, it is useless to us because he himself says that both construction and interpretation are methods of elaborating constitutional meaning. From Whittington's own use of the distinction, interpretation is mere discovery and application of noncontroversial constitutional provisions (like those relating to the frequency of elections and the ages of officials), while construction occurs when controversial ideas whose meaning cannot be reduced to uncontroversial legal rules (equal protection, due process, and the like) are elaborated and applied.[51] "Construction" (Whittington's approach to hard cases) thus does the work that "interpretation" does in this book. Whittington's "construction" seems equivalent to what we dub (in Chapter 11) the pragmatist view of interpretation—essentially a policy-making process of the kind one leaves to legislatures, which is precisely what Whittington wanted to do before the Bush White House and Senate populated the federal judiciary with conservatives. Finally, we've never seen anyone use the distinction between construction and interpretation consistently. The terms "construction" and "interpretation" are freely used as synonyms for each other in *The Federalist* and throughout constitutional history and commentary before Whittington. One need only recall Chief Justice John Marshall's famous statement in *McCulloch v. Maryland* (1819) that resolution of the question whether Congress had the power to establish a national bank depended upon "a fair construction of the whole instrument."[52]

B: Conclusion: Fidelity to the Constitution As Written

Originalism, old and new, would make a virtue of exiling moral philosophy from the activity of constitutional interpretation. But from what we have seen thus far, exiling philosophic choice from interpretation is impossible, and exiling responsible philosophic choice is indefensible.

[51.] *See* Whittington, *Constitutional Interpretation, supra* note 37, at 5–14.
[52.] 17 U.S. 316, 406 (1819).

Interpreting the Constitution with fidelity requires judgments of moral philosophy about how constitutional principles are best understood.

Originalism, old and new, misconceives fidelity in constitutional interpretation. Ironically, in the name of interpretive fidelity, originalists would enshrine an authoritarian constitution that defies justification and that the framers didn't write and the ratifiers didn't ratify—a constitution that, for these reasons, does not deserve our fidelity. The philosophic approach, because it accepts the Constitution's actual language and therewith the moral justification that the framers and the founding generation claimed for themselves, interprets and exhorts us to interpret the Constitution to make it the best it can be. The philosophic approach thus offers hope that the Constitution may deserve the fidelity that it claims to deserve.

From what we've seen so far, therefore, narrow or concrete originalism/intentionalism (whether old or new) has no successful argument against Dworkin's showing that the Constitution, as written, demands a fusion of constitutional law and moral philosophy. We'll have to see, in Chapter 7, whether originalism has still further arguments and whether yet another kind of originalism, *broad originalism*, can succeed where the others have failed.

CHAPTER 7

BROAD ORIGINALISM

We are distinguishing three kinds of originalism. The first is *abstract originalism.*[1] As we explained in Chapter 6, if a constitutional provision is written in general terms, abstract originalism construes those terms to refer to general ideas or concepts. Thus, "due process" is taken to refer to *due process*, not anyone's conception of due process. The abstract originalist accepts Ronald Dworkin's argument that fidelity to the Constitution as written calls for a fusion of constitutional law and moral philosophy.[2] This is due to the presence in the Constitution of moral terms like "justice" (in the Preamble) and "due process" (in the Fifth and Fourteenth Amendments), a kind of justice. Because the Constitution neither defines nor illustrates these or any of its terms, and because (recall Dworkin's thought experiment in Chapter 2) the moral authority of the founding generation (the Preamble's "We the People") depends on that generation's interest in the well-being of its posterity (as opposed to the arbitrary and narcissistic imposition of its authority and image on others), "due process" must refer to *due process itself*, not this or that conception of due process. And to cite examples of a different kind, regulations of commerce and wagings of war can be seen as constitutional only if they serve good-faith and arguably sound attempts to advance preambulary ends like the general welfare and the common defense. For those who think these terms refer to real things,

---

[1.] As stated in Chapter 6, note 7, we have terminological reservations about the locution abstract "originalism." In this book, however, we shall put those reservations aside.

[2.] Ronald Dworkin, *Taking Rights Seriously* (Cambridge, MA: Harvard University Press, 1977): 149.

"due process" and other kinds of justice along with "the common defense" and "the general welfare" mean what they ought to mean, as approximated through the give-and-take of philosophic and scientific reflection and debate. (Those who deny that these terms refer to real things in some sense may end up subscribing to the legal pragmatism that we discuss in Chapter 11. Pragmatists of this skeptical variety scoff at concerns with "interpretation" and "fidelity," as we shall see.)

There are important differences between moral philosophy standing alone and moral philosophy fused with constitutional law, and we outline those differences and their consequences for constitutional interpretation in Chapter 10. For now, we'll say that Dworkin has argued persuasively that fidelity to the Constitution as written demands what he calls the moral reading of the Constitution and what we are calling the philosophic approach to the Constitution.[3] The faithful interpreter will listen to others, look at the law and the general understanding of the law evident in historical materials and legal precedents, and think for herself about the best that concepts or ideas like due process can mean both generally and for the facts at hand.

The second kind of originalism is *concrete* or *narrow originalism*. We reviewed the problems with this kind of originalism in Chapter 6, and we'll say more about these problems in this chapter. Some writers claim that there is a third kind of originalism, one that is in some sense "between" abstract originalism and concrete originalism. In this chapter, we reject such an intermediate originalism. We call this third form *broad originalism*.

Broad originalism is actually a family of positions represented by some of the nation's most prominent constitutional theorists, including Bruce Ackerman, Lawrence Lessig, Cass Sunstein, Akhil Amar, Michael Perry, and others.[4] We simplify our treatment of this family here because in this book

---

3. Ronald Dworkin, *Freedom's Law: The Moral Reading of the American Constitution* (Cambridge, MA: Harvard University Press, 1996) [hereinafter Dworkin, *Freedom's Law*].

4. *See* Bruce Ackerman, *We the People: Foundations* (Cambridge, MA: Harvard University Press, 1991) [hereinafter Ackerman, *We the People*]; Lawrence Lessig, "Fidelity and Constraint," *Fordham Law Review* 65 (1997): 1365 [hereinafter Lessig, "Constraint"]; Lawrence Lessig, "Understanding Changed Readings: Fidelity and Theory," *Stanford Law Review* 47 (1995): 395; Lawrence Lessig, "Fidelity in Translation," *Texas Law Review* 71 (1993): 1165 [hereinafter Lessig, "Fidelity"]; Lawrence Lessig & Cass R. Sunstein, "The President and the Administration," *Columbia Law Review* 94 (1994): 1; Cass R. Sunstein, *Legal Reasoning and Political Conflict* (New York: Oxford University Press, 1996) [hereinafter Sunstein, *Legal Reasoning*]; Akhil Reed Amar, *The Bill of Rights: Creation and Reconstruction* (New Haven, CT: Yale University Press, 1998); Akhil Reed

we want to cover the basic and controlling questions, not variations that, while interesting in other contexts (like intellectual history), don't help to settle the question of how to decide what the Constitution means. The broad originalism we shall consider purports to be a position in the theoretical space between concrete originalism and abstract originalism. Our criticism of concrete originalism applies to any position that could claim to occupy such a middle ground.

I. Broad Originalism: Its Meaning, Motivation, and Premise

B road originalists seek a middle way between narrow or concrete originalism and abstract originalism or the philosophic approach. They agree that concrete originalism is, for various theoretical and practical reasons, unworkable and indefensible. But they also feel that the philosophic approach is incapable of being faithful to the Constitution.

Dworkin is a special target of the broad originalists; they complain about the content and scope of rights that he interprets the Constitution to protect. They place him on the left end of a spectrum whose right extreme is occupied by Robert Bork, Antonin Scalia, and William Rehnquist.[5] Though Lessig, a broad originalist, has little in common with Bork ideologically, he makes a Borkish comment when calling Dworkin an "infidel" of the law.[6] Lessig and Sunstein contend that Dworkin's moral reading of the Constitution is not a method of interpretation as much as a method for improving the Constitution in a left-liberal direction.[7]

Amar, "Intratextualism," *Harvard Law Review* 112 (1999): 747; Michael J. Perry, *The Constitution in the Courts* (New York: Oxford University Press, 1994). Other works illustrating the emergence of a form of broad originalism include Martin S. Flaherty, "History 'Lite' in Modern American Constitutionalism," *Columbia Law Review* 95 (1995): 523; William M. Treanor, "The Original Understanding of the Takings Clause and the Political Process," *Columbia Law Review* 95 (1995): 782.

5. *Compare* Ackerman, *We the People, supra* note 4, at 10–16 (criticizing Dworkin) *with* Bruce Ackerman, "Robert Bork's Grand Inquisition," *Yale Law Journal* 99 (1990): 1419 (reviewing and criticizing Robert H. Bork, *The Tempting of America* (New York: Free Press, 1990)); *compare* Sunstein, *Legal Reasoning, supra* note 4, at 48–53 (criticizing Dworkin) *with* Sunstein, *The Partial Constitution* (Cambridge, MA: Harvard University Press, 1993): 96–110 (criticizing Bork); *see also* Lessig, "Fidelity," *supra* note 4, at 1260 ("From the perspective of the two-step fidelitist, both the originalist [such as Scalia] and the Dworkinian are infidels.").

6. Lessig, "Fidelity," *supra* note 4, at 1260.

The broad originalist believes that Dworkin's chief problem is his emphasis on doing the right thing (as left-liberals see it) at the expense of what American constitutional history and traditions indicate the right thing is. Broad originalists believe the cure for Dworkin's abstract arguments for rights (especially rights of privacy or autonomy) is greater respect for historical beliefs and practices. They therefore recommend a "turn to history" in constitutional theory, and by a turn to history, they mean in part a turn away from Dworkin's philosophic approach. We shall see that a turn to history need not be and, understood correctly, cannot be a turn away from the responsibility of philosophic reflection and choice. The turn to history should be reconceived as being in service of, not an alternative to, the philosophic approach.

Unlike most narrow or concrete originalists, the broad originalists deny that a turn to history is a turn to the policies of the political right. In fact, a major motivation of the broad originalists discussed here is to rescue history from the political right. They believe (and we agree, as our analysis of *The Federalist* in Chapter 3 would suggest) that the nationalist and rationalist (i.e., secular) constitutionalism that prevailed at the founding is much closer to the constitutionalism of the New Deal and the Warren Court than to the (selectively) small-government, states'-rights, and anti-rationalist constitutionalism of figures like Bork, Scalia, and Rehnquist. Most broad originalists therefore urge their fellow liberals and progressives to acquaint themselves with a history that liberals and progressives often neglect on the (false) assumption that it is irrelevant to (or indeed a hindrance to) addressing modern problems.

Broad originalists identify the middle position they would assume between concrete and abstract originalism in terms of the "level of abstraction" at which they conceive and characterize constitutional provisions. To see what they mean by "level of abstraction," consider the Equal Protection Clause of the Fourteenth Amendment.[8] This clause prohibits the states from denying to "any person" "the equal protection of the laws." A concrete originalist might say (*might* say, for there's no canonical way to describe what happened when the Fourteenth Amendment was adopted) that the Equal Protection Clause was intended to enable the national government

---

[7.] Lessig & Sunstein, *supra* note 4, at 11 n. 35, 85 n. 336.

[8.] For an exposé of the ways in which narrow originalists vary the level of abstraction at which they conceive the Equal Protection Clause in order to justify the results they prefer on political grounds, *see* Ronald Dworkin, *Life's Dominion* (New York: Alfred A. Knopf, 1993): 132–43.

to stop the southern states from ignoring private violence against newly freed persons of African descent and to guarantee the freedmen the right to own property and to sue in civil courts.

An abstract originalist could find a great deal more in the Equal Protection Clause. Forming a judgment of the principle behind what the framers said and did, our abstract originalist might well see the Equal Protection Clause as a general protection against all discriminatory practices and acts that deny equal concern and respect and that are not justifiable as good-faith efforts to serve the common good of the entire community. Thus conceived, the Clause could protect voting rights and equal access to all public services, for whites as well as blacks, for women and for men, for homosexuals and for heterosexuals, and for persons of different religions and political persuasions. Abstract originalists might even claim that the principle that justifies protecting blacks from private violence also protects unborn persons from private violence and poor persons, especially children, from undeserved poverty and ignorance.

The broad originalists would end up somewhere in the middle on the ground that the historical beliefs of most Americans would probably not embrace judicially mandated protection for the unborn or welfare rights for the poor, though they would embrace some forms of protection for women and religious minorities and perhaps for homosexuals. "Person" in the abstract could cover whatever our best scientific or moral theory of personhood indicated a person to be. "Person" in the concrete would be "black person." And "person" at a middle level of abstraction would include "white person," "female person," and possibly "homosexual person," but perhaps not "poor person."[9]

With Dworkin, we shall argue eventually that the search for an intermediate theory is futile and that the philosophic approach, or the moral reading, is the only interpretative strategy that is faithful to the Constitution as written. At present, however, we shall look further into this self-described intermediate originalism. Before asking whether it really is an alternative to the philosophic approach, let's examine what has motivated constitutional theorists to develop it. Dworkin offers one reason for its emergence: its proponents are in the grip of an unfounded "majoritarian premise" that

---

9. Though they cast their interpretations differently, some broad originalists agree with the abstract originalists on the interpretation of the Equal Protection Clause with reference to homosexuals and poor persons.

leads them to reject the philosophic approach on democratic grounds.[10] This premise regards majoritarian democracy as presumptively justified and departures from it, like judicial review, as presumptively unjustified. We saw in Chapter 6, and we shall see later in this chapter and in subsequent chapters, that all forms of originalism except abstract originalism and mindset originalism (properly understood as a form of abstract originalism) actually insult democracy and leave it morally indefensible.

A second reason for this intermediate originalism can be called the "originalist premise."[11] This is the assumption that some form of originalism just has to be the only approach to the Constitution that is truly faithful to it. This premise functions as an axiom of originalist thought, and like most axiomatic beliefs, it is asserted, not argued for. Its basis seems to be a certain conception of law. Originalists stress the regulatory sense of law, law that regulates the conduct of its subjects despite the presumed disinclination of subjects to obey the law. This kind of law has an authority-subject property called "bindingness," and it is this bindingness that seems compromised or altogether denied by the philosophic approach. Fidelity to this kind of law is more on the order of dutiful or even pious submission or blind obedience to authority than thinking for yourself about the best that it can mean. Locate the Constitution's meaning in the prevailing opinions of the community, as consensualists do, and it is hard to see how the Constitution can function as a law that binds the community. If Dworkin is right about judges finding the Constitution's meaning in their best understanding of its terms—their understanding, not the specific or even broad understanding or expectation of the framers— then narrow and broad originalists find it hard to see how the Constitution binds judges. Yet they assume that the Constitution is supposed to bind everyone, including the judges who interpret it and including the community as a whole.

From this account of the originalist premise, it is evident that originalists beg two important questions. These questions are (1) what the Constitution is and (2) what its terms refer to. Here again, with respect to both questions, originalists just refuse to accept the Constitution as it is actually written. Regarding what the Constitution is, the Supremacy

---

10. Dworkin, *Freedom's Law*, *supra* note 3, at 15–19.
11. One of us has developed this argument elsewhere. *See* James E. Fleming, "Fidelity to Our Imperfect Constitution," *Fordham Law Review* 65 (1996): 1335.

Clause of Article VI declares the Constitution and the laws and treaties of the national government pursuant thereto the "supreme Law of the Land," contrary laws and constitutions of the states notwithstanding. This is clearly law in the regulatory sense. At the same time, the Preamble says the Constitution is "ordained and established" for the sake of ends like justice, the common defense, and the general welfare. And the Preamble expressly situates every other part of the Constitution within its broadly means-ends or instrumentalist framework. So, if we treat the Constitution and the laws and treaties of the national government pursuant thereto as supreme over the constitutions and laws of the state governments (as instructed by the Supremacy Clause), the Constitution says we are furthering the goals set forth in the Preamble. The Preamble thus announces the Constitution as something of a corporate charter or the enabling act of an agency dedicated to certain objectives. The authority-subject relationship that is part of the *regulatory* view is thus itself part of a broader relationship: the aspirational relationship of the *enabling* view—the view of the Constitution as establishing an agency to pursue desired ends. Originalists assume, without argument, that the Constitution's controlling property is its regulatory bindingness. But the constitutional text either elevates the enabling property to a controlling position or leaves the matter to be settled, if responsibly, by our best thought on the subject—that is, philosophically.

Originalists may claim, of course, that the best argument supports originalism for judges and that originalism makes the Constitution's regulatory aspect controlling. To any such claim we would have two responses. First, we would note, in originalist fashion, that this originalist response would reject the theory of interpretation outlined by James Madison himself in *Federalist* 40.[12] Here Madison responded to the Antifederalist complaint that the Constitutional Convention had disregarded the instructions of the Continental Congress. Congress had charged the delegates with "revising the [A]rticles of [C]onfederation" in ways that "render[ed] the Foederal Constitution [the Articles, in this case] adequate to the exigencies of government and the preservation of the Union." Instead of merely revising the Articles, however, the delegates proposed a wholly new set of institutions, with a fundamentally different operating principle

---

12. *The Federalist*, ed. Jacob E. Cooke (Middletown, CT: Wesleyan University Press, 1961), No. 40, at 259.

(legislation for individuals, not states), and a mode of ratification other than that prescribed by the Articles (by three fourths of the states, not unanimous agreement)—all justified by the famous argument in *Federalist* 10 that rejected the small-republic theory which was the public philosophy of the age in favor of the extended-republic theory discussed in Chapter 3.[13]

Here was a revolutionary act. Madison argued for its lawfulness by citing "two rules of construction, dictated by plain reason, as well as founded on legal axioms."[14] The first rule, he said, was to allow some meaning to every part of a legal instruction, so that all parts may "be made to conspire to some common end." The second rule was that where the parts "cannot be made to coincide, the less important should give way to the more important part; the means should be sacrificed to the end, rather than the end to the means." With this, Madison contended for a construction of the Articles that would "reconcile" that document and the changes proposed by the Convention. Madison's construction, however, was and is widely seen as patently disingenuous. His disclaimers notwithstanding, and for better or worse, he and his colleagues had proposed a new and fundamentally different constitution.

Yet Madison claimed, not unreasonably, that by sacrificing the Articles, the Convention had achieved a deeper fidelity to the Continental Congress. The delegates to the Convention believed, as did many in the country, that the Articles had failed—that they were not, and could not be made, adequate to the country's problems. Claiming this, Madison challenged his critics to deny what he assumed they wouldn't deny: that the "happiness of the people of America" was more important than the preservation of the Articles—which, after all, were but means to the people's happiness. Madison thus acted as if a rule of interpretation that assumes the law is serviceable to some common end—his first rule— treats interpreters of the law as participants in a common enterprise, something more than the unquestioning subjects of higher authority. The aspirational and participatory elements of this picture clash with the authoritarianism of the originalist premise.

This doesn't settle the question, for originalists can respond that fidelity to law is incompatible with Madison's first rule, because his first

---

[13.] *The Federalist* No. 10.
[14.] *The Federalist* No. 40, at 259–60.

rule justifies his second rule and, therewith, the sacrifice of legally binding means. And we would concede that sacrificing legally binding means, as Madison and his colleagues did, crosses the line between interpreting the Constitution and changing it. If irony didn't bother them, originalists could thus cite the revolutionary overthrow of the Articles in support of their claim that any but a regulatory view of law undermines fidelity to law. This poses a challenge for the philosophic approach that we try to meet in Chapter 10. We note in the meantime, however, that the originalist premise itself departs from the ends-oriented approach to interpretation defended by the most celebrated of the framers in *The Federalist*, the work widely regarded as the most important source of original intentions.

Our second response to the originalist claim that the regulatory aspect of law is controlling is that originalists themselves reject the regulatory aspect of the Constitution. If the Constitution commands (in regulatory fashion) that government accord its citizens due process, then the Constitution commands that agents of the government strive for the truth about or best understanding of what due process requires. As Dworkin has persuasively argued, fidelity to the law as written—fidelity, that is, to the positive law—requires a fusion of constitutional law and moral philosophy. Originalists resist or disregard this command because it conflicts with their axiomatic assumption about how law works— that is, how law ought to work. Now, this assumption may be right; no sensible person has ever claimed that the Constitution is either perfect or infallible.[15] But there are arguments, like Madison's, for a different view of how law works. And no one has successfully refuted Dworkin's argument that it is the Constitution itself as written that demands a fusion of constitutional law and moral philosophy. If originalists have the arguments, they should present them, instead of simply assuming— through the originalist premise—what has to be shown about what the Constitution is, what its terms refer to, and what fidelity to the Constitution consists of.

[15.] One of us has propounded a "Constitution-perfecting theory," that is, that we should interpret the Constitution so as to make it the best it can be. *See* James E. Fleming, *Securing Constitutional Democracy: The Case of Autonomy* (Chicago: University of Chicago Press, 2006): 4–6, 16, 225. But that is not to deny that there are many imperfections of our Constitution and constitutional scheme, or that "the best it can be" might be quite imperfect, if not evil. *Id.* at 220–22.

II. Does an Intermediate Position Exist?

Again, broad originalists claim to occupy a position between concrete (narrow) originalism and abstract originalism (the philosophic approach). They seek to avoid the unworkable constraints of narrow originalism and what they see as the unconstrained character of the philosophic approach. To accomplish this they would interpret constitutional words and phrases at "levels of abstraction" that are higher than concrete originalists want, yet not as high as the ordinary extension of the terms (the level of abstract originalism). We have illustrated this strategy by considering the word "person" in the Equal Protection Clause. An abstract originalist would protect any and all kinds of entities that our best theories of personhood indicate are kinds of persons. This would include female persons and homosexual persons, and it might even include unborn persons (assuming good-faith arguments within the limits of public reasonableness that establish the personhood of the unborn).[16] The narrowest of originalists would limit the protections of the Equal Protection Clause to black persons. The broad originalist would settle somewhere in between.

Now, from this it should be evident that the broad originalist must justify two things: why he takes the first step beyond the lowest level of abstraction and why, having taken that step, he doesn't include all persons. If he can justify the first step beyond the framers' concrete intentions, he recognizes the flaws of concrete originalism. But if he does recognize the flaws of concrete originalism, he has but one other option: abstract originalism, which in practice means the philosophic approach. If he steps beyond the lowest level of abstraction, he has to justify his stopping point, and he can't do so without a moral argument that his approach was supposed to avoid. He has to ask questions of the kind that the abstract originalist would ask—whether, for example, excluding women, homosexuals, and/or the unborn is consistent with our best understanding of personhood and/or equality or whether denying claims on their behalf is justified by some allegedly more compelling good of the community as a whole (like protecting the procreative family or the social goods that flow from

---

16. For the idea of public reason (or public reasonableness), *see* John Rawls, *Political Liberalism* (New York: Columbia University Press, 1993): 212–54; John Rawls, "The Idea of Public Reason Revisited," in John Rawls, *Collected Papers*, ed. Samuel Freeman (Cambridge, MA: Harvard University Press, 1999): 573–615.

enhanced economic and political participation and mobility for women). Since all such possibilities involve philosophic reflection and choice, there is no middle way between concrete and abstract originalism.

Writers who turn to the past turn either to words and sentences in the constitutional text that were written in the past or to past definitions and/or applications of those words and sentences. The meanings of those words and sentences are trans-temporal; they belong to the present and the future as well as to the past. What changes, and therefore belongs only to the past, are old definitions and applications—Dworkin's *conceptions*—of constitutional words and sentences. But since conceptions are conceptions *of* expressions whose meaning is trans-temporal, situating them in the past is a way of indicating that they have been replaced or are candidates for replacement by *better* conceptions—better conceptions of what the Constitution means. Writers who turn to the past do so for two kinds of reasons: (1) they believe the conceptions of the past are superior, or (2) they believe turning to the past is essential to their conceptions of values like democracy and the rule of law, which conceptions they believe are superior to their competitors. Philosophic reflection and choice are at work in either case, whether executed in publicly responsible fashion or not. Writers who pretend to turn to the past as such (that is, for no other reason) pretend to reject the philosophic quest for what the Constitution means in favor of past *conceptions* of what the Constitution means. These writers can be said to be narrow originalists, though in reality they are practitioners of deception (perhaps including self-deception). In any case, there is no option between abstract and concrete originalism because there is no option between what the words and sentences of the Constitution mean, on the one hand, and *conceptions* of what they mean, on the other.

III. Is the Turn to History a Turn to Real History?

B road originalists presume that a "turn to history" is a turn away from the philosophic approach that they associate chiefly with Dworkin. They seem motivated by a conception of law that separates legal questions from moral questions. This conception of law seems to reflect a certain understanding of the nation's constitutional culture. The thought seems to be that, in our constitutional culture, successful constitutional arguments have to put moral questions aside. As some have expressed this view: to persuade Justice Scalia, liberals must learn to make original-ist arguments.[17]

We offer several responses. First, our constitutional culture is not as originalist as the broad originalists (like the narrow originalists) seem to assume. It certainly requires constitutional lawyers and scholars as well as judges to respect tradition—that part of the past that we deem presently useful and in which we presently take pride. But this hardly makes our culture originalist in a sense that would exclude moral philosophy.[18] For we make moral choices when deciding which parts of our past are worth continuing. And everyone would agree that some parts of our past are clearly not worth continuing—not parts of our "tradition." Originalism is an *ism*, a conservative ideology that emerged in reaction against the Warren Court. Before Richard Nixon and Robert Bork launched their attacks on the Warren Court (and the right to privacy decisions of the early Burger Court), originalism as we know it did not exist.[19] Constitutional interpretation in light of original understanding[20] did exist, but original understanding was regarded as merely one source of constitutional mean-ing among several, not a general theory of constitutional interpretation, much less the exclusive legitimate theory. Indeed, history was regarded as secondary to, and merely as extrinsic evidence of, the meaning of text and structure.[21] Scholars wrote about the "uses of history" in constitutional interpretation rather than contending that enforcing original understand-ing was the only defensible conception of fidelity to the Constitution.[22] Moreover, original understanding, especially at a relatively specific level, was understood to be largely indeterminate and inconclusive. As Justice Jackson famously put it in *Youngstown Sheet & Tube Co. v. Sawyer*:[23]

---

17. One of us has heard Akhil Amar articulate a version of this position.
18. The Senate's rejection of the Bork nomination was at least in part a rejection of Bork's narrow originalism. *See* Dworkin, *Freedom's Law*, supra note 3, at 276–86, 287–305.
19. William W. Crosskey may be an exception, but he was roundly criticized as exceptional. *See, e.g.*, Henry M. Hart, Jr., "Professor Crosskey and Judicial Review," *Harvard Law Review* 67 (1954): 1456 (reviewing William W. Crosskey, *Politics and the Constitution in the History of the United States* [Chicago: University of Chicago Press, 1953]).
20. *See* Chapter 6, note 1, on the relationship between framers' intentions, original mean-ing, and original understanding.
21. *See* Jacobus tenBroek, "Admissibility and Use by the United States Supreme Court of Extrinsic Aids in Constitutional Construction," *California Law Review* 26 (1938): 287.
22. *See* Charles A. Miller, *The Supreme Court and the Uses of History* (Cambridge, MA: Harvard University Press, 1969); John G. Wofford, "The Blinding Light: The Uses of History in Constitutional Interpretation," *University of Chicago Law Review* 31 (1964): 502.
23. 343 U.S. 579 (1952).

Just what our forefathers did envision, or would have envisioned had they foreseen modern conditions, must be divined from materials almost as enigmatic as the dreams Joseph was called upon to interpret for Pharaoh. A century and a half of partisan debate and scholarly speculation yields no net result but only supplies more or less apt quotations from respected sources on each side of any question. They largely cancel each other. And court decisions are indecisive because of the judicial practice of dealing with the largest questions in the most narrow way.[24]

Regrettably, many constitutional lawyers and scholars as well as judges in recent years seem to have lost sight of this wisdom. Laura Kalman, in her intellectual history of recent constitutional theory, suggests that the best professional historians know better than to be originalists, but that some constitutional lawyers and scholars who have taken the turn to history do not.[25]

We should put the following question to the broad originalists: If our constitutional culture is as originalist as they assume, why do originalists characteristically complain that so many constitutional law cases and so many features of our constitutional practice deviate from original understandings?[26] The very fact of originalism as a movement indicates that our constitutional culture is not as originalist as the broad originalists have supposed. To the contrary, Dworkin is right in claiming that "[s]o far as American lawyers and judges follow any coherent strategy of interpreting the Constitution at all, they already use the moral reading," and that there is a confused "mismatch" between the role of the moral reading and its reputation. Though the moral reading *is* embedded in our constitutional practice, its reputation in many quarters is that it is illegitimate.[27]

[24.] *Id.* at 634–35 (Jackson, J., concurring).

[25.] *See* Laura Kalman, *The Strange Career of Legal Liberalism* (New Haven, CT: Yale University Press, 1996): 167–90; *see also* Jack N. Rakove, *Original Meanings* (New York: Alfred A. Knopf, 1996): 3–22.

[26.] *See* Bork, *supra* note 5; Henry P. Monaghan, "Stare Decisis and Constitutional Adjudication," *Columbia Law Review* 88 (1988): 723. For an analysis of the gap between originalist theory and our constitutional practice, *see* Michael C. Dorf, "Integrating Normative and Descriptive Constitutional Theory: The Case of Original Meaning," *Georgetown Law Journal* 85 (1997): 1765.

[27.] Dworkin, *Freedom's Law, supra* note 3, at 2, 4. For an argument that "modern" eras of judicial practice, symbolized by Lochner v. New York, 198 U.S. 45 (1905), Brown v. Board of Education, 347 U.S. 483 (1954), and Roe v. Wade, 410 U.S. 113 (1973), employ the same interpretive approach as the "classical" era dominated by John Marshall, see Sotirios A. Barber, *The Constitution of Judicial Power* (Baltimore: Johns Hopkins University Press, 1993): 68–73.

Second, broad and narrow originalists not only misdescribe our legal practice, they err more fundamentally in their view of human action and perception. Recall the thought experiment Dworkin used to introduce the distinction between general concepts and concrete conceptions of those general concepts (discussed in Chapter 2). He asked his readers to picture a father instructing his children to treat others fairly and the father's acceptance, as consistent with his original instructions, of the children's later improvements on the father's earlier conception of fairness. We, your authors, think this could be the most successful thought experiment in some two centuries of constitutional thought. The reason for its success is that it captures the multidimensional character of human action and perception.

This multidimensionality manifests itself in several ways. We all know that human beings generally want more than the satisfaction of their immediate desires, for example. They have first-order and second-order wants. They not only want what they want, they want to want what they want. Ask the habitual smokers you know; most of them will confirm that it's possible *not* to want what you want. The father in Dworkin's thought experiment displays another form of multidimensionality. He instructs his children to be fair to others because he thinks his instructions can make them better people than they might otherwise be. And he becomes better in their eyes—and in his own eyes—if he displays a willingness to learn from them how to be better than he would otherwise be. He knows that his authority—his good authorship, his good "makesmanship"—depends on preparing his children to rise above his authority. A third manifestation of this multidimensionality is our perception of human action. Often there has to be more than meets the eye in order for us to comprehend what we're seeing—in order for us to "see" what we're seeing, if you will. We would all be puzzled if, under normal conditions, someone suddenly jumped up and opened a window during a blizzard. We would be puzzled because we understand human action against shared background assumptions about what's good and, under normal conditions, we wouldn't see the point (i.e., the good) of letting in the cold.

Originalists who would exclude moral inquiry from constitutional law implicitly deny this multi-dimensionality or complicated structure of human action and perception. Their theory of interpretation implicitly rejects Dworkin's distinction between concepts and conceptions because they refuse to acknowledge the implication of that distinction: fidelity to the text as written calls for a fusion of constitutional law and moral philosophy. By effectively denying the distinction between concepts and conceptions, they reduce meaning to conceptions, flattening human action and understanding to one dimension. The result of this flattening is a distortion of linguistic practice that leaves definitions, examples, and applications to be definitions, examples, and applications of nothing at all. The result is also a distortion of history—ironically, in history's name.

To see this originalist flattening of history, consider the framers' attitudes toward slavery. These attitudes were not the simple matter described by Chief Justice Taney in *Dred Scott v. Sandford* (1857).[28] Reasoning in narrow originalist fashion from the historical facts regarding slavery in late-eighteenth-century America, Taney concluded that when the authors of the Declaration of Independence said "all men are created equal" they could not have included persons of African descent and, therefore, that the "We the People" who adopted the Constitution could not include persons of African descent—even African-Americans who were free, tax-paying citizens at the time of ratification and who had fought to win American independence from Great Britain.

We can't improve on what other writers have said about Taney's insult to the American founding.[29] Our point is that Taney distorted history by pretending that fidelity to the founding precluded a moral judgment on his part. Taney hinted that he and his generation had a different attitude than that of the framers toward "this unfortunate race."[30] But the attitudes of Taney's generation and those of the framers were not entirely different. The fact is that after the Revolution many white Americans joined the leading framers in viewing slavery as a source of national shame. Moral disapproval of slavery is recorded in *Federalist* 42.[31] In his only book, *Notes on the State of Virginia*, Jefferson famously says slavery threatens the nation's moral foundation and invites the "wrath" of a just God.[32] It is true that leading framers, Jefferson among them, held persons in slavery and that the Continental Congress

---

28. 60 U.S. 393 (1857).
29. Herbert J. Storing, "Slavery and the Moral Foundations of the American Republic," in *The Moral Foundations of the American Republic*, ed. Robert H. Horwitz (Charlottesville: University Press of Virginia, 1986): 313, 313–16.
30. Dred Scott, 60 U.S. at 407.
31. *The Federalist* No. 42, at 281–82.
32. Thomas Jefferson, *Notes on the State of Virginia*, ed. William Peden (New York: Norton, 1954): 163.

deleted criticism of slavery from Jefferson's draft of the Declaration of Independence. But the historical record clearly establishes that the nation as a whole and its leaders were at least ambivalent about slavery, and many who felt compelled to support the institution on economic and social grounds still saw it as a regrettable violation of the natural rights of all persons.

The historical record on slavery is mixed, in other words, and a responsible interpreter of that mixed record would offer an argument in either goodness or fairness for reading that record to support one normative conclusion over another. Taney pretended that the historical evidence concerning framers' intentions was a simple matter that compelled a decision against opening the federal courts to claims like Dred Scott's on behalf of his freedom. But neither the law as written nor the history of the founding compelled this result. How then do we explain Taney's decision? Christopher Eisgruber has answered this question by exposing the shared good Taney thought he was serving: the Union's survival.[33] Taney thought that the Union's survival depended on an accommodation with slavery, and (implicitly) that the Union's destruction was the greater evil.[34] Taney's decision included a moral choice after all, notwithstanding his originalist disclaimer.

IV. The Broad Originalists' Obsession with Ronald Dworkin

We have noted narrow originalists' obsession with the Warren Court. Broad originalists are obsessed with Ronald Dworkin. They suspect the motives behind his approach to constitutional interpretation. They fault him because they think the results of his analyses of particular constitutional controversies patently conform to his political beliefs. They think the cure lies in a "turn to history." Having discussed the illusory and deceptive nature of this proposal, we offer a few thoughts on targeting Dworkin.

The first thought goes almost without saying, so we won't dwell on it. Many agree with T. M. Scanlon's description of Dworkin as the nation's

---

[33.] Christopher L. Eisgruber, "*Dred* Again: Originalist's Forgotten Past," *Constitutional Commentary* 10 (1993): 37.
[34.] For an insightful recent analysis of the Constitution's concessions to evil and the lessons of *Dred Scott*, see Mark A. Graber, *Dred Scott and the Problem of Constitutional Evil* (New York: Cambridge University Press, 2006).

leading public philosopher.[35] Being a special target of criticism is an honorific that goes with this role, and no one seems to appreciate the honor and enjoy the role more than Professor Dworkin himself.

Second, it should go without saying that Dworkin's own use of the interpretive method that he defends says nothing conclusive about the soundness of the method. Some critics might object that Dworkin himself does not adequately ground his interpretations in historical materials. No method can guarantee its good-faith use. Nor is it clear that Dworkin has used his method in a partisan way. Each of the authors of this book has his disagreements with Dworkin, running from his moral metaphysics and the Constitution's basic normative structure to specifics in his theory of constitutional rights. Yet we know of no one who has shown that any of Dworkin's constitutional interpretations is beyond a reasonable elaboration of principles in our constitutional tradition (for example, Locke's teaching that by nature each of us owns his or her own body, Jefferson's vision of the separation of church and state, and Publius's support of an independent judiciary for protecting rights). That the framers did not enumerate or even discuss rights to reproductive freedom and sexual autonomy doesn't begin to prove that these rights are inconsistent with beliefs about liberty reasonably attributable to the framers or the concept of liberty embodied in the Constitution.[36] The historical lack of protection for such rights during the founding period proves they don't exist only if you read the Ninth Amendment out of the Constitution (recall Chapter 5) and if you also assume what we have seen to be an untenable proposition: that liberty's meaning lies solely in the way historical authorities defined and/or applied the term.

V. Conclusion: The Turn to History in Service of the Philosophic Approach

Far from needing a special turn to history, the philosophic approach to constitutional meaning is itself an approach to history. It concerns itself with the meaning of a text whose provisions were written in the past, and as it seeks the meaning of that text it elaborates principles that

---

[35.] T. M. Scanlon, "Partisan for Life," *New York Review of Books*, July 15, 1993, at 45, 45 (reviewing Dworkin, *Life's Dominion, supra* note 8).

[36.] *See* Jack M. Balkin, "Abortion and Original Meaning" (August 28, 2006), available at SSRN: http://ssrn.com/abstract=925558.

are traditional in our constitutional order. Broad originalists would do better to reconceive their turn to history as being in service of, not an alternative to, the philosophic approach. By resisting the falsification of reality in the minor premises of constitutional decisions (as discussed in Chapter 6), the philosophic approach represents a traditional faith in reason, science, and the power of law to cope with reality. It continues that tradition in the manner personified by the good father in Dworkin's thought experiment: a tradition of cultivating citizens who can live together while thinking self-critically for themselves about the meaning of their important commitments.

By limiting themselves to the putative definitions and the applications of the framers and/or the founding generation, narrow originalists represent a different kind of father: the authoritarian father who knows best and who wants his children to remain subservient to his will. But narrow originalism is simply unworkable; one-dimensional history just doesn't exist, much less speak univocally for itself. So narrow originalism is no more than a shield for insulating power from scrutiny (as Justice William Brennan famously described it, "arrogance cloaked as humility").[37] In our time the power in question is that of the Supreme Court; a majority of the justices become the willful, authoritarian father presumed by narrow originalism.

No middle way exists between narrow originalism and the philosophic approach. No middle way exists because the words and phrases of the Constitution can refer either to (1) general ideas or concepts or (2) concrete conceptions thereof. If your theory of meaning falls into the first group, you accept the distinction between concepts and conceptions and what that distinction implies about constitutional interpretation. If your professed theory of meaning is of the second type, you profess a narrow originalism and prepare the way for irresponsible authority under constitutional cover.[38]

So-called broad originalists are free to decide whether to associate themselves with one group or the other. This decision determines whether they will accept or avoid the burdens of defending controversial moral choices. What they can't do is avoid the controversial moral choices.

---

[37] William J. Brennan, Jr., "The Constitution of the United States: Contemporary Ratification," *University of California at Davis Law Review* 19 (1985): 2, 4.

[38] *Compare* Abner S. Greene, "Constitutional (Ir)responsibility," *Fordham Law Review* 71 (2003): 1807, 1825 (criticizing certain theories of constitutional self-government—theories that are more open to explicit moral philosophizing than is broad originalism—for seeking to deflect the responsibility for interpreting the moral concepts in the Constitution).

CHAPTER 8

STRUCTURALISM

None of the approaches we've considered has successfully avoided the need for a fusion of constitutional law and moral philosophy. Neither textualism, consensualism, nor originalism (whether narrow or broad) can deny that good-faith reflection, debate, and moral judgment constitute at least part of the process of deciding constitutional meaning in hard cases. But our story can't end here. There may be other ways to deny a significant role for philosophic methods and attitudes in constitutional decision. We'll attend to defending the philosophic approach eventually, but we shall first consider the remaining approaches.

The remaining approaches include structuralism and doctrinalism (to be considered in the next chapter). Can either of them help us avoid the burdens and responsibilities of philosophic reflection and choice in hard cases? Can interpreters avoid moral judgment by reflecting either on the structures of government or on bodies of judicial doctrines developed through a process of deciding one case at a time? For guidance in hard cases, the structuralist looks to the overall constitutional arrangement of offices, powers, and relationships, or what used to be called "the meaning of the Constitution as a whole." The Constitution's leading structural principles include *federalism, separation of powers,* and *democracy.* "Structuralism" is a capacious term, though—so much so that the most famous proponent of structuralism, Charles L. Black, Jr., invokes structural norms not just to assess institutional practices but also to identify individual and minority rights claimed to be essential to full citizenship.[1]

[1.] *See* Charles L. Black, Jr., *Structure and Relationship in Constitutional Law* (Baton Rouge: Louisiana State University Press, 1969), together with his *A New Birth of Freedom: Human Rights, Named and Unnamed* (New York: Grosset/Putnam, 1997). Many scholars follow

According to one of the best-known structuralists, John Hart Ely, a woman does not have a constitutional right to abortion, for example, because the Constitution's "open-ended" provisions ("due process," "equal protection," and the Ninth Amendment) should include only those "unenumerated" rights essential to representative democracy, which he argues is the Constitution's leading structural value.[2] But Ely's position on this question is not uncontroversial, nor is his conception of democracy uncontested. A structuralist who disagrees with Ely on the right to abortion could cite the joint opinion in *Planned Parenthood v. Casey* (1992), which states that the availability of abortion has enabled women increasingly to participate as equals with men in the nation's government, economy, and society.[3] And such a structuralist might argue that the right to abortion is essential to women's full citizenship in a constitutional democracy.

Disagreements like this reflect the fact that Americans have always disagreed on structural questions and their implications for the constitutional rights of individuals. This fact holds for the three structural principles we'll discuss here: federalism, separation of powers, and democracy. We'll see in *McCulloch v. Maryland* (1819) differences of opinion about the nature of American federalism (national federalism versus states' rights federalism) that persist to this day and reflect fundamental disagreements on the basic normative properties of the Constitution. The debate between

---

Black's lead: for example, James E. Fleming, *Securing Constitutional Democracy: The Case of Autonomy* (Chicago: University of Chicago Press, 2006): 90–91 (arguing for carrying forward "the unfinished business of Charles Black" by constructing a structure of basic liberties integral to free and equal citizenship). Unlike many structuralists, Black did not see elaborating structures as an approach whereby interpreters can avoid making substantive decisions about what the Constitution means.

2. *See* John Hart Ely, "The Wages of Crying Wolf: A Comment on *Roe v. Wade*," *Yale Law Journal* 82 (1973): 920; John Hart Ely, *Democracy and Distrust* (Cambridge, MA: Harvard University Press, 1980): 15–21, 98–101 [hereinafter Ely, *Democracy and Distrust*].

3. Planned Parenthood v. Casey, 505 U.S. 833, 856 (1992); Cass R. Sunstein, *The Partial Constitution* (Cambridge, MA: Harvard University Press, 1993): 283–84 (analyzing *Casey*). Ely's famous criticisms of *Roe* in "The Wages of Crying Wolf" and *Democracy and Distrust* were not his final words on the legitimacy of *Roe*, however. After the Supreme Court reaffirmed *Roe* in *Casey*, Ely wrote what he described as a "fan letter" to the three justices who authored the joint opinion in that case. Ely praised their opinion as "excellent": "not only reaching what seem to me entirely sensible results, but defending the refusal to overrule *Roe v. Wade* splendidly." John Hart Ely, *On Constitutional Ground* (Princeton, NJ: Princeton University Press, 1996): 305. Ely added in commentary on the letter: "*Roe* has contributed greatly to the more general move toward equality for women, which seems to me not only good but also in line with the central themes of our Constitution." *Id.*

departmentalism and judicial monopoly concerning who may interpret the Constitution—whether each branch or department of government shares in the responsibility of constitutional interpretation or instead the courts are the exclusive interpreters—is part of a larger debate between different theories of the separation of powers (reflecting disagreements between positive and negative constitutionalists) and different theories of democracy (as conceived by majoritarians, on the one hand, and constitutionalists, on the other).[4] So there are no uncontroversial theories of the Constitution's structural principles. The question is not what the Constitution means as a whole; it is what we ought to say it means. We cannot elaborate structures as a way of avoiding substantive philosophic choices; we can elaborate structures only by making substantive philosophic choices.

The same holds for doctrinalism, the approach that conflates constitutional meaning with what courts are interpreting the Constitution to mean in concrete cases. That doctrinalism offers no escape from philosophic reflection and choice is evident enough in the different interpretations of virtually any long-standing judicial doctrine, like the "separate but equal" doctrine (discussed further in Chapter 9) and the "clear and present danger" test in First Amendment cases (whose interpretation has ranged from relatively weak to quite stringent protection of freedom of expression).[5] We know in advance of any such inquiry that if doctrinalism could relieve us of philosophic responsibilities, it would come with the same costs as those associated with concrete originalism/intentionalism. Instead of locking us into the framers' definitions and applications of constitutional provisions, and thus their view of the world, doctrinalism would lock us into the views of old judges, which would eventually lead constitutional law and discourse to a false view of reality. Under precedents like *Plessy v. Ferguson* (1896), forced segregation of the races would not be harmful to racial minorities as a matter of constitutional law, for example, regardless of whether it was harmful as a matter either of

---

[4.] For fuller discussion, *see* Walter F. Murphy, James E. Fleming, Sotirios A. Barber, and Stephen Macedo, *American Constitutional Interpretation*, 3rd ed. (New York: Foundation Press, 2003): 43–59, 274–89, 448–54.

[5.] *Compare* Whitney v. California, 274 U.S. 357 (1927) (bad tendency test that is not very protective of First Amendment freedoms), *with* Dennis v. United States, 341 U.S. 494 (1951) (weak version of clear and present danger test), *and* Brandenburg v. Ohio, 395 U.S. 444 (1969) (strong version of clear and present danger test that is quite protective of freedom of expression).

scientific fact or common sense. We saw in Chapter 6 that concrete intentionalism founders on the shoals of *Brown v. Board of Education* (1954).[6] We shall see the same fate for doctrinalism in Chapter 9.

I. Structuralism

A s we have seen, some writers propose that judges can avoid or minimize the need for philosophic methods, attitudes, and choices in hard cases by reasoning from the Constitution's structural principles.[7] The phrase "constitutional structures" usually refers to the constitutional relationships between the national government and the states, the branches of the national government, the government and the people and, in sum, the general arrangement of offices, powers, and relationships allegedly manifest in the Constitution's text and the settled facts of constitutional history. A strong concern for elaborating and maintaining proper governmental structures has been a prominent feature of constitutional debate in America. And few will deny that American judges should exercise their power in ways that maintain constitutional structures. But structuralism can hardly remove the need for philosophic methods and attitudes in hard cases, for constitutional text and history contain relatively few uncontroversial structural messages. Structurally, for example, America is manifestly a democracy of some sort, where people are related to governments at least partly as principals to agents, and decisions are processed through separate institutions whose parts check each other in limited ways, formal and informal. But that alone does not resolve what form of democracy the Constitution establishes—for example, whether we have a majoritarian representative democracy, as Chief Justice Rehnquist assumed (Chapter 2), or a constitutional democracy imposing substantive limitations upon what majorities may do to people, as Ronald Dworkin and *The Federalist* argued (Chapters 2 and 3).

The same holds for "federalism" and "separation of powers." What good are appeals to "federalism" in the face of a long-standing debate about the best understanding of federalism? If constitutional text or tradition had sent a clear message regarding "separation of powers," we

---

6. 347 U.S. 483 (1954).
7. *See, e.g.,* the works by Ely cited *supra* note 2.

shouldn't have experienced two centuries of debate over the nature and scope of judicial power—the very debate of which the present discussion of interpretive approaches is often seen as but a part. If the cases manifesting "structuralism" show anything, they show a history, perhaps a tradition, of disagreement over structural questions. They show that judges can't solve structural questions by pointing to structures. At some point responsible judges must ask what they've always asked: what ought we to conceive our structures to be? That is, what is the best understanding of our institutional structures and inheritance? And that is at least partly a philosophic question. To support this general conclusion, we'll take a brief look at some of the important cases touching on major structural issues of American constitutional history, including the nature of American federalism, the best understanding of the form of democracy embodied in the Constitution, and the division of responsibility between courts and legislatures in protecting structural norms.

II. The Basic Structure of Federalism: From *McCulloch* to *Garcia* and Beyond

McCulloch v. Maryland (1819)[8] is paradigmatic for the structuralist thesis that judges can reason from constitutional structures to conclusions regarding congressional power, states' rights, and, by extension, individual rights. In *McCulloch*, Chief Justice Marshall answered two questions, regarding (1) Congress's power to incorporate a national bank and (2) Maryland's power to tax that bank. The first question emerged partly from the fact that the Constitution gives Congress no express power to incorporate a bank or anything else. Marshall handled this problem with a complex and subtle argument. He began with the theory that the people (not the states) had established the Constitution for the sake of general ends like economic prosperity and national security. Next he conceived the specific powers of Congress listed in Article I, § 8 as means to these general ends. He then construed the Necessary and Proper Clause of Article I, § 8 and the Tenth Amendment to permit Congress unlisted or implied powers as needed to pursue authorized national ends.[9]

---

8. 17 U.S. 316 (1819).
9. *Id.* at 411–15.

Marshall didn't say that Congress could choose whatever means it wanted. He said that the means couldn't be "prohibited" by or inconsistent with "the letter and spirit" of the Constitution. He said that they had to be "appropriate" and "plainly adapted" to some authorized end.[10] Marshall may have planted these general words as hedges against his main thrust should future congressional excesses demand judicial checks. But Marshall's principal message seemed clear: Congress was free to consult its own judgments regarding convenience in deciding how to pursue its authorized ends; Congress didn't have to worry about encroaching on areas reserved to the states. The same didn't hold for state power, however. For in deciding against Maryland on the second legal question in *McCulloch*, Marshall held that the states could not use their otherwise lawful power to tax in ways that obstructed a congressional policy.[11] Mere conflict with state policies wasn't enough to void a congressional act; conflict with federal policies was sufficient to void state acts.

The full significance of what Marshall wrought in *McCulloch* may not have been generally appreciated until the Court decided *Heart of Atlanta Motel v. U.S.* in 1964.[12] *Heart of Atlanta* upheld the public accommodation section of the Civil Rights Act of 1964, an act in which Congress used its power to regulate interstate commerce to outlaw racial discrimination in certain classes of business, including hotels and restaurants. The Court upheld this act without disturbing precedents that left racial discrimination of the kind in question a matter to be regulated only by the states. These precedents were viable then, and they remain so today. So the Court permitted Congress to use the Commerce Power to supplant a state's policies in an area that the Court's own precedents left to the control of the states. *Heart of Atlanta* thus registered what *McCulloch* had implied a hundred and forty-five years earlier: Congress's version of economic health (and other national ends) is a more important constitutional objective than state autonomy in areas (like race, education, and public morality) that are not (directly) within Congress's powers. The upshot of *McCulloch*, as the Civil Rights Act would dramatize, was that virtually all aspects of American life would eventually have to conform

---

10. *Id.* at 421.
11. *Id.* at 425–37.
12. 379 U.S. 241 (1964). Marshall's famous opinion in Gibbons v. Ogden, 22 U.S. 1 (1824), is also an important foundation for *Heart of Atlanta*.

to—because they could not conflict with—Congress's views of economic well-being.

Marshall did not read the Constitution in the way he did because he could read it no other way. Maryland had its reading, and by that reading Congress could act in areas left to the states only when absolutely necessary to advance national objectives, narrowly conceived. Maryland's reading would have favored a nation of states with significantly diverse styles of life, with Congress ensuring minimal and largely uncontroversial levels of national security and interstate commercial intercourse. Marshall rejected Maryland's view of the structure of federalism because he rejected the Jeffersonian vision of America that motivated Maryland's argument. Marshall favored Alexander Hamilton's vision of America at a time when the country still may have been able to go Jefferson's way. (These visions correspond roughly to the visions of the small republic and the large commercial republic discussed in Chapter 3.) Marshall presumably preferred Hamilton's vision because it reflected what Marshall considered a true teaching, the political philosophy of John Locke. Marshall's Lockean assumptions supported the theory of federal-state relations sct forth in *McCulloch*.[13]

Later decisions of the Court, beginning with *Dred Scott v. Sandford* (1857)[14] and maturing in *Hammer v. Dagenhart* (1918),[15] experimented with a *dual-federalist* theory of state-federal relations which held, contrary to Marshall, that state prerogatives did constitute limits on national power. For example, in *Hammer*, the Court held that Congress could not regulate child labor because to do so would exceed its limited powers and encroach on state sovereignty. When the Court overruled *Hammer* in 1941,[16] Marshall's views triumphed again and dominated until the Court returned to dual federalism in *National League of Cities v. Usery* (1976).[17] There, as indicated in Chapter 1, the Court held that Congress may not regulate the hours and wages of employees of state and local governments because to do so would invade state sovereignty. The regulatory needs of

---

[13.] *See* Robert K. Faulkner, *The Jurisprudence of John Marshall* (Princeton, NJ: Princeton University Press, 1968): 102–13; Walter Berns, "The Meaning of the Tenth Amendment," in *A Nation of States: Essays on the American Federal System,* ed. Robert A. Goldwin, 2nd ed. (Chicago: Rand McNally, 1974): 139, 150–58.

[14.] 60 U.S. 393 (1857).

[15.] 247 U.S. 251 (1918).

[16.] United States v. Darby, 312 U.S. 100 (1941).

[17.] 426 U.S. 833 (1976).

an integrated national economy made *Usery* difficult to live with, and within a decade, the Court overruled it in *Garcia v. San Antonio Metropolitan Transit Authority* (1985).[18] Even that was hardly the end of substantive disagreement about what structure of federalism the Constitution embodies, for the Court to some degree has revived the dual federalist vision in a series of cases represented by *New York v. United States* (1992) and its progeny[19] together with *United States v. Lopez* (1995) and its progeny.[20] Clearly, the structure of federalism is not a matter of consensus among American jurists and theorists, and so it provides no escape from philosophic reflection and judgment.

Garcia is an important case for structural issues beyond and even more basic than federalism, and we shall return to it. But lest you miss our point about structuralism generally and federalism in particular, we want to analyze one more classic case, *The Slaughterhouse Cases* (1872).[21] *Slaughterhouse* demonstrates part of the structuralist position, the part that says judges can reason from structuralist premises to conclusions in hard cases involving individual and minority rights. At the same time, *Slaughterhouse* illustrates our argument against another part of the structuralist view, the part that would present structuralist reasoning as a way to avoid the burdens of philosophic reflection and choice. The *Slaughterhouse* Court did reason from structural premises to important conclusions about constitutional rights. But those premises were controversial then and later, and as the debate unfolded over the years, the Court abandoned some of them.

The legal questions in *Slaughterhouse* were whether a slaughterhouse monopoly granted to a company by the city of New Orleans and the legislature of Louisiana violated the rights of other butchers protected by (1) the Privileges or Immunities Clause of the Fourteenth Amendment, (2) the Amendment's Due Process Clause, (3) the Amendment's Equal Protection Clause, or (4) the Thirteenth Amendment's ban on involuntary servitude. For the majority, Justice Samuel F. Miller answered that the Due Process Clause protected procedural rights, not substantive rights like the right to practice one's trade claimed by the independent butchers;[22] that the Equal Protection Clause was reserved for cases

---

18. 469 U.S. 528 (1985).
19. 505 U.S. 144 (1992); Printz v. United States, 521 U.S. 898 (1997).
20. 514 U.S. 549 (1995); United States v. Morrison, 529 U.S. 598 (2000).
21. 83 U.S. 36 (1872).
22. *See id.* at 80–81.

involving "discrimination against the negroes as a class, or on account of their race";[23] and that forcing butchers to use a particular slaughter-house or quit slaughtering was not what the framers of the Thirteenth Amendment had in mind by "involuntary servitude."[24] On the pivotal first question of the case, Miller held that the Privileges or Immunities Clause protected only certain narrow rights like access to the services and facilities (courts, seaports, capital) of the national government, not fundamental human rights guaranteed in all free governments, like (arguably) the rights to acquire property and practice one's trade.[25]

In the view of the dissenting justices, Miller's opinion deprived the Civil War and the Civil War Amendments of their broader institutional promise—to change the basic structure of federalism—and left the states largely free to violate those fundamental human rights not connected with a narrow conception of racial justice. For the dissenters, especially Justice Stephen J. Field, those rights were "natural and inalienable,"[26] not merely conventional rights. For his part, Miller made no effort to hide his motivation. He wanted an opinion that would minimize the constitutional impact of the Civil War and the Civil War Amendments upon the basic structure of federalism. The antebellum system had regarded federal constitutional rights as rights mostly against the national government, with the state governments largely free to treat their citizens as they wished. This aspect of the old system suggested the kind of majoritarianism that led Stephen Douglas (in the Lincoln-Douglas Debates) to insist that state and territorial majorities had a right to mandate slavery[27]—ultimately the view that human convention or community (not "self-evident truths" or "nature" or "nature's God") fully determines the difference between political right and wrong. Because Abraham Lincoln opposed majoritarianism thus conceived, the nation could have construed the Civil War together with the Civil War Amendments as implying that majorities can be wrong and that democracy no less than other forms of government should strive to honor fundamental human rights.

---

23. *Id.* at 81.
24. *Id.* at 68–72.
25. *Id.* at 75–80.
26. *Id.* at 96 (Field, J., dissenting).
27. Abraham Lincoln, "Address of October 16, 1854, Peoria, IL," reprinted in *The Collected Works of Abraham Lincoln*, ed. Roy P. Basler (New Brunswick, NJ: Rutgers University Press, 1953): 2: 247–83.

The *Slaughterhouse* majority saw things differently. Miller wanted to preserve as much state power over civil rights as possible. He thought that he had a clear view of "the structure and spirit of our institutions," and he charged that the minority's view of federally protected privileges and immunities departed from that structure.[28] As he put it: "[w]e do not see in those amendments any purpose to destroy the main features of the general system" or structure of federalism as it had existed before the Civil War and Civil War Amendments.[29]

Whether the dissenting justices had a better understanding of "the structure and spirit" of federalism is not as important here as the fact that there were conflicting understandings and that at least one view of the founding supports the dissenting justices. Recall *Federalist* 10 (discussed in Chapter 3). Madison argued that the national government would be a better government than the state governments for controlling the effects of majority faction, and thus for honoring rights that any just government would respect. Accordingly, Madison proposed to the First Congress that certain freedoms of conscience and the right to a trial by jury be guaranteed against state governments as well as Congress.[30] The defeat of this proposal in the Senate is not as important here as the fact that Madison proposed it. For that fact suggests that federally guaranteed rights against the states are at least consistent with and arguably implicit in the theory of *Federalist* 10—the most influential account of American constitutional structure. The Senate's rejection of Madison's proposal may well have departed from the assumptions of *Federalist* 10. And if so, the Civil War Amendments, as understood by the *Slaughterhouse* minority, turned back toward that theory—the view that rights are inalienable and real, not just conventional; that they should not be defined by the prejudices of local majorities; and that when it comes to honoring fundamental human rights, the organization or structure of the national government makes it more trustworthy than the state governments.

Later courts abandoned Miller's reading of the Due Process Clause and the Equal Protection Clause, and the federal courts now use those clauses to guarantee a broad range of fundamental rights against the states, including

---

28. 83 U.S. at 78.
29. *Id*. at 82.
30. James Madison, "Speech in the House of Representatives, June 8, 1789," reprinted in *The Mind of the Founder*, ed. Marvin Meyers (Indianapolis, IN: Bobbs-Merrill, 1973): 210, 217.

most of the Bill of Rights and rights of privacy. These developments in effect have reversed, without formally overruling, Miller's narrow reading of the Privileges or Immunities Clause.[31] Critics of the modern Court have kept some life in the question of whether Miller was right regarding both the basic structure of federalism and the content of fundamental constitutional rights.[32] A responsible answer demands a careful development and examination of the arguments for preferring one over another theory of constitutional rights in our federal system. And those arguments are partly philosophic because they inevitably combine legal with historical, moral, and scientific considerations.

This brings us back to *Garcia*, a case which features still another conflict between conceptions of federalism, with implications for that most basic of structural questions: the nature of our form of democracy. Justice Harry Blackmun's opinion for the 5-4 majority in *Garcia* achieved a lot for one case. It overruled *Usery*, turned the law of state-federal relations back in Marshall's general (if not precise) direction in *McCulloch*, and held that the interests of the states are guaranteed best by the states' participation in the national political processes, not by judicial restrictions on national policy in the name of states' rights.

As Blackmun saw it, states' rights were *process* rights, not *substantive* rights or guarantees against specific results.[33] States could no longer claim judicially enforceable substantive rights like the right to determine the hours and wages of state employees. They could claim only those rights of representation in the national policy-making process that determines what those hours and wages would be. This, said Blackmun, was principally how the framers intended to protect the states within the structure of federalism and, he added, a lengthy history of federal grants (of land and money) to the states proved the effectiveness of the framers' strategy.

In the theoretically richest of the three dissenting opinions in *Garcia*, Justice Lewis Powell said that by making the states' role a matter of congressional grace, not judicially enforceable constitutional law, the majority was abandoning two centuries of judicial responsibility for maintaining

---

31. Many scholars have criticized *Slaughterhouse* and called for overruling it and reviving the Privileges or Immunities Clause as a ground for fundamental rights. The Supreme Court has left some life in the Clause by invoking it as a ground for the right to travel. *See* Saenz v. Roe, 526 U.S. 489 (1999).
32. *See, e.g.*, Robert H. Bork, *The Tempting of America* (New York: Free Press, 1990): 180–83.
33. *Garcia*, 469 U.S. at 550–51, 554.

the proper state-federal balance.[34] Powell charged that leaving Congress to judge the extent of its power vis-à-vis the states went against the framers' expectation that the states would function as a counterpoise to national power. He also decried the more abstract suggestion that policy-making "*processes* . . . are the proper means of enforcing constitutional limitations." And he suggested that weakening state control over state governmental functions weakened democracy because it "disregard[ed] entirely the far more effective role of democratic self-government at the state and local levels."[35]

This cursory account suffices to show that the debate between Blackmun and Powell (as well as Marshall) runs to deep and choppy waters that force us to ask: How should we read the framers' intentions regarding issues like state power as a counterpoise to federal power and the virtues of large republics relative to small? What form of democratic self-government does the Constitution establish? Framers aside, what's the best conception of democracy, and has democracy in fact flourished better in small areas (e.g., in state and local governments) as opposed to large (in the national government)? What are the basic differences and relationships between procedural and substantive rights, and can there be good reasons for judicially protecting one kind but not the other? What are the respective roles of legislatures and courts in protecting rights as well as in protecting structures of government? (For example, are there good reasons for judicial "underenforcement" of structural norms and for leaving their fuller enforcement to the national political processes outside the courts?)[36] What, exactly, are rights, and do principled differences separate states' rights from individual and minority rights? If legislatures can be trusted with the definition of substantive states' rights, why not trust them with deciding the content of substantive individual and minority rights? Such are the cross-cutting historical, philosophic, and scientific issues in the Blackmun-Powell debate in *Garcia*.

Blackmun's reduction of states' rights to process rights warrants further discussion, for it has affinities to a broader structuralist project of reducing individual and minority rights to process rights. Although they

---

34. *Id.* at 560–61 (Powell, J., dissenting).
35. *Id.* at 566 (emphasis in original), 576.
36. For the idea of judicial "underenforcement" of certain constitutional norms, and for leaving their fuller enforcement to legislatures and executives, *see* Lawrence G. Sager, *Justice in Plainclothes: A Theory of American Constitutional Practice* (New Haven, CT: Yale University Press, 2004): 93–128.

generally oppose reducing states' rights to process rights, many ideological conservatives would reduce individual and minority rights to process rights because they believe, with Bork, that the most important right of individuals and groups is the right to participate in choosing representatives who will vote to enact their constituents' social, economic, and even moral preferences into law.[37] Thus, a woman's right would be the right to vote for pro-choice candidates, not the right to act contrary to a legislature's view restricting abortion. At the same time, many liberals would reduce states' rights to process rights, while they oppose reducing individual and minority rights to process rights.

Blackmun's position on the right to abortion in *Roe v. Wade* (1973)[38] reveals him to be a liberal who opposes reducing individual rights to process rights, but other liberal justices and theorists have embraced this structuralist reduction of individual rights as a way out of two difficulties facing defenders of the New Deal and the Warren Court. These difficulties involve (1) the post-New Deal "double standard" between human rights and property rights and (2) the perceived conflict between strong courts and democracy.

III. *Carolene Products* Footnote 4 and "Democracy"

In *American Constitutional Interpretation*, we together with Walter Murphy and Stephen Macedo discuss the "double standard" between judicial deference to legislatures concerning property rights and stringent judicial protection of human rights in connection with Justice Stone's famous footnote 4 in *United States v. Carolene Products Co.* (1938).[39] The word "liberty" in the Due Process Clause of the Fourteenth Amendment once was interpreted to protect "liberty of contract" against state interference, as in *Lochner v. New York* (1905).[40] By 1938, stringent judicial protection for liberty of contract was a thing of the past. The Court now limited its protection of substantive liberties under the Due Process Clause to freedoms of speech, press, assembly, and religion (which were

---

37. *See, e.g.*, Bork, *supra* note 32, at 121–26.
38. 410 U.S. 113 (1973).
39. Murphy, Fleming, Barber, and Macedo, *supra* note 4, at 683–91 (discussing United States v. Carolene Products Co., 304 U.S. 144, 152–53 n. 4 [1938]).
40. 198 U.S. 45 (1905).

said to be "incorporated" into the word "liberty"). Yet the Clause expressly refers to "property" as well as to "liberty," and if the Court is to protect the liberties of speech and press, why not also the liberty to contract? What could justify not according similar protection to property rights—especially in a "large commercial republic"?

Footnote 4 was an attempt to answer this question. In its three paragraphs, Justice Harlan Fiske Stone described three situations that might warrant "more searching" judicial scrutiny of legislation than the deferential scrutiny courts generally apply. Paragraph 2 of the footnote indicates special judicial concern for freedoms of speech, press, and assembly as aspects of "those political processes which can ordinarily be expected to bring about repeal of undesirable legislation." Paragraph 3 calls for "more searching" judicial scrutiny of laws embodying racial and religious prejudice, "which tends seriously to curtail the operation of those political processes ordinarily thought to be relied upon to protect minorities."[41] If these were the only paragraphs, the footnote would exclude special judicial protection for property rights while protecting favored substantive rights and certain freedoms from discrimination in the guise of protecting process rights (in a broad sense of process). But Chief Justice Charles Evans Hughes, apparently wanting greater recognition that the Court was operating under a constitutional text, insisted on a reference to specific constitutional guarantees, and Stone thought he needed Hughes's vote. So Stone rewrote the draft footnote, and paragraph 1 now indicates special judicial concern not just for process rights but also for "specific" constitutional prohibitions, which include substantive rights.[42] Stone evidently felt the reference to "specific" rights would exclude rights "forbidden only by the general words of the Due Process Clause," rights like the liberty to contract.[43] But the redrafted footnote frustrated this expectation for three reasons: it restored substantive rights as a category of protected rights (since many "specific prohibitions" are substantive); specificity would remain in the eye of the beholder; and the Due Process Clause expressly refers to "liberty" and "property." Stone's efforts to alter these facts went for naught: the Court would continue to protect and expand "unenumerated" substantive liberties in the area of human rights.

---

41. 304 U.S. at 152–53 n. 4.
42. *See* Murphy, Fleming, Barber, and Macedo, *supra* note 4, at 684 (reprinting letter from Hughes to Stone).
43. *See id.* at 685 (reprinting reply from Stone to Hughes).

Footnote 4 failed as the foundation of an exclusively structural or process-oriented constitutionalism.

Ely tried in his well-known book, *Democracy and Distrust*, to revive the structuralist jurisprudence of *Carolene Products* footnote 4 by de-emphasizing the substantive implications of paragraph 1 and reducing its protections (along with those of paragraphs 2 and 3) to process rights.[44] Ely argued that notwithstanding its references to substantive rights, the Constitution exists primarily to ensure fair representation in policy formation for all political interest groups, a goal he conceived as including results that don't discriminate against relatively powerless racial, ethnic, and religious minorities. An interest was a real right for Ely primarily to the extent of its derivation from his baseline commitment: the structure of representative democracy. Though specified in the First Amendment, freedoms of speech and press, for example, were genuine rights for a reason beyond their presence in the text: their role in democratic processes. By the same reasoning, Ely argued, abortion and liberty to contract were not genuine rights: they were not essential to the operation of the political processes of representative democracy. Ely thought, in sum, that judges could minimize the philosophic risks and burdens of deciding which rights deserve judicial protection by deriving rights from the Constitution's democratic structure.

As a theorist, Ely failed to show why his conception of democracy is better than other conceptions, like the constitutionalist conception that stresses substantive rights limiting what majorities may do to individuals and minorities even when the democratic processes are otherwise working properly.[45] Because he could not have shown any of these things without a major philosophic effort, he could not avoid fusing constitutional *theory* and moral philosophy, notwithstanding his objections to

---

44. Ely, *Democracy and Distrust, supra* note 2, at 73–101. Each of us has criticized Ely's theory elsewhere. *See* Fleming, *supra* note 1, at 19–36; Sotirios A. Barber, *On What the Constitution Means* (Baltimore: Johns Hopkins University Press, 1984): 19–37.

45. For constitutionalist conceptions of democracy, and of our form of government as a constitutional democracy instead of a majoritarian representative democracy, *see* Murphy, Fleming, Barber, and Macedo, *supra* note 4, at 43–59; Walter F. Murphy, *Constitutional Democracy: Creating and Maintaining a Just Political Order* (Baltimore: Johns Hopkins University Press, 2007): 1–19; Fleming, *supra* note 1, at 10, 61–85; Stephen Macedo, *Liberal Virtues* (New York: Oxford University Press, 1990): 163–202; Ronald Dworkin, *Freedom's Law: The Moral Reading of the American Constitution* (Cambridge, MA: Harvard University Press, 1996): 15–26; Frank I. Michelman, *Brennan and Democracy* (Princeton, NJ: Princeton University Press, 1999): 3–62.

the contrary.[46] Nor did he show how judges can avoid fusing constitutional *law* and moral philosophy.

Judges can't avoid philosophic responsibilities through noncontroversial inferences from the Constitution's democratic structure, for they have to decide whether to conceive that structure as constitutionalist or majoritarian and, if constitutionalist, whether positive or negative (as we saw in Chapters 2 and 3). Indeed, the clash between constitutionalist and majoritarian conceptions of our scheme of government is one way to encapsulate the unresolved difficulties of constitutional thought. Nor can judges avoid the fusion of constitutional law and moral philosophy by simply declaring the Constitution's structure to be basically majoritarian, for there is no one majoritarian conception of the Constitution. A majoritarian like Ely thus can disagree with a majoritarian like Bork concerning the Warren Court's reforms in voting rights and state legislative apportionment (Ely justified them while Bork condemned them).[47] Even Ely's inference from constitutional structures against the right to abortion requires a philosophic justification that he doesn't supply. Why would it be wrong to conceive anti-abortion legislation as discriminatory against women (we'll consider such arguments in Chapter 9) or as imposing sectarian religious beliefs about the moral status of fetuses?[48] Why would these kinds of prejudice be different from the kinds of race- and religion-based legislation that Ely's structuralism (paragraph 3) would prohibit?[49] By asking these questions, we're not suggesting they can't be answered; we're underscoring what we see as a constitutional duty to try to answer them.

The unavoidability of such questions makes structures seem as controversial as plain words, consensus, intentions, and the rest. The question

---

46. Indeed, there are deep affinities between Ely's constitutional theory and that of Dworkin, which unmistakably fuses constitutional law and moral philosophy. *See* Fleming, *supra* note 1, at 24–26.

47. *Compare* Ely, *Democracy and Distrust, supra* note 2, at 88–104, *with* Bork, *supra* note 32, at 194–96.

48. *See, e.g.,* Ronald Dworkin, *Life's Dominion* (New York: Alfred A. Knopf, 1993): 148–68 (arguing that restrictive abortion laws not only violate women's procreative autonomy but also violate their liberty of conscience because such laws involve government forcing women to conform to an official view about what the sanctity of life requires); Sunstein, *supra* note 3, at 257–61, 270–85 (arguing that such laws discriminate against women).

49. For Ely's final words on the right to abortion, approving *Casey*'s reaffirmation of *Roe* despite his famous criticism of *Roe*, see *supra* note 3.

is not only why process and structure and not substance, but also what structures. All structural decisions proceed from answers to such questions. The choice that interpreters face is whether to take responsibility for their answers. A responsible approach to structural questions demands a fusion of historical, philosophic, and scientific inquiry. It cannot avoid philosophic reflection and choices. Nor can a doctrinal approach or a "minimalist" approach that seeks, in a shallow and narrow way, to decide "one case at a time," as we'll see in the next chapter.

CHAPTER 9

DOCTRINALISM AND MINIMALISM

I. Doctrinalism

Cases like *McCulloch v. Maryland* (1819)[1] and *The Slaughterhouse Cases* (1872)[2] (discussed in Chapter 8) come along only once in the life of a legal system, for they are the first judicial applications of specific constitutional provisions. The more a constitutional system matures, the more its lawyers and judges look at its constitutional provisions not directly but through layers of interpretations in previous cases. These past interpretations purport to articulate constitutional principles in the form of rules or precedents that bind future courts. An example of such a rule or precedent would be the "separate but equal" doctrine of the Equal Protection Clause, announced in *Plessy v. Ferguson* (1896),[3] and courts that followed *Plessy* would refer to that case as a "precedent."

Precisely why an old case should ever be a precedent case and its holding a rule or precedent for future cases is a difficult question to answer fully or satisfactorily.[4] It becomes more difficult in constitutional law, an area where it is generally agreed that courts can err about constitutional meaning and later courts may legitimately cancel the precedential value of old cases by overruling them. (Indeed, it is commonly said that precedent has less weight in constitutional law than in law generally, because the only alternative to a court's overruling a mistaken precedent interpreting the Constitution is for the people to amend the Constitution through the

---

[1] 17 U.S. 316 (1819).
[2] 83 U.S. 36 (1872).
[3] 163 U.S. 537 (1896).
[4] *See* Michael S. Moore, "Precedent, Induction, and Ethical Generalization," in *Precedent in Law,* ed. Laurence Goldstein (Oxford: Oxford University Press, 1986): 183, 186–87.

formal procedures of Article V, and that is a very cumbersome process.) But there are reasons for honoring old cases (concern for consistency, stability, and predictability, for example), and we needn't go into those reasons fully to recognize that American constitutional practice includes a limited policy of stare decisis—letting the precedent stand as decided— which makes old cases important though not conclusive in judicial determinations of constitutional meaning.

The fact that a body of old cases can gloss a constitutional provision with much more detail than is found in the spare language of the constitutional document might tempt you to think that a relatively strict adherence to stare decisis can substantially reduce the burdens of philosophic reflection and choice in hard cases. You might believe, for example, that the Warren Court could have avoided a controversial philosophic choice concerning the meaning of our commitment to "equal protection of the laws" by following *Plessy* when deciding *Brown v. Board of Education* (1954).[5] If you believe this, and if you believe also that fusing constitutional law and moral philosophy is indeed un-American and dangerous (recall the objections to the philosophic approach in Chapter 5), you might support a doctrinal approach in constitutional interpretation— even though that would mean practically entrusting the correction of judicial mistakes to the very cumbersome process of amending the Constitution, since a strict approach to precedent (assuming we could ever be sure about the meaning of precedent cases) would disable future courts from correcting the mistakes of past courts.

A doctrinal approach would raise many questions in addition to that of the wisdom of making judicial mistakes very hard to change. But more fundamental to our concerns here is whether the doctrinalist's central assumption is correct: Is it true that a doctrinal approach can actually reduce the burdens of philosophic choice in hard cases? Could the Court have avoided a difficult choice in *Brown* by following *Plessy*? Let's see.

Precedents typically come in lines of decision or series, and judges who would follow precedent typically ask what a whole series says about the law. Such was the situation as the Court considered *Brown*; stare decisis pointed not just to *Plessy*, but also to intervening cases elaborating the doctrine of "separate but equal," especially *Sweatt v. Painter* (1950).[6]

[5.] 347 U.S. 483 (1954).
[6.] 339 U.S. 629 (1950).

In *Sweatt*, a unanimous Court held that Texas couldn't satisfy the Equal Protection Clause simply by equalizing the library and other "tangible facilities" of two law schools: a newly established law school for blacks and the well established University of Texas School of Law, reserved for whites. The Court's central reason was that the black law school could not offer a professional preparation equal to that available from the white law school, because the black law school excluded 85% of the state's population and therewith most of the future judges and lawyers with whom its graduates would have to deal as professionals. This reasoning made it all but impossible for segregated law schools to satisfy the Constitution, and *Sweatt* was widely seen as a threat to *Plessy's* doctrine of "separate but equal" in other areas of public education. Read this way, *Sweatt* imparted ambiguity to the series of precedents beginning with *Plessy* and forced the Court into a difficult choice.

This example doesn't prove that conflict in a series of precedents is inevitable, however. A defender of the doctrinal approach can argue that *Sweatt* doesn't belong to the *Plessy* family of cases, that *Sweatt* was a departure from precedent, and that *Sweatt* was therefore a mistake. If *Sweatt* seems morally better and therefore attractive, he might add, "Then you should consider the reasons why democracy needs stare decisis. You might then appreciate the costs in correcting such mistakes."

But our doctrinalist can't prove that *Sweatt* rejected *Plessy* just by asserting that it did. In his opinion for the Court in *Sweatt*, Chief Justice Fred M. Vinson didn't say the Court was deviating from *Plessy*. In fact, Vinson seemed to accept *Plessy's* framework by making the decision in *Sweatt* turn on a comparison of the facilities in the two law schools. As Vinson understood it, *Plessy* said the facilities could be separate as long as they were equal. Because Vinson agreed, he concentrated on the quality (and equality) of the facilities. So even though *Sweatt* had a different assessment of a different set of *facts* in a different time and place, *Sweatt* followed the *rule* of *Plessy*.

Does honesty require us to conclude that Vinson's respect for *Plessy* in *Sweatt* was superficial and disingenuous? That depends on how you read *Plessy*. The *Plessy* doctrine is fairly described in terms of "separate but equal facilities." Justice Henry Brown's opinion for the *Plessy* majority contains no analysis of "facilities" or equivalent concepts. Nor is it clear from his opinion that he would have excluded "intangible facilities" from "facilities." But, even if we assume that by "facilities" he would have meant "tangible facilities only," our problems aren't over. For he still could have counted teachers as tangible facilities, and it's easy to assume that he would have done so.[7]

Imagine a racist municipality erecting a state-of-the-art school building for blacks while leaving the building totally unstaffed with teachers. Would a court clearly depart from a doctrine of equal tangible facilities by declaring such a ploy unconstitutional? Now imagine the municipality meeting such a declaration by hiring "teachers" with no certification or actual ability to teach. Would that count as equal tangible facilities if teachers in the white school were qualified teachers? Would precedent demand accepting this second ploy? Suppose the municipality's next move is to certify the incompetent teachers as competent. Could a court honor the *Plessy* rule by approving this last move?

Not if the rule were really a rule. A municipality that could make incompetent teachers competent simply by issuing certificates of competence could equalize other unequal facilities in similar fashion. Neither "separate but equal" nor any other rule of law could ever be a problem for this municipality, because it could comply simply by declaring itself in compliance. And what would be true of this municipality would be true of state agencies generally. Under these conditions, the *Plessy* rule wouldn't be what we could recognize as a legal rule. It wouldn't be a legal rule because it couldn't bind its admitted subjects (states and their subunits) against their will. And pronouncements that cannot possibly bind subjects against their will don't fall into the category of legal rules.

At some point, therefore, a court that would honor *Plessy* would have to decide what level of teacher competence to require for constitutional purposes. To determine a minimum standard of teacher competence would require some attention to the goals of education since competence is an agent's capacity to achieve its purpose, and to achieve it with relative efficiency. Treating *Plessy* as a precedent therefore would involve a court in no little amount of reflection, debate, and choice. Letting state agencies themselves decide what constitutes equal facilities would hardly honor *Plessy* as a precedent.

From this it follows that fidelity to *Plessy* required the Vinson Court, when deciding *Sweatt*, to form a responsible opinion on what constitutes

---

7. To be sure, it is not obviously wrong to conclude that Cumming v. Board of Education of Richmond, 175 U.S. 528 (1899), Berea College v. Kentucky, 211 U.S. 45 (1908), and a widespread pattern of unequal tangible facilities were consistent with *Plessy*.

equal faculties. The Court assumed, safely, that attending law school is not an end in itself and that people typically go to law school to become lawyers. It also assumed, again safely, that law schools aren't equal if they can't give equally capable and motivated law students equal preparation for professional success. The Court assumed further—controversially now, but still responsibly—that being a successful lawyer meant success in places like courts, professional associations, and governmental agencies. The Court assumed, in other words, that professional success was success in institutions of the politically and economically dominant culture, which was white. So the Court concluded that equal preparation required teachers with reputations and connections in the politically and economically dominant culture. Classmates from that culture were also needed if minority law students were to develop the personal contacts that enhance success in any field. That the assumptions and choices here are controversial is unmistakable, but does that fact alone make *Sweatt* inconsistent with *Plessy*?

You might continue to insist that it does on the theory that, even though *Plessy* didn't expressly say so, it stood not just for "separate but equal" but also for "separate *over* equal" if the two can't be reconciled. You *can* read *Plessy* that way, but does fairness to Justice Brown's opinion compel you to do so? Does *Plessy* read: Equalize to the extent permitted by the greater desideratum of segregation? Or does it read: Segregation is permissible to the extent that it doesn't treat blacks and whites unequally? That this last statement is a possible reading of *Plessy* may explain why Vinson felt no compulsion to overrule that case in *Sweatt*. It may also explain why the opinion in *Brown* concentrates not on *Plessy's* reading of the Constitution, but on *Plessy's* view of the world (as we saw in Chapter 6). *Brown* makes a factual finding that segregation is actually harmful to minority students, and what *Brown* rejects in *Plessy* is "[a]ny language . . . contrary to this finding."[8] (There are affinities between our analysis and that of the joint opinion in *Planned Parenthood v. Casey* (1992), which analyzed *Brown's* overruling of *Plessy* in terms of a change in understanding of the facts.)[9]

Read *Plessy*, *Sweatt*, and *Brown* with all of this in mind. Then consider two widely supported propositions in jurisprudence: (1) courts in hard cases can't phrase their conclusions in ways that yield uncontroversial

---

8. 347 U.S. at 494–95.
9. 505 U.S. 833, 862–63 (1992).

answers to all future cases and (2) there's rarely only one way to read an old case. If your reading of these cases makes these propositions plausible, you'll agree that stare decisis can't eliminate controversial choices in hard cases. Thus, doctrinalism cannot avoid the burdens and responsibilities of philosophic reflection and choice in such cases.

II. Minimalism: A Pragmatic Variation on Doctrinalism

Cass R. Sunstein proposes what he calls a "minimalist" approach to constitutional interpretation, a pragmatic variation on doctrinalism whereby judges would narrowly decide "one case at a time."[10] Sunstein's "minimalism" is best understood in terms of what motivates it: the concern that "theoretically ambitious" federal judges are removing too many issues (for example, abortion and sexual orientation) from the purview of elected legislatures and therewith popular choice. Sunstein's principal target is Ronald Dworkin's approach to constitutional meaning or what we're calling the philosophic approach.[11] This approach, he says, invites theoretically ambitious decisions (like *Roe v. Wade* (1973) and *Lawrence v. Texas* (2003)) that rob popular majorities of the opportunity to deliberate about, and through deliberation to reach consensus about, divisive moral issues. Sunstein proposes "minimalism," therefore: "the view that judges should take narrow, theoretically unambitious steps" in deciding constitutional questions.[12]

We'll attempt a clearer picture of minimalism momentarily, but we note first something that isn't always clear in Sunstein's argument: his

---

[10.] Cass R. Sunstein, *Legal Reasoning and Political Conflict* (New York: Oxford University Press, 1996) [hereinafter Sunstein, *Legal Reasoning*]; Cass R. Sunstein, *One Case at a Time: Judicial Minimalism on the Supreme Court* (Cambridge, MA: Harvard University Press, 1999) [hereinafter Sunstein, *One Case at a Time*]. In this section, we partly draw upon analyses in other work: James E. Fleming, *Securing Constitutional Democracy: The Case of Autonomy* (Chicago: University of Chicago Press, 2006): 142, 160–67 [hereinafter Fleming, *Securing Constitutional Democracy*]; James E. Fleming and Linda C. McClain, "In Search of a Substantive Republic," *Texas Law Review* 76 (1997): 509, 514, 538–46; James E. Fleming, "The Incredible Shrinking Constitutional Theory: From the Partial Constitution to the Minimal Constitution," *Fordham Law Review* 75 (2007): forthcoming.

[11.] *See, e.g.,* Sunstein, *Legal Reasoning, supra* note 10, at 7 (criticizing Ronald Dworkin, "The Forum of Principle," *New York University Law Review* 56 [1981]: 469 [hereinafter Dworkin, "Forum"], reprinted in Ronald Dworkin, *A Matter of Principle* [Cambridge, MA: Harvard University Press, 1985]: 33).

[12.] Cass R. Sunstein, "Second-Order Perfectionism," *Fordham Law Review* 75 (2007): forthcoming, available at SSRN: http://ssrn.com/abstract=948788, at 3.

position on interpretation is a two-part affair. Only one of these parts proposes anything fairly described as "minimalist." The minimalist part, moreover, does not deal with *constitutional interpretation* in our sense: it does not advise interpreters how to find what the Constitution means. The minimalist part is rather a theory of *judicial strategy*. Its explicit audience is judges. Sunstein says his focus is "constitutional interpretation by the judiciary." While he advises judges to adopt minimalism, he leaves "citizens and their representatives" free to adopt what he calls a "first-order perfectionism"[13]—which is what Dworkin calls the moral reading and what we're calling the philosophic approach to constitutional meaning. Instead of advising judges and other interpreters how to find what the Constitution means, minimalism tells judges what to do *after* they've decided that question. In other words, minimalism tells judges the kind of thing they should say to the public in constitutional cases, not how to decide what the Constitution means.

Sunstein, however, does have a theory of how to decide what the Constitution means. That theory comprises the second part of his position. But this second part is not minimalist; it is in fact a version of what we're calling the philosophic approach, as we shall see. Unraveling and then recombining the two parts of Sunstein's position leaves us with the following advice to judges: (1) find what the Constitution means essentially as Dworkin does, then (2) tell the people what it's best for them to hear. Sunstein's position raises many issues about the role of judges and the nature of constitutional democracy, especially the theory of *responsibility* in constitutional democracy (Recall Chapter 3.) But our present interest in his position is limited. We seek to show only that (1) his approach to constitutional interpretation is philosophic in nature, and (2) his "minimalism" is a theory of what judges should do or say to the public *after* they've decided what the Constitution means.

That Sunstein's approach to constitutional interpretation is philosophic in nature is indicated in a preliminary way by his choice of labels. He calls Dworkin's approach (our "philosophic approach") "first-order perfectionism" and minimalism "second-order perfectionism," which is enough to suggest that minimalism is some diminished form of what we're calling the philosophic approach. Looking behind these labels to what they stand for, we see that Sunstein distinguishes four strategies of judicial conduct in constitutional cases. The first strategy (associated with

---

[13.] *Id.* at 5.

James Bradley Thayer) is that judges should let legislation stand unless legislation "is plainly in violation of the Constitution" — i.e., a "clear mistake," in violation beyond reasonable question. The second (associated with Raoul Berger and other originalists) is that judges should ground their judgments in "the original public meaning of the [constitutional] document." The third strategy (Sunstein's approach) is minimalism, in which judges should "build modestly on their own precedents" instead of ruling "broadly or ambitiously." And the fourth strategy (associated with Dworkin) is that judges should represent the Constitution as the best it can be morally, "and in that sense perfect[] it." None of these strategies is "ruled off the table by the Constitution itself," Sunstein says, and therefore each "must be defended by reference to some account offered by the interpreter."[14] These accounts, moreover, must be "perfectionist" in nature —that is, moral or philosophic.

Sunstein is clear and emphatic about this last point. We quote him in full:

> Any approach to the founding document must be perfectionist in the sense that it attempts to make the document as good as it can possibly be. Thayerism is a form of perfectionism; it claims to improve the constitutional order. Originalism, read most sympathetically, is a form of perfectionism; it suggests that constitutional democracy, properly understood, is best constructed through originalism. Minimalism is a form of perfectionism too; it rejects Thayerism and originalism on the ground that they would make the constitutional system much worse. It would appear that the debate among Thayerians, originalists, minimalists, and perfectionists must be waged on the perfectionists' own turf. And if this is so, perfectionists are right to insist that any approach to the Constitution must attempt to fit and justify it. Perhaps the alternatives to perfectionism are all, in one or another sense, perfectionist too.[15]

Though this is an important passage, it should be an uncontroversial one at this stage of our discussion. For here Sunstein simply recognizes that a philosophic argument is needed to defend any general approach to constitutional meaning or judicial strategy. Sunstein's observation falls short of our main point, however. Here Sunstein says something about

---

14. *Id.* at 2–4.
15. *Id.* at 4.

his activity as a constitutional theorist. *He* has to offer a philosophic argument for minimalism, just as other theorists have to offer philosophic arguments for their positions. But this proves nothing about the activity of judges deciding concrete constitutional questions. Armed with Sunstein's philosophic argument for minimalism (whatever it may be) can *judges* (or any other interpreters) utilize the tenets of minimalism to decide concrete constitutional questions in a manner free of controversial philosophic choices? To see why the answer is no—to see, in other words, why minimalism is no answer to Dworkin's call for a fusion of constitutional law and moral philosophy—we shall consider Sunstein's further observations about minimalism and we shall examine Sunstein's commentary on some important cases involving rights of personal liberty or autonomy.

Sunstein says that "[n]o approach to constitutional interpretation makes sense in every possible world," and that the case for each approach "must depend, in part, on a set of judgments about institutional capacities."[16] Thus, where "democratic processes work exceedingly fairly and well" on their own—where there's no racial segregation, for example, and "political speech is not banned," and "federalism and separation of powers are safeguarded, and precisely to the right extent," all without "judicial intervention"—then "it would make a great deal of sense" for judges to adopt Thayer's approach to constitutional adjudication. On the other hand, when representative institutions are behaving badly and "the original public meaning is quite excellent" from the standpoint of honoring constitutional rights and institutions, then an originalist approach "would seem best." Where original meanings are inadequate and courts are more competent, morally and intellectually, than representative institutions, then Dworkin's approach is best. And minimalism is best when "original meaning is not so excellent" for protecting rights and institutions, "the democratic process is good but not great," and "judges will do poorly if they strike out on their own, but very well if they build modestly on their own precedents."[17]

From this it appears that before a judge can decide to go minimalist, she must decide (1) the best view of constitutional rights and/or institutions; (2) whether the original meaning comports with the best view of

---

16. *Id.* at 2.
17. *Id.* at 2–3.

rights/institutions; (3) how well present democratic processes are progressing toward the best view of rights/institutions; and (4) whether judges are presently likely to do a better job than the democratic processes in serving the best view of rights/institutions. The complexity and theoretical ambition of these moral and non-moral judgments require no elaboration. They are at least as ambitious as anything Dworkin has ever attempted. The minimalist judge may pretend otherwise to the public. She may say, for example (more of this below), that a particular prosecution of homosexual intimate conduct is unconstitutional simply because prosecutions under the relevant statute are too rare for the public to know what to expect, and that knowing what to expect is a hallmark of the rule of law. But what she says to the public is one thing, and what she's thinking to herself is another. What she's thinking is that public opinion on homosexuality is heading in the right direction without her help, and that she risks mucking things up if she boldly steps ahead of public opinion and flatly declares a constitutional right of homosexuals to intimate association. If there's minimalism here, it's not in how the judge understands the Constitution, it's in how she presents herself to the public as a matter of judicial strategy.

We now assess Sunstein's call for judicial minimalism by reviewing his analysis of cases protecting a right of privacy and intimate association from *Griswold v. Connecticut* (1965) to *Lawrence v. Texas* (2003). At the outset, we emphasize that we are not here taking positions on the substantive issues to be discussed, including contraception, abortion, and homosexuality. Instead, we are examining Sunstein's minimalism, his view that even though (on his own account) the Constitution embodies substantive moral principles that protect the rights in question, courts should refrain from fully elaborating those principles and protecting those rights.

Sunstein believes that the Court was too ambitious in *Griswold*. For him, judicial enforcement of a broad right to privacy is too "adventurous," because a broad right to privacy under the Due Process Clause invites judges to declare specific rights of privacy that popular majorities might oppose, and for Sunstein this means that a broad right to privacy is undemocratic.[18] Not that Sunstein would have dissented in *Griswold*; he would have taken a different route to the result in that case. He would

---

[18.] *See, e.g.*, Cass R. Sunstein, "Liberal Constitutionalism and Liberal Justice," *Texas Law Review* 72 (1993): 305, 312 (suggesting that reliance upon equal protection principles could provide a narrower and more secure basis for judicial decisions than due process).

have built upon and invigorated the idea of "desuetude" (a government's long-standing neglect to enforce a policy) as a constitutional basis for courts to invalidate statutes. Rather than recognizing a right of privacy, he says, the Court should have struck down Connecticut's ban on contraceptives on the ground that "citizens need not comply with laws, or applications of laws, that lack real enforcement and that find no support in anything like common democratic conviction."[19] Sunstein contends that enforcement of the statute against a married couple would have lacked contemporary democratic support and that the real function of the statute was to deter birth control clinics from assisting poor people.[20] He argues that a decision based on desuetude would have left open broader questions of a right to privacy. This strategy might have earned the agreement of people "who reject any 'right of privacy' or are uncertain about its foundations and limits."[21] Sunstein justifies his "minimalist" approach on democratic grounds: when courts decide the case before them on the narrowest ground available, they minimize restraints on popular majorities.

Sunstein's position on *Griswold* recalls Michael Perry's position on *Roe*, which we discussed in Chapter 5. Both writers belong to a modern tradition that includes Justice Stone (discussed in Chapter 8), Justice Rehnquist (discussed in Chapter 2), and Professor Bickel (mentioned in Chapter 3). This tradition treats an undefended conception of democracy as our Constitution's supreme value and conceives constitutional rights in a manner consistent with that conception. One of its tenets is that when elaborating the "liberty" mentioned in the Due Process Clauses, courts should limit themselves to liberties that enjoy popular support. Yet this position itself may well lack popular support. As we've observed in previous chapters, it conflicts with constitutional language and tradition tracing back to *The Federalist*, and it puts its defenders in the difficult position of explaining why and how "democracy" can refer to a real value that the public is not at liberty to define while "liberty" can be no more than what the public wants it to be.

Another problem with minimalism is that desuetude, by definition, cannot justify invalidating laws that are regularly enforced. Restrictive abortion laws prior to *Roe v. Wade* (1973)[22] offer an illustration. Sunstein's

---

[19.] Sunstein, *Legal Reasoning, supra* note 10, at 156.
[20.] *See id.* at 155.
[21.] *Id.* at 156.
[22.] 410 U.S. 113 (1973).

approach to abortion suggests just how much his commitment to deliberative democracy would shape legal reasoning and constrain courts. Sunstein believes that the Equal Protection Clause incorporates a principle of opposition to castes that condemns laws that reduce certain classes of persons, like African-Americans or women, to the status of second-class citizenship. As he interprets it, therefore, the Equal Protection Clause forbids discrimination on the basis of sex.[23] Restrictive abortion laws, Sunstein argues, selectively impose upon women a duty to devote their bodies to aid the vulnerable (i.e., fetuses), a burden that the state does not impose upon men (e.g., parents are not required to donate kidneys to their children).[24] This selective imposition stems from stereotyped "conceptions of women's proper role" and perpetuates women's "second-class citizenship."[25] Thus, abortion restrictions are a form of sex discrimination. By reaching this conclusion in this way, Sunstein, as constitutional theorist, performs an act of interpretation whose implications seem at least as broad as the implications of *Griswold* and *Roe*. Compared to a principle of liberty-as-privacy (in *Griswold* and *Roe*), there's nothing "minimalist" about Sunstein's principle of non-discrimination against women and others who might constitute a "caste."

Nonetheless, Sunstein concludes that courts should proceed incrementally, narrowly, and cautiously. Thus, he criticizes *Roe* as an ambitiously "maximalist" decision that in effect invalidated the abortion laws of almost every state. He suggests that a properly incremental approach would have begun by striking down laws that did not permit abortion in cases of rape and incest.[26] This would have given democratic bodies time to wrestle with the broader moral questions and (perhaps) ultimately to protect a more expansive right to reproductive freedom, rooted in sex equality, rather than the right to liberty or privacy recognized by the Court in *Roe*.[27] Sunstein thus confounds the substance of a right with the pace of its enforcement. *Eventually*, he hopes or assumes, the equal protection right to abortion will protect a right as expansive as the due process right to abortion. What he fails to show is why or how an incremental pace is

---

[23.] *See* Sunstein, *Legal Reasoning, supra* note 10, at 180–81; Cass R. Sunstein, *The Partial Constitution* (Cambridge, MA: Harvard University Press, 1993): 270–75, 402 n. 17 [hereinafter Sunstein, *Partial Constitution*].

[24.] *See* Sunstein, *Legal Reasoning, supra* note 10, at 180.

[25.] *Id.*

[26.] Recall our discussion in Chapter 5 of Michael Perry's similar consensualist approach to *Roe*.

[27.] *See* Sunstein, *Legal Reasoning, supra* note 10, at 180–81.

connected more to one of these grounds for rights than to the other. Can't a court develop the idea of liberty as cautiously as it can develop the idea of equality? Nor does he show how the equal protection right is any less controversial than the due process right. No less than Justice Blackmun's conclusions in *Roe*, Sunstein's conclusions turn on controversial philosophic choices, like the personhood of a fetus and the moral equivalence of terminating a pregnancy and refusing to donate a kidney.

As for Sunstein's approach to the rights of homosexuals, he says that courts should not rob the people of their right to deliberate, through the democratic processes, the moral issues involved in the legal treatment of sexual orientation. He generally applauds the Supreme Court's decision in *Romer v. Evans* (1996), which invalidated Colorado's Amendment 2, a categorical proscription of state and local laws aimed at protecting gays, lesbians, and bisexuals from discrimination.[28] *Romer* avoids deciding whether discrimination on the basis of sexual orientation is as wrong (or "suspect") constitutionally as racial discrimination. *Romer* holds instead that the Equal Protection Clause does not permit a state to make a class of citizens a "stranger to its laws." It holds that the very sweep of Amendment 2 belied any assertion of legitimate governmental interests, indicating rather "animus" against or "a bare ... desire to harm a politically unpopular group."[29] Sunstein suggests that, by its "narrow and shallow" decision, the Court proceeded incrementally, in recognition of the need for democratic rather than judicial conclusions, and left unanswered the question whether a more closely tailored prohibition justified in terms of legitimate public purposes could pass muster.[30]

Sunstein offers a different assessment of *Lawrence v. Texas* (2003).[31] Here, he argues, the Court should have avoided declaring that a right of privacy or autonomy protects homosexuals as well as heterosexuals. Instead, he says, the Court should have struck down the Texas law banning same-sex sodomy (but not opposite-sex sodomy) on the ground of desuetude. Yet the principle that justifies Sunstein's void-for-desuetude rule is itself a controversial principle. As applied to same-sex sodomy, the

---

[28.] 517 U.S. 620, 635 (1996). Sunstein discusses *Romer* in Sunstein, *One Case at a Time, supra* note 10, at 137–62.

[29.] *Romer*, 517 U.S. at 634, 635 (quoting United States Department of Agriculture v. Moreno, 413 U.S. 528, 534 (1973)).

[30.] *See* Sunstein, *One Case at a Time, supra* note 10, at 151, 156–67.

[31.] 539 U.S. 558 (2003).

principle is: "Without a strong justification, the state cannot bring the criminal law to bear on consensual sexual behavior if enforcement of the relevant law can no longer claim to have significant moral support in the enforcing state or the nation as a whole."[32] As formulated, this principle implies (1) a right to "consensual sexual behavior" that is (2) a right against elected officials but not against public opinion. That there should be any right to "consensual sexual behavior" is a matter of controversy that implicates issues of liberty and privacy. That elected officials cannot act independently of public support in a given policy area (sexual morality) compounds the liberty-privacy question with a question about the nature of representation in a democracy. (We recall here from Chapter 3 that *The Federalist* favors a government that to some extent can and should act independently of public opinion.) And whether public opinion can legitimately determine the content and strength of any right is a question about the nature of rights. All of these questions are questions of moral and political philosophy.

Sunstein holds that the methods of moral and political philosophy are simply not in the judge's tool box of lawyerly methods. Sunstein's view seems to be that, so long as deliberative democracy will *eventually* vindicate constitutional principles, courts should defer to the democratic processes. In contrast with, say, Dworkin's liberal model of courts as a "forum of principle" vindicating constitutional rights,[33] Sunstein's model of judicial minimalism comes perilously close to sacrificing such rights for the sake of deliberative processes. Yet the question for Sunstein remains: How long should the courts stay their hand? What of the human cost to the individuals who may have legitimate claims to constitutional protection but whose rights are underenforced by the courts and who must await protection in the democratic arena? Justice delayed is not, for Sunstein, justice denied. Or justice delayed, all things considered (especially the benefits to deliberative democracy of such a delay), is justifiably denied.

---

32. Sunstein, "What Did *Lawrence* Hold? Of Autonomy, Desuetude, Sexuality, and Marriage," *Supreme Court Review* (2003): 27, 30. For criticism of Sunstein's minimalist analysis of *Lawrence* along with the other cases protecting a right of privacy, *see* Ronald Kahn, "Why *Lawrence v. Texas* Was Not Expected: A Critique of Pragmatic Legalist and Behavioral Explanations of Supreme Court Decision Making," in *The Future of Gay Rights in America*, ed. H.N. Hirsch (New York: Routledge, 2005): 229.
33. Dworkin, "Forum", *supra* note 11.

Sunstein does recognize that the democratic processes may have flaws and that courts have an appropriate role in protecting persons who are disadvantaged in those processes.[34] Yet his commitment to judicial minimalism leads to a judicial incrementalism that appears to undercut that protection for the sake of democratic processes. To return to the example of abortion, women, he argues, are a group who suffer disadvantage in the democratic processes, and the courts should play a role in striking down restrictive abortion laws. But Sunstein suggests that judicial incrementalism (e.g., beginning with invalidating laws that prohibited abortion even in cases of rape and incest) would have been a better course than the "maximalist" approach of *Roe*, and he wagers that judicial incrementalism might have led to legislatures fashioning a broader and more accepted right of sex equality and reproductive freedom than did the Court in *Roe*.[35] It is a point of considerable controversy whether, without *Roe*, state legislatures would have done so.[36] In any event, abortions sought because of rape and incest are a tiny portion of all abortions, and such a limited right would leave most women who seek to terminate their pregnancies with no legal recourse. And here, justice delayed, given the temporal nature of pregnancy, would certainly be justice denied. If there are, as Sunstein contends, strong arguments for abortion rights rooted in an anticaste principle of sex equality (under the Equal Protection Clause), why must women wait for democratic vindication? No answer to this question can be anything but "theoretically ambitious."

As for the "minimalism" in *Romer*, it hardly represents avoidance of controversial philosophic questions. *Romer*'s utter silence about *Bowers v. Hardwick* (1986), in which the Court had concluded that the majority's "presumed belief" in the immorality of homosexual sodomy afforded a rational basis for its criminal proscription,[37] can be taken, and was taken, to say a great deal. *Lawrence* subsequently overruled *Bowers*, and cited

---

34. Sunstein, *Partial Constitution, supra* note 23, at 142–44.
35. *See* Sunstein, *Legal Reasoning, supra* note 10, at 180–81.
36. *Compare* Mary Ann Glendon, *Abortion and Divorce in Western Law* (Cambridge, MA: Harvard University Press, 1987): 47, 47-50 (arguing that a "decision leaving abortion regulation basically up to state legislatures would have encouraged constructive activity by partisans of both sides"), *with* Laurence H. Tribe, *Abortion: The Clash of Absolutes* (New York: Norton, 1990): 49–51 (stating that "the history of abortion law reform in the United States seriously undermines [Glendon's] claim").
37. 478 U.S. 186, 196 (1986).

Romer together with *Planned Parenthood v. Casey* (1992) as undermining *Bowers*.[38] Yet that ending was by no means a foreordained conclusion. *Romer* may be read either as implicitly overruling *Bowers* or as postponing the evident conflict between these two cases. For, as Justice Scalia pointed out in dissent, the "mere animus" against homosexuals that the Court condemns as inadequate to justify civil disabilities in *Romer* was the very moral condemnation that justified criminal penalties in *Bowers*.[39] Sunstein seeks to reconcile these cases by drawing an unpersuasive distinction (which, he suggests, a minimalist decision in *Romer* could have drawn) between the "forward looking" or critical function of the Equal Protection Clause (it criticizes even long-standing historical practices that deny equal protection) and the "backward looking" or status-quo preserving function of the Due Process Clause (it protects long-standing historical practices against short-term or ill-considered departures).[40] But surely Dworkin has a point; for the sake of principle and integrity in constitutional interpretation, the Court in *Romer* should have reached more directly the underlying question whether moral condemnation of homosexuals justifies treating them unequally despite constitutional promises of liberty and equality.[41] Making that judgment requires philosophic choices.

Sunstein's commitment to judicial minimalism cannot be understood simply as entailed by his theory of legal reasoning, with its advocacy of reasoning by analogy. To the contrary, minimalism would constrain even the process of analogical reasoning. As Sunstein explains, the crucial step in analogical reasoning comes at the point where a court must formulate the rule that justifies the result in the prior case and apply that rule to the new case. This is an act of judgment involving choice among alternative formulations of the old rule, for there is often no uncontroversial formulation of the rule of an old case. How do we know, for example, exactly

---

[38] 539 U.S. at 573–74.

[39] *Romer*, 517 U.S. at 644.

[40] *See* Sunstein, *One Case at a Time*, *supra* note 10, at 155–56. For criticism of Sunstein's distinction between due process and equal protection along these lines, *see* Fleming, *Securing Constitutional Democracy*, *supra* note 10, at 56–59.

[41] *See* Ronald Dworkin, *Sovereign Virtue: The Theory and Practice of Equality* (Cambridge, MA: Harvard University Press, 2000): 49–50 [hereinafter Dworkin, *Sovereign Virtue*]; *see also* Ronald Dworkin, "The Arduous Virtue of Fidelity: Originalism, Scalia, Tribe, and Nerve," *Fordham Law Review* 65 (1996): 1249, 1268 (criticizing *Romer* for not overruling *Bowers* and criticizing pragmatic approaches to distinguishing those cases: "Lives don't pause while the passive, pragmatic virtues drape themselves in epigrams and preen in law journal articles").

what *Brown v. Board of Education* stands for? Does it promise no racial classifications of any kind, regardless of the objective? Or does it promise equal educational opportunity and therewith racially integrated schools, through quotas if need be? And how do we know that one social practice is analogous to another? Sunstein holds that sex discrimination is analogous to race discrimination and that, therefore, the state may not force women to continue a pregnancy unless it is prepared to force men to give up spare kidneys to their children. But what tells him or a "minimalist" judge that it is wrong to hold that women have a special role in childbearing and that special obligations attend this role? Since none but a moral argument can responsibly answer any of these questions, and since Sunstein defines minimalism as avoiding moral arguments, no responsible judge can be a minimalist. A responsible judge might *profess* minimalism, perhaps, but only if there's a good reason (vouchsafed to whom?) to pretend to the public what isn't so: that she's deciding constitutional questions in a manner that avoids controversial moral choices.

Sunstein recognizes the moral judgments in analogical reasoning when he says that the "meaning of an analogous case may be inexhaustible."[42] It is this very choice among alternative interpretations that allows for what some call "moral evolution" within the law in light of new facts and ideas. Whether analogical reasoning takes a conservative or a critical view of social practices depends, he says, not on the method itself, but on the "principles brought to bear on disputed cases."[43] Yet Sunstein concludes that while a court could use analogical reasoning to conclude that bans on abortion are unconstitutional, courts should avoid the full deployment of such analogies and decide cases as narrowly as possible. This constraint upon the use of analogy is puzzling given that Sunstein approves courts' applying high-level principles of equal protection in drawing analogies between race and other classifications such as gender.

Sunstein invokes an anticaste principle as a theory of equality's proper scope,[44] while Dworkin applies a principle of equal concern and respect.[45] Neither principle is less "adventurous" than privacy or autonomy as a constitutional ground for invalidating statutes. We can see an anticaste

---

[42.] Sunstein, *Legal Reasoning, supra* note 10, at 194.
[43.] *Id.* at 95.
[44.] Sunstein, *Partial Constitution, supra* note 23, at 139, 270–85, 338–45.
[45.] Ronald Dworkin, *Taking Rights Seriously* (Cambridge, MA: Harvard University Press, 1977): 180–83, 272–78 [hereinafter Dworkin, *Taking Rights Seriously*]; Dworkin, *Sovereign Virtue, supra* note 41, at 1–7.

principle together with a right of autonomy at work in the joint opinion of *Casey*, for example.[46] Here the full participation of women in the nation's economic and political life was cited as a good that justifies a right to abortion much broader than Sunstein thinks it proper for judges to declare. That Sunstein would apply the principle differently is due to the greater weight that he places on his conception of democracy, a conception whose controversial nature is established by his disagreement with Dworkin and a tradition of judicial protection of fundamental rights now in its third century.[47] If Sunstein is to defend his conception of democracy and the weight he attaches to it as something more than his arbitrary preference, he will need a philosophic argument.

Sunstein justifies his judicial minimalism with a claim about legitimacy—that judicial resolution of pressing moral conflicts robs the people of their right to deliberate about them. But if you believed that you had a right to choose your political affiliation or your religion or your spouse or your mode of sexual expression, you would not accept Sunstein's categorical assertion that the people have a right to deliberate about the scope of your right, for your right would be a personal right against the people. Your right would be a limitation on the agency that collects, formulates, and enforces the people's will, namely, the government. If Sunstein is to support his claim about the people's right to deliberate your (apparent?) personal right, he will need a complex argument about the nature of rights, and that, of course, would be a philosophic argument.

Though we contest Sunstein's suggestion that constitutional theorists and judges in constitutional cases can avoid philosophic choices by minimally deciding one case at a time, there is an element of Sunstein's position that we need not contest. He argues for judicial minimalism partly because he claims that courts will often get things wrong and that they lack any special qualities that would make them better suited than ordinary citizens or legislatures to resolve moral conflicts.[48] He embraces Gerald Rosenberg's "hollow hope" argument that courts usually cannot

---

[46] 505 U.S. 833 (1992).

[47] *See* Sotirios A. Barber, *The Constitution of Judicial Power* (Baltimore: Johns Hopkins University Press, 1993): 68–73.

[48] Sunstein, *Legal Reasoning, supra* note 10, at 177 (pointing out that judges confront only small-scale pieces of systemic controversies, that they are drawn from relatively narrow segments of society, and that they generally lack any philosophical training or other unique bases for moral evaluation).

effectively bring about social change and that, even if they seek to vindicate constitutional rights, political and social resistance will weaken those rights and render their efforts ineffectual.[49] Thus, judicial minimalism is appropriate given the relative institutional capacities of courts as compared with those of politically elected officials. This part of Sunstein's position concerns judicial conduct, and we can concede arguendo that it may be right—under some circumstances, will be right. Judicial activism, as Dworkin has shown (recall Chapter 2), does "presuppose[] a certain objectivity of moral principle";[50] but moral objectivity need not imply judicial activism in all circumstances.[51] Assume judges obligated to secure moral rights against the state as best they can, and it may well be that they can do better sometimes by moving cautiously, one small step at a time. This is a contingent question of strategy, a question of judicial prudence and statesmanship; it is not a question of what the Constitution means or how to seek that meaning.

There are two opposed traditions in constitutional theory concerning the relative institutional capacities of courts and legislatures. On one account, the independence of courts from politics disqualifies them from elaborating and protecting substantive constitutional freedoms against encroachment by elected officials. Sunstein defends a version of this view. On the other account, the independence of courts from politics uniquely qualifies them for discharging such a responsibility. Dworkin defends a version of this view.[52] We won't attempt to resolve the long-standing dispute between these traditions here, for we, individually, have taken positions on this question elsewhere,[53] and our present concern is approaches to constitutional meaning, not the strategies for progress toward constitutional states of affairs—as transcendently important as these questions of strategy may be. But it may be worth recalling Justice Robert H. Jackson's formulation in the second flag salute case (invalidating a requirement that school children salute the flag), responding to Justice Felix Frankfurter

---

49. *Id.* at 176. Here Sunstein endorses the argument made in Gerald N. Rosenberg, *The Hollow Hope: Can Courts Bring About Social Change?* (Chicago: University of Chicago Press, 1991).

50. Dworkin, *Taking Rights Seriously, supra* note 45, at 138.

51. *See, e.g.,* Robert P. George, "Natural Law, the Constitution, and the Theory and Practice of Judicial Review," *Fordham Law Review* 69 (2001): 2269.

52. *See, e.g.,* Dworkin, *Taking Rights Seriously, supra* note 45, at 131–49; Dworkin, "Forum," *supra* note 11, at 516–18.

53. *See* Barber, *supra* note 47, at 38–40, 54–57, 208–13; Fleming, *supra* note 10, at 61–74, 167.

in the first flag salute case (which had upheld such a requirement): Rather than deferring to the "vicissitudes" of the political processes, courts vindicate constitutional freedoms, "not by authority of [their] competence but by force of [their] commissions."[54] If the commission of courts is to preserve the Constitution, including substantive liberties, against encroachment by elected officials, courts would be abdicating their responsibility were they to side with Sunstein and against Dworkin on this dispute. In neither case, however, would responsible jurists avoid fusing constitutional law and moral philosophy.

---

[54] West Virginia State Board of Education v. Barnette, 319 U.S. 624, 638, 640 (1943) (Jackson, J., for the majority), *overruling* Minersville School District v. Gobitis, 310 U.S. 586 (1940) (Frankfurter, J., for the majority).

CHAPTER 10

THE PHILOSOPHIC APPROACH

I. The Philosophic Approach Revisited

Let's take stock. The failure of the plain words textualist and consensualist approaches indicated that the question in hard cases is not what the words mean to us, but how we ought to interpret them in trying to approximate their true meaning or the best interpretation of them, and that argued for a fusion of constitutional law and moral philosophy, the philosophic approach. But then (in Chapter 5) we acknowledged objections to the philosophic approach, namely, that it might prove undemocratic, un-American, dangerous, and/or fruitless. So we resumed the quest for an approach that might steer us away from controversies about what we ought to interpret the Constitution to mean. We've considered originalist/intentionalist, structuralist, doctrinal, and minimalist approaches, and we've seen that none of them can avoid the burdens and responsibilities of philosophic reflection and choice in hard cases. These considerations bring us back to the philosophic approach. Can we escape its burdens and responsibilities? Because we have yet to find a way to do so, it's time to ask whether the philosophic approach really is undemocratic, un-American, dangerous, or fruitless. As we consider those questions, let's be clear about what the philosophic approach, properly conceived, is and is not.

We have characterized the philosophic approach in rough and common sense terms: thinking for yourself about what constitutional provisions seem to refer to—like equal protection *itself* and due process *itself*, not anyone's specific *conceptions* of equal protection and due process. This thinking for yourself must be conducted with an attitude of self-criticism. The good-faith interpreter is trying to find out what the

Constitution means; she's not trying to use the Constitution as a cover for imposing her beliefs on other people. Because she's adopting a posture of fidelity to the law, she appreciates the inclinations of all subjects of law to disobey the law. She's trying to do the *right* thing by the Constitution, not necessarily *her* thing. She appreciates her fallibility. For these reasons, she sees constitutional interpretation as a self-critical quest for truth about or the best understanding of the Constitution which, given her limitations—and the limitations of the Constitution itself (a document made by humans, after all)—can only mean an interpretation of the Constitution that tries to redeem its expressed claim to be an instrument of justice, the general welfare, and the other goods listed in the Preamble. The reason for calling this a philosophic approach is that philosophy is the perfected form of thinking for yourself.

In practice, good-faith constitutional interpretation (after some two centuries of American constitutional interpretation) requires a willingness to change our minds about the major and the minor premises of past constitutional interpretations. We strive for (1) morally and/or scientifically sound understandings of constitutional provisions that appear in the major premises of legal syllogisms, and (2) true or sound accounts of the world that appear in minor premises. Consider, again, applications of the Equal Protection Clause of the Fourteenth Amendment in *Plessy v. Ferguson*[1] and *Brown v. Board of Education*[2] (discussed in Chapters 6 and 9). The change from *Plessy* to *Brown*, and other important changes in constitutional interpretation to be discussed, illustrate the philosophic approach at work.

Both *Plessy* and *Brown* agreed on the proposition of law that occurred in the major premise, which we paraphrase roughly as: *No state shall harm blacks in special ways. Plessy*'s minor premise can be phrased as: *Segregation doesn't harm blacks any more than it harms whites.* And *Brown*'s minor premise is: *Segregation is especially harmful to blacks.* So, the conclusions of the two cases differ, with *Plessy* saying that segregation is constitutionally permissible if transportation facilities are equal, and *Brown* saying that segregation is unconstitutional even if tangible educational facilities are equal.

Our question is, which minor premise represented a truer or sounder account of the world? This question, in essence, is a scientific question.

---

[1] 163 U.S. 537 (1896).
[2] 347 U.S. 483 (1954).

But it is made relevant by an assumed answer to a prior question that is at least partly a moral question: What is the Constitution's purpose? Is the Constitution supposed to enable us to pursue our aspirations in a real world that we can control (to a limited extent) only by understanding realities not entirely of our making? Or is the Constitution's purpose to enable us to legitimate our preferences (no matter what they are) by "creating" a world that flatters our pretensions to be a praiseworthy people? This question in turn presupposes answers to questions like: Is there a real world beyond what we believe about "it"? Can we approximate the truth of that (those?) world(s)? How do we know we're getting closer to the truth or better understandings?

At some level in constitutional theory, all of these questions must be answered, if only tentatively and/or implicitly. The *Brown* Court's assumptions about the nature of the Constitution justified the justices' concern with what they saw as a question of fact: the social conditions necessary for equal educational opportunity. The Court therefore asked how segregation actually affected black children. The Court's answer might have been wrong when the case was decided, and it might be wrong today, just as anyone can be wrong about complex matters of fact. But the aim of the *Brown* Court was truthfully to describe a slice of reality and to attain a sound understanding of the world, in this case the real effects of state-mandated segregation on the life chances of black children. The *Plessy* Court, although it invoked a conception of "the nature of things,"[3] aimed at something other than a true description of reality. It sought to reaffirm the traditions and practices of a racist, unequal way of life for blacks and whites. The clearest indication of the *Plessy* Court's concern with something other than the truth was its statement that the Louisiana statute requiring segregated railroad cars was not intended to imply the inferiority of black people. The Court wrote: "We consider the underlying fallacy of the plaintiff's argument to consist in the assumption that the enforced separation of the two races stamps the colored race with a badge of inferiority. If this be so, it is not by reason of anything found in the act, but solely because the colored race chooses to put that construction upon it."[4] The historical record proves that this was false when the Court said it and that people generally knew that it was false. Here we need only recall

---

[3.] 163 U.S. at 544.
[4.] *Id.* at 551.

Justice John Marshall Harlan's argument in dissent that everyone knew the "real meaning" of enforced segregation: to affix a "badge of servitude" and a "brand of inferiority" upon blacks.[5] Those who welcomed the Court's statement might have done so because it gave constitutional legitimacy to their racial beliefs. They might have done so also because they wanted constitutional legitimacy for an unhappy social situation they considered beyond the power of popular government to remedy. As the *Plessy* Court put it: "Legislation is powerless to eradicate racial instincts or to abolish distinctions based upon physical differences, and the attempt to do so can only result in accentuating the difficulties of the present situation."[6] Either way, the majority justices in *Plessy* were falsifying reality; they were saying that *for constitutional purposes*, segregation doesn't imply racial inferiority, even though everyone knows that it does as a matter of social-scientific fact. (As noted in Chapter 9, there are affinities between our analysis and that of the joint opinion in *Planned Parenthood v. Casey* (1992), which analyzed *Brown*'s overruling of *Plessy* in terms of a change in understanding of the facts.)[7]

Turning now from the minor premise of the legal syllogism (a factual premise) to the major premise (a proposition of law), the history of the Equal Protection Clause provides numerous examples of changed interpretations. The Fourteenth Amendment says that *no state* shall deny equal protection, and several nineteenth-century cases said that the Clause applied only to the state governments, not the national government. The Court changed its mind about this in *Bolling v. Sharp* (1954),[8] a companion case to *Brown*. The *Bolling* Court found that the idea of equal protection was embodied in the Due Process Clause of the Fifth Amendment, which is applicable to the national government. The guarantees of equal protection and due process both expressed what Chief Justice Warren called "an American ideal of fairness." Precisely because of this ideal, said Warren, "it would be unthinkable that the same Constitution would impose

---

5. *Id.* at 560 (Harlan, J., dissenting).
6. *Id.* at 551.
7. 505 U.S. 833, 862–64 (1992). For an insightful analysis of dramatic Supreme Court reversals like that in *Brown* that emphasizes changed factual conditions and the process of social construction, see Ronald Kahn, "Social Constructions, Supreme Court Reversals, and American Political Development: *Lochner, Plessy, Bowers,* But Not *Roe*," in *The Supreme Court and American Political Development,* ed. Ronald Kahn and Ken I. Kersch (Lawrence: University Press of Kansas, 2006): 67.
8. 347 U.S. 497 (1954).

[a duty on the states to end segregation and] a lesser duty on the Federal Government."[9] What probably made this "unthinkable" to the Court was that there seemed no way to justify letting the national government violate "an American ideal of fairness." If segregation by the states offended this ideal, how could segregation by the national government offend it any less?

In *Pace v. Alabama* (1883), the Court accepted an "equal application" theory of the Equal Protection Clause.[10] According to that theory, a statute punishing fornication between persons of different races more than fornication between persons of the same race did not deny equal protection because the same penalty applied to each member of the interracial couple. The state of Virginia relied on *Pace* in defense of its law against interracial marriages. In *Loving v. Virginia* (1967), the Court overruled *Pace* and struck down that law.[11] In rejecting the "equal application" theory of *Pace*, the *Loving* Court started with a statement of the Fourteenth Amendment's "clear and central purpose": to "eliminate all official state sources of invidious racial discrimination."[12] To achieve this end, the Court would treat all statutes containing racial classifications as constitutionally "suspect" and demanding the "most rigid scrutiny" to determine if they served some "permissible state objective, independent of racial discrimination."[13] The Court found that Virginia's purpose of preserving "racial integrity" or "White Supremacy" failed this test.[14] A fundamental right to marry a person of one's choice protected by the Due Process Clause provided the Court with a second reason for invalidating the Virginia law.[15] The state may not exercise its traditional power to regulate marriage in a way that abridged this fundamental freedom of interracial couples.

In *The Slaughterhouse Cases* (1872), the Court stated that the Equal Protection Clause protected newly freed African-Americans. Indeed, the Court wrote: "We doubt very much whether any action of a State not directed by way of discrimination against the negroes as a class, or on account of their race, will ever be held to come within the purview of

---

9. *Id.* at 500.
10. 106 U.S. 583 (1883).
11. 388 U.S. 1 (1967).
12. *Id.* at 10.
13. *Id.* at 11.
14. *Id.* at 7, 11.
15. *Id.* at 12.

this provision."[16] This would have excluded protection under that clause for women, religious groups, homosexuals, the unborn, and others. But *Slaughterhouse*'s restrictive view of the Equal Protection Clause was untenable from the beginning for precisely the reason that motivated adoption of the Clause: the sense that blacks share a common humanity with whites. If this justifies the Equal Protection Clause, then all who share that common humanity (all classes of innocent persons) have claims under it.[17] The Court eventually responded to that principle, and today it finds protections in that clause for women, religious groups, homosexuals, and other (though not yet all) classes of innocent persons. All of the foregoing changes of mind, concerning understandings of both fact and law, illustrate the philosophic approach.

II. The Philosophic Approach and the Teachings of Famous Philosophers

In their willingness to reconsider the major and minor premises of past constitutional interpretations, practitioners of the philosophic approach are expected to think self-critically for themselves. They have to think self-critically about the best interpretation of our constitutional text, history, and structure. They have to reflect critically upon our aspirations in striving for the interpretation that makes the Constitution the best it can be. In doing this, they may well find themselves influenced by the great thinkers of the past or the present. After all, judges and others actively interested in the problems of constitutional meaning are usually educated people, with some exposure to the great thinkers—writers known to be such precisely because of the persuasive quality of their thought. But the goal of the philosophic approach is *truth* or best understanding as distinguished from *opinion*—anyone's opinion, including the opinions of great philosophers. The truly philosophic judge, therefore, would not

---

[16.] 83 U.S. 36, 81 (1872).

[17.] *See* Baker v. State, 170 Vt. 194, 228 (Vt. 1999) (justifying extending common benefits of legal protections afforded to intimate human relationships to gay and lesbian couples on the basis of their "common humanity"); Goodridge v. Department of Public Health, 440 Mass. 309, 323 (Mass. 2003) (likewise invoking a conception of "common humanity" in striking down a law that did not extend the rights, responsibilities, and benefits of civil marriage to gay and lesbian couples).

apply the teachings of any of the great thinkers in a doctrinaire fashion. She would never find herself saying something like "Locke says government is established to protect property, not the natural environment, therefore environmental regulations are constitutionally suspect." Or "Aristotle says the fetus has no soul before quickening, therefore a woman has the right to an abortion in the first trimester of a pregnancy."

Think about these two examples and you'll see that they represent a kind of *concrete intentionalism*.[18] They put particular philosophers in the place of the Constitution's framers, and they try to reach conclusions in hard cases from the definitions or applications of those philosophers. Thus conceived, the philosophic approach would be no more defensible than the forms of concrete intentionalism criticized in Chapter 6. Reasoning from a philosopher's past applications of general ideas would lock us (no pun) into a particular view of reality that would in turn force us into falsifying reality, just as the *Brown* Court would have done had it reaffirmed *Plessy*. The same holds for a philosopher's definitions. They would be just like anyone else's definitions: mere versions of the things defined and, as such, correctable in light of better theories of those things. And adopting the mindset of a particular philosopher would reject the philosophic aspect of that very mindset, since philosophers typically claim an interest in truth, not any particular slant on truth, including their own. Philosophers as philosophers think for themselves, and a judge who adopted the mindset of a philosopher would adopt that aspect of the mindset which makes the philosopher a philosopher: a willingness to think for oneself in self-critical quest for the truth or the best account.

III. Would the Philosophic Approach Require Replacing Judges with Philosophers?

The answer to this question is a clear no, and for several reasons. To begin with, judges have a job to do, a job they're paid to do. They work for and are responsible to people other than themselves. They do not

---

18. It should not come as a surprise, therefore, that intentionalists like Robert Bork and Gary McDowell tend to conceive the philosophic approach this way. *See* Robert H. Bork, *The Tempting of America* (New York: Free Press, 1990): 211; Gary McDowell, *The Constitution and Contemporary Constitutional Theory* (Cumberland, VA: Center for Judicial Studies, 1985): 23, 29.

live lives that are as free as that which Plato describes in the *Apology of Socrates*, the classical account of the philosophic life in its purest form.[19] The job of judges, moreover, involves fidelity to the law, and the law can proceed from beliefs about moral and scientific reality that are far from true, maybe even far from a reasonable approximation of the truth. Take the Fugitive Slave Clause of Article IV, § 2 of the Constitution. It basically required that escaped or fugitive slaves be returned to their owners. If this clause proceeded from a false conception of justice, a philosopher as such could not deny that it did; a judge held to an oath of fidelity to the law (including this unjust clause) might have to deny that it did or in any event enforce it nonetheless. Probably the best that our philosophic judge could do would be to give the Fugitive Slave Clause that interpretation which came as close to her best conception of justice as the Clause might admit, like requiring full due process and a presumption of freedom in any proceeding for returning alleged fugitive slaves to their masters.[20] But because even the best interpretation of the Clause would be forced to honor the false conception of justice embodied in it, the philosophic judge would still be participating in injustice. An obligation of fidelity to the law is essential to judging, not to philosophy. In fact, where conditions permit, philosophic inquiry will go as far beyond law and other forms of social convention as the imagination, skills, insight, and courage of individual philosophers will reach, as Socrates proved in *The Republic of Plato* when he proposed the destruction of the family and the outrageous community of wives and children.[21]

But if philosophers can't be judges, that doesn't mean that judges can't adopt philosophic methods and attitudes. Following the law does not preclude thinking self-critically about the best that the law could mean within the limits of the law's language and what the community will accept. (Even a philosophic judge could have approved of the Court's prudential delay of more than ten years after *Brown* before overruling *Pace* in *Loving*.)[22] Judges certainly cannot follow the law of the American

---

19. Plato, *Apology of Socrates*, 21c–23c, 30d–31e.
20. *See* Robert M. Cover, *Justice Accused: Antislavery and the Judicial Process* (New Haven, CT: Yale University Press, 1975): 201–25.
21. Plato, *The Republic*, 457d–466d.
22. Shortly after *Brown*, the Supreme Court itself delayed invalidating Virginia's law prohibiting interracial marriage. *See* Naim v. Naim, 197 Va. 734, 90 S.E.2d (Va. 1955), *appeal dismissed*, 350 U.S. 985 (1956).

Constitution without thinking for themselves. This is precisely what Dworkin has argued and our analysis in this book has confirmed. Plain words force judges to think for themselves because the words refer to concepts like due process itself and equal protection itself, not to anyone's specific conception of due process and equal protection. We've seen that consensus can't help us in hard cases because, in such cases, there is no consensus. We've seen that all admissible conceptions of originalism (abstract originalism, mindset originalism, and broad originalism) force judges to think for themselves in hard cases. And we've seen that neither constitutional structures nor old judicial doctrines can free judges from a responsibility to think for themselves. Judges can think for themselves covertly, as Justice Black did in dissent in *Griswold v. Connecticut* (1965) when he construed the Ninth Amendment into insignificance for the sake of his (controversial) notion of democracy.[23] Or they can think for themselves openly, as Black did when he joined a unanimous court in *Brown*. But they can't avoid thinking for themselves. Thus, they can't responsibly avoid the philosophic approach.

We emphasize again that the philosophic approach does not involve judges or other interpreters doing moral and political philosophy without regard to the commitments of our constitutional order. But it does involve judges making philosophic choices in elaborating the meanings of our constitutional commitments. In doing so, judges strive for the true meaning or best account of those commitments. Some jurists and scholars have objected that judges simply are not capable of discharging this responsibility: that, under the philosophic approach, judges must be Platonic philosopher-judges living on Olympus.[24] In fact, all the philosophic approach requires is that judges take responsibility for the kinds of philosophic choices that they have been making all along down here in the U.S.A.

---

[23] 381 U.S. 479, 507–26 (1965) (Black, J., dissenting) (discussed in Chapter 5).

[24] *See* Learned Hand, *The Bill of Rights* (New York: Atheneum, 1974): 73 ("For myself it would be most irksome to be ruled by a bevy of Platonic Guardians, even if I knew how to choose them, which I assuredly do not."); Cass R. Sunstein, "Second-Order Perfectionism," *Fordham Law Review* 75 (2007): forthcoming, available at SSRN: http://ssrn.com/abstract=948788, at 3 (claiming that judges are not capable of making the kinds of judgments called for by "first-order perfectionism" or the philosophic approach and imagining a society "proudly called Olympus" where such an approach would be "entirely appropriate").

IV. The Charges Against the Philosophic Approach

As you assess the charges raised in Chapter 5—that the philosophic approach is undemocratic, un-American, and dangerous (we'll leave the charge of fruitlessness for the discussion of pragmatism in Chapter 11)—consider the following questions. Constitutional law has involved controversial philosophic choices throughout American history. Is it undemocratic and un-American for judges to be open and responsible about what they're doing in making such choices? Is it undemocratic and un-American to believe that when the Constitution refers to things like "liberty" and "justice" it refers to real things and that the American people can be genuinely concerned with pursuing and honoring these things?

Only some meaning-as-application approaches—doctrinalism and one form of concrete intentionalism—could even pretend to minimize judges' thinking for themselves. And constitutional applications combine propositions of law and fact. Are ends like justice and domestic tranquility best served by approaches that would force interpreters either to falsify reality or to say that there are two classes of truth—one truth for constitutional purposes, the other truth for scientific purposes—that may conflict with one another? Would it be more democratic or less democratic, more American or less American, more dangerous or less dangerous to disable constitutional government from dealing with the realities of life outside constitutional discourse? Would it be more or less undemocratic, un-American, and dangerous to pretend that the world as described for constitutional purposes can replace the real world? Would it be more or less undemocratic, un-American, and dangerous to deny that there is a "real world" beyond our opinions of "it"? Would it be more or less undemocratic, un-American, and dangerous to deny that there are ways to bring these opinions closer to the truth or to better understandings, even if we can never fully close the gap?

We, your authors, have our answers to these questions. But we ask the questions for more than rhetorical purposes. We want our readers to confront these questions honestly. Readers who do so will see the great conundrum facing all who attack the philosophic approach from a concern for the values of democracy, Americanism, and safety. These attacks on the philosophic approach quickly undermine the very values that motivate them. This in itself is not enough to establish the soundness of the philosophic approach. It does show, however, that values like democracy,

Americanism, and safety cannot serve as grounds for coherent attacks on the philosophic approach.[25]

V. The Philosophic Approach and Other Approaches

The philosophic approach is a kind of textualism, albeit not Justice Black's plain words textualism (criticized in Chapter 5). For the philosophic approach describes the text as what it facially appears to be: an ends-dedicated scheme of institutional rules, enabling rules, powers, and rights, phrased more often than not as referring to general goods and principles. On its face, the Constitution is not a detailed code of conduct or an enumeration of definitions or concrete illustrations and examples. Justice Black saw textualism as an antidote to philosophic reflection and choice; to the contrary, Dworkin has shown how fidelity to this particular text as written necessitates a fusion of constitutional law and moral philosophy. And we have confirmed that position.

But our argument for the philosophic approach doesn't exclude considerations associated with other approaches, as we acknowledged in Chapter 4 in calling for a fusion of philosophic and other approaches.

[25.] Another objection to the philosophical approach focuses on the fact of disagreement about moral concepts. We acknowledge that judges and other interpreters will disagree in their first-order judgments about moral concepts, such as what conceptions are best (just as they will disagree about legal concepts generally). Our focus is on second-order questions of interpretive method. We defend (as true) a second-order claim about constitutional interpretation, that it cannot avoid philosophic methods and choices. The test of any second-order claim can hardly be agreement on any first-order claim. Constitutional jurists and theorists have mistakenly assumed that the correct interpretive method should eliminate reasonable differences on the first-order questions of constitutional law, such as whether a fetus is a person (Roe v. Wade, 410 U.S. 113 (1973)), and whether homosexuals like heterosexuals have a right to intimate association (Lawrence v. Texas, 539 U.S. 558 (2003)). They also err in assuming that agreement on questions in constitutional law is always a good thing. Our position is that the truth about or best understanding of general concepts can be approximated only through elaborating conflicting conceptions in a spirit of self-critical striving and public-regarding reasonableness. A second-order theory can influence first-order disagreement by indicating the kinds of questions to be asked, the evidentiary protocol to be followed, and the spirit of the debate to be conducted. But originalists will continue to debate whether Madison meant this or that, and proponents of the philosophic approach will continue to debate whether a fetus is a person and what is the best understanding of "liberty" in the Due Process Clauses. We therefore deny that a successful theory of interpretation (a second-order theory) will or should end debate on first-order questions like those addressed in Roe and Lawrence.

The philosophic approach embraces structuralism, for example, both because structuralism is a kind of textualism (looking to structures suggested by the text) and because philosophic judges understand that questions of moral and political philosophy must be answered in elaborating constitutional structures. This is clear when elaborating the basic structure of federalism, the character of separation of powers, and the form of democratic self-government embodied in the Constitution.[26] This is especially clear when deciding on the basic normative qualities of the Constitution taken as a whole: whether it is to be conceived as a charter of positive benefits the government is obligated to pursue, like national security and the general welfare, or as a charter of negative liberties against the government.[27]

The philosophic approach is also fully compatible with, if not equivalent to, abstract originalism and mindset originalism, properly understood. We have seen that it can encompass broad originalism, at least as some have described that position. The philosophic approach is clearly opposed to the remaining concrete forms of originalism as well as to conventional understandings of consensualism and doctrinalism. As these positions are usually understood, they share a feature that is antithetical to the philosophic approach: they posit some sort of authority as the source of moral truth. The concrete originalist sees the truth about justice and fairness, for example, to lie in the authority of some original definer or applier of these terms. The consensualist finds truth about these terms in public opinion, and the doctrinalist finds it in the definitions and applications of old courts. These positions see authority as the source of truth; the philosophic approach takes truth or best account and its responsible quest as the source of authority. That said, consensus and doctrine may well be understood to embody truths or best accounts without being viewed as their source. If so, they can be consulted in a manner that is compatible with the philosophic approach.

VI. Implications for Ordinary Citizens

The philosophic judge is a judge with a certain attitude: a public-spirited and self-critical concern for doing her duty under the Constitution as written. The good citizen of the Constitution will support judges of this kind and the institutions that produce them.

---

26. *See* Chapter 8.
27. *See* Chapter 3.

As for what the people expect from judges, some evidence may lie in the facts of public behavior. The public permits judges to think for themselves without depriving them of their right to be judges—even when their critics say they have ignored the law or made it meaningless. (Calls to strip courts of jurisdiction to hear claims asserting certain rights or calls to impeach judges who interpret the Constitution to protect certain rights almost always fail and are met with reaffirmations of judicial independence.) You could easily agree with Justice Miller's critics that he ignored the Privileges or Immunities Clause or rendered it meaningless in *Slaughterhouse*.[28] You could say that Justice Black defied the Ninth Amendment and tried to make it meaningless in *Griswold*.[29] And by their own lights Miller and Black would have flouted other constitutional principles, like federalism and democracy, had they done what their critics wanted. So no matter how Miller would have gone in *Slaughterhouse* and Black in *Griswold*, they would have thought for themselves to what their critics would have called fundamentally objectionable conclusions, and they would have expressed what they regarded as fidelity to the law.

We don't deny that Miller and Black were unfaithful, respectively, to the Privileges or Immunities Clause and the Ninth Amendment. We're saying that their views of the larger principles of the Constitution—and their fidelity to those principles—may have forced them to see these particular constitutional provisions as mistakes.[30] Of course, American judges openly pronounce statutes unconstitutional and precedents mistakes, even when they enjoy popular support, as statutes segregating public schools along with precedents like *Plessy* did among southern whites at the time of *Brown*. So the public has accepted judges who think for themselves to the detriment of convention—including convention that takes the form of established constitutional provisions and long-standing statutes

---

[28]. *See, e.g.*, the dissenting opinions in *Slaughterhouse* itself; Walter F. Murphy, "*Slaughter-House*, Civil Rights, and Limits on Constitutional Change," *American Journal of Jurisprudence* 32 (1987): 1, 2.

[29]. *See* John Hart Ely, *Democracy and Distrust* (Cambridge, MA: Harvard University Press, 1980): 34–41; Randy E. Barnett, "Introduction: James Madison's Ninth Amendment," in *The Rights Retained by the People: The History and Meaning of the Ninth Amendment*, ed. Randy E. Barnett (Fairfax, VA: George Mason University Press, 1989): 1.

[30]. *See* Murphy, *supra* note 28, at 6, 9. For the general idea of "mistakes" in constitutional inter-pretation, *see* Ronald Dworkin, *Taking Rights Seriously* (Cambridge, MA: Harvard University Press, 1977): 118–23.

and precedents. The public has thus accepted judicial conduct that has some parallels to philosophic conduct.

Judges can think for themselves covertly—as when Black pretended in *Griswold* that his position flowed from plain words rather than a controversial conception of democracy. Or judges can think for themselves openly—as when the *Brown* Court set forth its arguments and evidence that compulsory segregation hurts black children. Which way is better from the perspective of fidelity to the law?

When Black pretended to be following plain words in *Griswold*, he in effect pretended that his conceptions of due process, "unenumerated" rights, and democracy were the law rather than what they actually were: controversial and possibly wrong versions of the law. Had Black been more interested in *the law* than in his theories of the law, he would have been sensitive to the difference, and he would have found a way to present his conceptions as just that: things submitted to the kind of public-spirited debate that brings us closer to the truth or to better understandings of constitutional principles. Black did better by the law when he joined his brethren in *Brown*.

As we have seen, the *Brown* decision turned on a simple proposition: segregation hurts blacks (by reducing them to or maintaining them in the status of an inferior caste). When the Court supported that proposition by citing common sense experience and scientific evidence, it implicitly offered its pivotal proposition as a factual proposition. Scientific evidence and common sense experience agree that the truth about segregation depends not on what the speaker believes about its truth, but on the state of the world the speaker purports to describe. If a speaker's beliefs about the world are faulty, or if the world changes, his description is or will be false. The *Brown* Court displayed this understanding of truth when it measured the factual premise of *Plessy* against the world of the 1950s and found it defective.

We can summarize the argument in *Brown* as follows: The best available evidence shows that *Plessy* is wrong about the impact of segregation on minority children in the modern world; segregation harms those children. This argument implicitly affirms not only its result but also the method through which one establishes its result, the method of continually testing old propositions against fresh evidence. That very method could one day reverse the factual proposition of *Brown*, for the world could change again. In recent years, a group of educators (including black educators) has claimed that special teaching methods in racially and sexually segregated inner-city schools can improve the education of black males without harming whites or black females. The issues surrounding this claim are difficult and complex, but should the best arguments and evidence support the claim, *Brown* can stand for a method that should entail an adjustment in its holding (or at least the evident implications of its holding). The methodological message of *Brown* is that the Court's doctrines are but theories of the law, not the law itself, and that the law itself prohibits those practices that actually harm minority groups in special ways. The justices who joined in *Brown* were not philosophers, but they displayed the attitude of philosophers by using a method that implicitly distinguishes doctrine from truth and subordinates doctrine to truth. *Brown* illustrates what fusing constitutional law and moral philosophy should mean in practice.

When Dworkin called for a fusion of constitutional law and moral philosophy, he called not for compromising the Constitution, but for honoring its commitments as faithfully as possible. Since the Constitution delivers its messages in written words and sentences that refer, among other things, to authors ("We the People"), addressees ("ourselves and our Posterity"), purposes ("Justice," "Domestic Tranquility"), and institutions ("The Executive Power shall be vested in a President"), a philosophic approach is essential to being faithful to the Constitution itself. The philosophic approach incorporates a proper concern for plain words, intentions, and structures. To see this, we need only review what we've already covered: The Equal Protection Clause plainly refers to equal protection—that is, to equal protection itself. And though the demands of equal protection may not be evident to us, we can hope to improve our understanding through a self-critical and responsible quest for the best available arguments and evidence concerning its meaning and application. The same holds for our conceptions of constitutional structures, which the Preamble describes as instruments of abstract ends, like "Justice," intended by "We the People." The practical meaning of these ends and structural means is very far from clear to us, but here again, we can hope to improve our conceptions through an open and self-critical quest for the best evidence and arguments on these matters. And whoever the framers and ratifiers were, it's hard for an originalist to conclude that they intended or meant something less than that to which the ratified document refers: justice, equal protection, and other things whose practical meaning we can pursue only through philosophic methods, attitudes, and choices. For if we say the framers and ratifiers consciously intended something less—like their concrete conceptions of justice, whether really just or not—we are attributing a fraud to them, and that's not something the typical originalist wants to do.

CHAPTER 11

PRAGMATISM

If we've guessed correctly about your tentative answers to the questions in Chapter 10 concerning whether the philosophic approach is undemocratic, un-American, or dangerous, that leaves one last charge against the proposal for fusing constitutional law and moral philosophy: the fusion would be *fruitless* because moral philosophy is a fruitless activity. This is the central charge of some leading contemporary legal pragmatists. We've saved pragmatism for last because it is not so much an approach to constitutional interpretation that seeks to avoid the philosophic approach as it is a challenge to the entire enterprise of constitutional interpretation.

Writers who use the term "pragmatism" in discussions of constitutional matters agree that it is an "umbrella term" that covers different views about law.[1] Our interests here do not involve all that pragmatism can mean and has meant or what the proper use of the term might be. We are not rejecting every idea associated with "pragmatism." One of these ideas, perhaps the leading one, is *legal instrumentalism*—that law generally is instituted to serve social purposes and that it should be interpreted in that way.[2] One understanding of this general idea is that the Constitution is what it says it is: an instrument of ends like justice, the general welfare, and national security, and that it should be interpreted to facilitate these ends. There's hardly anything new or revolutionary about this instrumentalist outlook, as Richard Posner, among others, recognizes,[3] and as our discussions of *The Federalist* and Chief Justice John Marshall's

---

[1.] Steven D. Smith, "The Pursuit of Pragmatism," *Yale Law Journal* 100 (1990): 409, 409–11; Richard A. Posner, "What Has Pragmatism to Offer Law?," *Southern California Law Review* 63 (1990): 1653, 1653–54.

[2.] Posner, *supra* note 1, at 1656–57.

[3.] *Id.* at 1657.

opinion in *McCulloch v. Maryland* (1819) have shown.[4] Far short of a general discussion of pragmatism and the varieties of legal instrumentalism, therefore, our interest here is focused on the challenge that some self-styled pragmatists pose to the philosophic approach to the meaning of the Constitution as a whole and to such constitutional expressions as due process, equal protection, liberty, property, the common defense, and the general welfare. The pragmatist tenet with which we are concerned is that a public-spirited, self-critical and open-minded quest for true constitutional meaning or best interpretation is fruitless, because there is no true constitutional meaning or best interpretation to be sought.

Many writers offer variations on this skepticism about constitutional meaning, and relatively few of these writers call themselves pragmatists. William Rehnquist and Michael Perry aren't known as pragmatists, yet skepticism about values is explicit in Rehnquist's originalism and Perry's consensualism, as we have seen.[5] But no contemporary constitutional theorists have elaborated skepticism about values with the intellectual thoroughness and rhetorical flair of Posner and Stanley Fish. These writers are self-styled pragmatists, and they have set themselves firmly against Ronald Dworkin's moral reading of the Constitution and, therewith, what we call the philosophic approach. In this concluding chapter, we concentrate on their specific claim that the philosophic approach is fruitless.

I. The Assumptions Underlying Constitutional Interpretation

The philosophic approach, properly understood, holds that the Constitution itself exercises a constraint on what interpreters can say about it. To appreciate the Constitution's capacity to constrain interpreters, we need only recall points that should be familiar by now. If you accept an obligation of fidelity to the law, and if you also assume that, say, "liberty" (the word) refers to liberty itself (the thing), then you assume (1) a gap between your conception of liberty and liberty itself; (2) the possibility that your conception of liberty may be wrong; (3) an obligation under the law to liberty itself, not your conception of liberty; and (4) the possibility of progress toward the truth about liberty or better understandings of it.

---

4. Chapter 3; Chapter 8.
5. Chapter 2; Chapter 5. As noted in Chapter 5, note 7, Perry's subsequent work may be less skeptical about values than the work we examine there.

These four assumptions combine to mandate an attitude of self-criticism, and this attitude excludes a willful reading of one's personal preferences or values into the Constitution. The four assumptions combine to demand suspensions of judgment pending a full airing of contending arguments and evidence about what the law means and what the facts are. Deny any of these four assumptions and you deny what they jointly amount to: an obligation to seek a sound interpretation of the law, as opposed to using the law as a cover for willful impositions on other people. These four assumptions of the philosophic approach constitute an intrinsically legal constraint on interpreters because philosophic attitudes, methods, and assumptions are constituent parts of following the law in hard cases. The prospect of better theories about concepts like liberty and equal protection is not opposed to law and legal constraint, for without this prospect there would be no legal constraint on judges in hard cases. All that would restrain judges would be their own calculations of what they could get away with politically.

To deny the aspiration to truth or better understandings about matters like the meaning of equal protection and whether segregation hurts people is to deny the possibility of legal constraints in hard cases. Contemporary legal pragmatism ridicules any suggestion of truth beyond convention regarding normative concepts like equal protection and liberty. (In its pure form, pragmatism even rejects the possibility of scientific truth beyond convention.)[6] That's why Posner once entitled a speech summarizing his position as "Pragmatism *versus* the Rule of Law."[7]

We have listed pragmatism among the approaches to constitutional meaning in hard cases. It would be more accurate to conceive it as a position in the field of constitutional theory, not as an approach to constitutional meaning. For pragmatism rejects the possibility that the Constitution means something beyond what some population believes or, more importantly for pragmatists, what some population can be brought to believe— and, according to Fish and Posner, brought to believe by whatever rhetorical devices work.[8] That's why we've saved pragmatism for last. The other

---

6. Stanley Fish, "Almost Pragmatism: Richard Posner's Jurisprudence," *University of Chicago Law Review* 57 (1990): 1447, 1448–49 [hereinafter Fish, "Almost Pragmatism"] (reviewing Richard A. Posner, *The Problems of Jurisprudence* (Cambridge, MA: Harvard University Press, 1990) [hereinafter Posner, *The Problems of Jurisprudence*]).

7. Richard A. Posner, "Pragmatism versus the Rule of Law," American Enterprise Institute, Bradley Lecture, January 7, 1991 (emphasis added).

8. *See* Fish, "Almost Pragmatism," *supra* note 6, at 1450–51.

approaches try to accommodate the common sense faith in the rule of law, namely: (1) that the Constitution can mean something; (2) that what the Constitution means is the aim of constitutional interpretation; and (3) that the Constitution provides a standard for determining whether concrete interpretations are right or wrong. The pragmatism we're discussing tries to make a clean break with this common sense faith.

Contemporary legal pragmatists deny some or all of the foregoing assumptions underlying constitutional interpretation. They deny that there is a moral reality beyond social convention. They assert that social convention is a creation of political power (physical force, ultimately).[9] And they deny that the law—or indeed reason and logic—can restrain interpretation. What restrains interpretation are the prudential calculations of interpreters regarding what they can get away with politically. Those are the only restraints. Thus, there are no legal or moral restraints on interpretation.[10] And there is no real reason not to get away with whatever willful imposition one can get away with. According to pragmatists, the "rule of law" is a myth, and talk about the proper approach to the meaning of laws (including the Constitution) proceeds from illusions about meaning and reality. That's why pragmatism is something other than an approach to constitutional interpretation.

II. Pragmatists' Claim to Expose the Myths of the Rule of Law

By exposing what they call the myths of the rule of law, pragmatists challenge our sense of ourselves as persons who can do the right thing at the expense, if need be, of what seems our immediate interest. If we were to abandon this self-image as meaningless or illusory, we could not see ourselves as members of the "We the People" who aspire to public purposes like justice and the general welfare. In that case, the most we could aspire to would be justice and well-being, for ourselves individually, as each of us conceives those ends. The Constitution's Preamble would be mere window dressing for arrangements that we accepted or to which we acquiesced from thoughtless habit, fear, or self-serving grounds, not public-spirited grounds. The public-spirited voice of the

---

9. *Id.* at 1452.
10. *Id.* at 1449–50.

Constitution and political life generally would be illusory—expressive of myths needed by people who are too weak emotionally to face the realities of the human condition.

This skeptical view of law is often associated with Jerome Frank, a legal theorist of the early twentieth century cited by Posner as a forerunner of contemporary pragmatism.[11] We sketch a different view of Frank here. But first we should ask the reader to reflect on the motive of those who claim that the Constitution's references to ideas like justice and the general welfare and our concern for true or better conceptions of such ideas manifest empty illusions born of our insecurities and weaknesses. Why would anyone want to express such a skeptical view of legal-moral life in a written work produced for the educated general reader? What good comes from publishing such a view?

You might think the answer to this last question is obvious: Exposing myths in the law and about law is implicitly claimed to be speaking the truth, and speaking the truth about most things is usually a self-justifying good. Your authors agree that speaking the truth is usually a good thing. We find it hard to deny, at least, that truth is the aim of scholarly enterprises generally, including the present one. Don't you, the reader, have a right to assume that we, your authors, to the best of our abilities, write what we believe approximates the truth or best understanding about matters at hand? If you had arguments and evidence that we're wrong about something, wouldn't you expect us to hear you out? Wouldn't you want your proffer of contrary arguments and evidence to be taken as expressing more than your personal distaste for our position? If you answer these questions in the affirmative, as we wager you will, you implicitly agree that truth or objectivity in some sense[12] is an aim of this engagement between readers and writers. But agreement about the value of pursuing and reporting truth is not a straightforward matter for the pragmatists we're discussing here. As Posner says at one point, "'[T]ruth' is going to be a problematic concept for the pragmatist."[13] Were Posner to admit that he publishes his position not because the best available evidence and arguments favor it, but because publishing it benefits him in some manner disconnected from the truth, he would leave us wondering why we should even consider his views, much less accept them.

---

[11] Posner, *supra* note 1, at 1654.
[12] *See* Ronald Dworkin, *Taking Rights Seriously* (Cambridge, MA: Harvard University Press, 1977): 138 (discussed in Chapter 2).
[13] Posner, *supra* note 1, at 1655.

Frank, like Fish and Posner, also spoke about the myths of law. But Frank's motive was expressly connected not only to the truth about judicial behavior, but also to the truth about goods like justice and the general welfare. Frank's message was published in the public-spirited voice of a legal reformer. He wrote about the myths of law in hopes of exposing the pretenses that bad judges used to avoid moral responsibility for unjust decisions.[14] At least part of his thought was fully consistent with what we're calling the philosophic approach, for Frank was interested in justice as an object or end of human aspiration—something more than unreflective personal or community preference. Frank thus urged judges to quit pretending that decisions were "mechanical deductions" from uncontroversial premises. He urged them instead to adopt the self-critical ways of scientists at their best by keeping an open mind in pursuit of truth about the meaning of legal provisions (like the Equal Protection Clause) and the facts to which they applied (like whether segregation hurts people), even if that meant "breaking up tradition." He thus assumed that there was a truth about justice and other values to pursue, and that he and others had an obligation to pursue that truth.[15]

Posner assumes the same reformist posture as Frank did, but Posner tries to deny that there is a truth about justice and other moral values.[16] Posner is skeptical about *moral reality* but not *non-moral reality*.[17] In fact, he accepts the scientific objectivity of economic theory as the theory of how best to satisfy human wants. He believes that by facing the facts of constitutional interpretation, judges can rid themselves of its myths, and proceed in an untroubled way to manipulate the law to facilitate what science (principally economics) discloses about the conditions for human happiness. Posner's pragmatism thus culminates in a pragmatist program: a general plan to make people happier. His motive can therefore fairly be described (though he might put it differently) as legal reform for the common good or at any rate for the general welfare.

---

14. Jerome Frank, *Law and the Modern Mind* (Garden City, NY: Anchor, 6th printing, 1963): 139–48, 172–82.
15. *Id.* at xx–xxi, 172–73.
16. *See, e.g.*, Posner, *supra* note 1, at 1655–56; Posner, *The Problems of Jurisprudence, supra* note 6, at 459–60; Richard A. Posner, *The Problematics of Moral and Legal Theory* (Cambridge, MA: Harvard University Press, 1999): 3–90 [hereinafter Posner, *The Problematics of Moral and Legal Theory*].
17. Posner expresses this idea spiritedly in his polemic, *The Problematics of Moral and Legal Theory, supra* note 16.

Fish rightly observes a conflict between Posner's reformist program and Posner's moral skepticism. Posner cannot act the reformer consistently with what he sees as essential to pragmatism: the denial of real truths about right and wrong to be pursued in a scientific spirit. Hope for legal "reform" presupposes truth or better understandings about right and wrong and the possibility of moving one's opinions closer to the truth or better understandings.[18] Deny the existence of truth or the possibility of improving our conceptions of the truth, and the reformer's talk about institutional pathology and reform expresses no more than his or her personal likes and dislikes. Yet Posner thinks he expresses more than his personal likes and dislikes; he urges judges and the larger legal community to adopt his views of law and legal practice, implicitly in the public interest.[19] He thus assumes possibilities regarding moral truth that he purports to deny, and in doing so, he justifies Fish's judgment that he is not a full-blooded pragmatist, but a mere "almost pragmatist."[20]

Fish is not altogether critical of Posner's position, however. Fish calls Posner an "almost pragmatist," rather than a flat-out anti-pragmatist, because Fish accepts one part of Posner's position even as he rejects the other part. Fish rejects the *practical* or *programmatic* part of Posner's position—the part that urges the legal community to conform its actual conduct to what Posner says about the nature and functions of law. Fish rightly holds that a pragmatist can't have a practical program without sacrificing his position on moral truth.[21] All such programs assume that (1) there's a truth about what's good and/or right for the community as a whole; (2) the practices of the community as a whole presently fall short of that truth; (3) the community ought to do better; and (because "ought" implies "can") (4) the community can do better. These propositions taken together assume what Dworkin calls "a certain objectivity of moral principle"[22]—that is, truths that refer either to an objective moral reality or to beliefs that seem objective because they are uncontested in a given community at a level deeper than the community's contested beliefs.[23]

---

18. Fish, "Almost Pragmatism," *supra* note 6, at 1457–59.
19. Posner, *The Problems of Jurisprudence*, *supra* note 6, at 122–23.
20. Fish, "Almost Pragmatism," *supra* note 6.
21. *Id.* at 1456–61.
22. Dworkin, *supra* note 12, at 138.
23. As stated in Chapter 1, we have written this book to be agnostic between moral realism and constructivism (or deep conventionalism).

An example of such a deeper belief would be "slavery is wrong." That slavery is wrong would almost surely be held by both sides of any debate (among us) over how to define or apply the word "slavery"—whether, for example, carrying an unwanted pregnancy to term under compulsion of law is a form of slavery.[24]

These considerations entitle us to conclude that no one who proposes legal reform can successfully maintain that the philosophic approach to constitutional interpretation is fruitless. A *practical* pragmatist (i.e., one who has something relevant to say about how the community ought to conduct its affairs) therefore cannot consistently oppose the philosophic approach. This leaves opposition to the philosophic approach to a rather oxymoronic figure: the *impractical* pragmatist—the pragmatist who claims that his understanding of law and morality can have no practical effect on legal/moral life. Constitutional theorists associate the claim that "pragmatism changes nothing" chiefly with Fish. As he understands it, pragmatism is purely theoretical or explanatory, not at all practical or prescriptive: "there is absolutely nothing you can do with it."[25] He claims that pragmatists can do no more than *explain* law and legal practice.[26]

Fish's position might tempt us abruptly to end the present debate and declare victory for the philosophic approach. We might say that the incoherence of practical pragmatism (Posner's pragmatism) and the admitted practical impotence of purely theoretical pragmatism (Fish's pragmatism) ends the argument about how to conduct the political practice called "constitutional interpretation." We might say that since the philosophic approach held the field of debate when pragmatism entered with the final challenge to it, the philosophic approach wins because pure pragmatism—the only coherent form of pragmatism—admits that pragmatism had no business entering the debate in the first place. The debate, after all, is a debate over how to approach constitutional meaning, and how to approach constitutional meaning is a question of how to understand and conduct a practice of the community—how we ought to do something. Pure pragmatism says pragmatists can't answer such questions.[27]

---

24. *See, e.g.*, Andrew Koppelman, "Forced Labor: A Thirteenth Amendment Defense of Abortion," *Northwestern University Law Review* 84 (1990): 480.

25. Fish, "Almost Pragmatism," *supra* note 6, at 1464.

26. *Id*. at 1464–66.

27. *Id*. at 1462–63, 1464–66.

III. Pragmatism's Claims to "Change Nothing" and to "Explain" Law

Your authors can't end the debate this way, however. For, alas, Fish errs when he claims that purely theoretical pragmatism leaves legal practice unchanged—that it leaves the myths of legal/moral life intact to serve social functions like shielding people from the unsettling truths of the human condition.[28] We'll also see reason to doubt that pragmatism can succeed even in its theoretical goal of explaining legal/moral practice.

Let's see how pragmatism changes things in spite of its claims. Pure pragmatism of the kind defended by Fish holds that words like "justice," "liberty," and "equality" refer to nothing beyond our (or our community's) arbitrary preferences, and that constitutional interpreters manipulate such terms to achieve results that they just happen to prefer.[29] If this is true, fidelity to the Constitution is somewhere between an outright fraud and an empty illusion. Yet neither the fraud nor the illusion could succeed unless some people believed for various reasons (an oath of office, say, or the benefits of constitutional government) that they ought to be faithful to the Constitution. Those who believe this must believe at the same time that they can be faithful to the Constitution, for people generally deny that they ought to do what they also believe they cannot do. People who took pragmatism to heart, and came to believe that fidelity to the Constitution really is a hopeless aspiration, could no longer believe that they could be faithful to the Constitution. Believing this, they could acknowledge no duty of fidelity to the Constitution.

At present, however, many in the legal community and the public at large do seem to acknowledge duties under the Constitution. And in doing so they assume beliefs that pragmatism consigns to myth. If they saw the myths as myths—if they believed, for example, that fidelity to the Constitution was altogether an empty aspiration—they would feel no obligation to try to be faithful to the Constitution. They might therefore pretend to listen with respect to "arguments" and "evidence" against the conclusions that they arbitrarily favored (about whether segregation hurts people, for example) but in the end they'd go with their gut (suitably rationalized for others), because they would believe that, ultimately, there's

---

[28.] *See id.* at 1462–63.
[29.] *See id.* at 1449–53.

nothing else they could go with. So pragmatism can't successfully claim that one can demythologize legal practice without changing it. Pragmatism could leave legal/moral practice untouched only if pragmatism were a teaching tightly held among an initiated few who occupied a figurative closet in some location outside the political community—a group of philosophers, perhaps, whose burning interest in cosmic questions left no motivation to broadcast their destructive views about the world of human affairs. (Here we remind the reader of two points in Chapter 10: (1) fusing constitutional law and moral philosophy does not mean delegating our affairs to philosophers and (2) it's very doubtful that genuine philosophers could be forced or induced to take the job of ruling us.)

Because pragmatism's account of law and morality, if widely accepted, could indeed affect legal/moral practice, writers who would save the possibility of fidelity to the Constitution have no choice but to confront pragmatism's claim to "explain" law. As we interpret this claim, we believe it is false. We interpret "explaining law" as giving reasons why people would choose to live under law and giving those reasons to someone—a community, a readership, or an audience of people. These people on the receiving end of the reasons would make up the general public, for as far as we know pragmatists like Fish and Posner publish their works for anyone who is interested in what they write about. We can assume, as do Fish and Posner when they set out to deflate widespread myths about law, that the general public is composed of ordinary men and women who entertain the illusions that pragmatism would expose. If pragmatism's explanation of law is to be successful with its targeted audience—the interested public—pragmatism must tell what that audience would regard as a likely story about why people accept what pragmatism calls the myths of law—why people believe, in the present context, that the Constitution guarantees "equal protection of the laws" and that despite our disagreements about the meaning of this term, it does refer to something other than our conception "of it" or anyone else's conception "of it." Those of us who accept an obligation under the Constitution have an obligation to pursue that meaning in a spirit of self-critical striving.[30]

The kind of explanation we have in mind differs from explanations in physics and those social sciences that take physics as a model. If ordinary men and women observe over and over again through a lengthy

---

30. Chapter 2.

period of time that white-hot heat applied to metal is followed by the metal melting, and if a steel beam is found twisted and bent in the ruins of a building destroyed by fire, they can say (absent evidence to the contrary) that the heat of the fire caused the beam to bend. This, on any given occasion of bent-beam-in-burned-building, may be an incorrect explanation of the bent beam, but it is a plausible one under normal circumstances because the story of what happened fits what people have repeatedly observed when heat is applied to metal.

We might try to "explain" human happenings in the same way simply by observing juxtapositions of events over lengthy periods of time. If we just happened to notice, for example, that moderate Republicans voted repeatedly and overwhelmingly for Democrats who are running against conservative Republicans within two weeks of a blue moon (the second full moon in a month), but that moderate Republicans voted for conservative Republicans at other times, we might say that the blue moon causes moderate Republicans to vote Democratic. We shouldn't expect this putative explanation to leave people talking about Blue Moon Democrats, however; for the explanation would be no explanation at all of human action as ordinarily understood. At best it would provide an utterly coincidental correlation of events or mere happenings in the world. But mere events (changes in the world from one state of affairs to another) are simpler than that species of event called *human actions*. The latter do involve changes in the world, but they also involve intentions to effect those changes, and these intentions are regularly understood in terms of some goods.

Aristotle says in the first sentence of the *Nicomachean Ethics* that "every art and every inquiry, and similarly every action and pursuit, is thought to aim at some good."[31] Consider Aristotle's proposition carefully: It doesn't explicitly say (though it doesn't deny) that every action, art, inquiry, and pursuit *in reality does aim at some good*; it says rather that every action, etc., *is thought to aim at some good*. Understood in this narrow, ecumenical way, Aristotle's proposition is difficult to deny. Test this for yourself by trying to deny it. Try thinking about someone consciously doing something (anything at all) without assuming that she does it for the sake of something she thinks is good. Try doing this and we predict that you'll come up with examples of unconscious and/or involuntary movement of some sort. Someone under hypnosis might be said to open a

---

31. Aristotle, *The Nicomachean Ethics*, in *The Basic Works of Aristotle*, ed. Richard McKeon (New York: Random House, 1941): 935, 935.

window, for example, when so directed by a hypnotist. Or someone under threat of death might be directed to do something, like shoot a friend, that she would never ordinarily do. But in such cases we could as easily say that the real actor was the person pulling the strings, and that the person whose hand was on the sash or whose finger was on the trigger was a mere instrument of someone else's intentions. We can say, in any case, that to speak unequivocally of someone's doing *x*, we have to see her as effecting a change in the world for two reasons: (1) because she intends it, and (2) because she thinks it a change for the better. Opening a window can be a change for the better when it's hot inside and cooler outside; accepting slavery can be thought to improve your prospects when the alternative is death at the hands of an invading military force. These and all other acts can be interpreted as actors trying to change things or the likely course of events for the better.

In everyday discourse we call the "good for the sake of which" someone does something a *reason* for what she does, and we regularly treat such a reason as a *cause* of the action—a thing that moves her to act or that motivates the act. If we who are describing an action hope to give a plausible account of it, we have to relate the actor's physical movements to a result that our audience can appreciate as something the actor regards as a good. Opening the window would make sense (to us and to the actor, as we see her) under some conditions of internal and external temperature. Even something we would not normally do, like accepting slavery, would make sense if the alternative were worse or if we could see how someone might think it worse. This doesn't mean every member of the audience would do the same thing under the circumstances. (The Patrick Henrys among us would sooner die than submit to slavery.) It means only that our audience can see how someone could think that the result of the action is good. If the actor's reason is completely beyond the range of anything we can recognize as a good connected to the changes to be explained, the action is beyond our capacity to explain. That's why the mere occurrence of a blue moon typically fails to explain an act of voting. We know of no connection between blue moons and the goods or apparent goods that provide familiar reasons for voting. Though the possibility of a connection remains—the blue moon might be a sign from God concerning how to vote—we presently see no connection.

How, then, would anyone "explain" our ordinary propensity to accept what pragmatism calls the myths of law and morality? The answer lies in goods or values widely connected to the rule of law by pragmatists and non-pragmatists alike. The rule of law is generally credited with giving people a sense (albeit perhaps false) of predictability and security.[32] If the state governs by laws that apply to everyone, including the legislators who enact them, and if judges apply laws faithfully, then people can hope to predict the consequences of their behavior and free themselves from the arbitrary rule of men and women in positions of power, or so it is generally argued on behalf of the rule of law. Law thus gives one a sense of control over one's life, and that is widely regarded as a good thing; indeed, Publius suggests in *Federalist* 1 that it may be the best thing.[33]

Frank ridiculed the idea that judges deciding hard cases bear no personal responsibility for the outcomes because the outcomes are preordained by (follow deductively from) legal rules.[34] This was the myth of "legal formalism" or "mechanical jurisprudence." We know that decision in hard cases at constitutional law is far from a formal matter of deductive logic. Deductive inference can't begin until major and minor premises are formulated and in place, and it takes more than logic to formulate and position these premises. We know that provisions like the Equal Protection Clause and the Due Process Clause (in major premises) attract a range of incompatible conceptions. And we know that the social facts (in minor premises) to which these provisions apply can be described in different and incompatible ways. Though Frank strongly denied that patterns of legal decisions were as stable as commonly assumed, he explained that people believed the contrary because they wanted to. They wanted to believe in stable patterns of decision because they thought that such patterns would improve their power to plan for the future, and that power was crucial to their sense that they had some control over their lives.[35] Frank's explanation looks like an explanation to us because even the risk takers among us know that a sense of security through control is thought to be good by many people, and all of us can see how the myth of mechanical judging enables us to plan for the future believing that lawsuits with similar facts will have outcomes in the future similar to their outcomes in the past. We accept that myth because we want to believe it: good things would come of it, if it were true.

---

32. *See* Fish, "Almost Pragmatism," *supra* note 6, at 1462–63.
33. *The Federalist,* ed. Jacob E. Cooke (Middletown, CT: Wesleyan University Press, 1961), No. 1.
34. *See* Frank, *supra* note 14, at 127–58.
35. *See id.* at 3–23.

By this account, *explaining action is a social practice that presupposes communities of shared perceptions about what's good*. Frank could tell his readers why the myth of mechanical judging was attractive because he, like them, believed that some things were objectively good (in his case, reporting the truth and facing the realities of the human condition), and because he shared with his readers a belief that security through control is really a good thing. And since the "us" to whom Frank sought to communicate was the world at large, he assumed, with Publius, that security through control was an aspiration of mankind as such—either a real good or something widely assumed to be a real good.

The pragmatist who would explain our legal practices and beliefs thus suffers a handicap: he denies presuppositions of any community of shared beliefs about what's good, namely, (1) that there are truths about what's good, (2) that there are real goods, and (3) that the closer we approximate knowledge and enjoyment of real goods, the better. We cannot have beliefs about what's good without presupposing true beliefs or best understandings about what's good. Without shared beliefs about what's good—and therewith the possibility of real goods or goods objective in some sense[36]—we cannot conceive, much less explain, actions as a special class of human event. Because actions are changes in the world brought about for the sake of some good, because a belief that something is in some way good must be present whenever there is unequivocal action, and because belief about what's good presupposes that some things are truly good, the possibility of human action as we know it depends upon the possibility of real or objective goods.

Pragmatists would consider none of what we've said to be effective criticism of their position. All that our criticism amounts to, they might say, is that pragmatism is hard to swallow—hard, that is, for us and the average reader to swallow. But what's easy to swallow may not be a good test of what's true, and pragmatists already know that their position is hard to swallow. In fact, the unpalatable nature of their position helps account for its attractiveness. We all know that what's hard to swallow is largely determined by conventional wisdom and self-images that we're comfortable with. What's hard to swallow is what goes against conventional wisdom and flattering self-images. We need the rule of law because it flatters and comforts us. It proceeds from the notion, flattering to most

---

[36.] *See* Dworkin, *supra* note 12, at 138.

people, that no one is so much better than anyone else that one can in justice govern the other without the other's consent. And it comforts most of us by sparing us the rule of persons whose laws apply to others but not to themselves. Attacks on the very possibility of fidelity to law are attacks on the rule of law, and attacks on the rule of law undermine our democratic beliefs and implicitly invite consideration of alternatives besides democracy. This invitation is something no sensible person can dismiss out of hand, for the problems of modern life (global warming, terrorism, deepening class and sectarian divisions, and the like) may be just too much for popular governments to handle.[37] And a constitution fails its duty to promote the general welfare if it leaves its people incapable of regime change when conditions call for it.[38] We have no good reason to believe that conventional wisdom and our comfort level are adequate to our needs. We value, or we should value, the thinker whose message is hard to accept precisely because we appreciate or should appreciate our fallibility.

But fallibility is a notion that makes sense only if we assume that there are truths about which we can be wrong. So, defending pragmatism as an antidote to intellectual complacency is not something that pragmatists should welcome. This defense of pragmatism values it for its skepticism and the role of skepticism in a process that would replace opinion with better opinion and, ideally, truth. As Fish realizes, any defense of pragmatism—any submission of reasons for valuing pragmatism—is itself anti-pragmatist because it relies on assumptions like the possibility and the value of truth that pure pragmatism purports to deny.[39]

IV. An Instrumental Reading of the Constitution and the Philosophic Approach

We conclude by elaborating a point made at the beginning of this chapter. "Pragmatism" is a capacious term, and the line separating pragmatism from other positions is not easy to locate. Posner has

---

[37] *See* Walter F. Murphy, *Constitutional Democracy: Creating and Maintaining a Just Political Order* (Baltimore: Johns Hopkins University Press, 2007): 68–107.

[38] *See* Sotirios A. Barber, *Welfare and the Constitution* (Princeton, NJ: Princeton University Press, 2003): 153–55.

[39] *See* Fish, "Almost Pragmatism," *supra* note 6, at 1474–75.

suggested that the chief characteristic of legal pragmatism is its instrumentalist or result-oriented view of how judges do and ought to decide
cases. Our quarrel with contemporary legal pragmatism in this book lies
solely with the skepticism of its leading figures about constitutional
meaning and the duty of judges and other interpreters to pursue that
meaning through a self-critical process best represented by the philosophic approach. We have no quarrel with pragmatism as instrumentalism because instrumentalism, without more, is perfectly compatible with
the philosophic approach to constitutional meaning. We've already noted
how the Constitution's Preamble and the argument of *The Federalist* support an instrumentalist reading of the Constitution.[40] We've noted John
Marshall's instrumentalist reading (in *McCulloch*) of the powers of Congress
vis-à-vis the prerogatives of the states.[41] Abraham Lincoln read the "take
care that the laws be faithfully executed" clause to facilitate his power to
preserve the Union.[42] These and countless other instrumentalist interpretations of the Constitution are far from denying that (1) the Constitution
means something independently of what interpreters might want it to
mean; (2) a process of reflection and debate can hope to approximate that
meaning in concrete situations; (3) a duty of fidelity to the Constitution
is a duty to employ that process in good faith; and (4) it's psychologically
possible for interpreters to accept this duty and act accordingly.

A result-oriented approach to constitutional meaning may be consistent with fidelity to the Constitution if the Constitution itself is the
source of results that interpreters seek to advance. We see no reason to
deny this possibility. We see no reason to deny that preserving the Union
is a constitutional end and that Lincoln could legitimately read his powers
with that end in view without compromising his sworn duty to the
Constitution. We see no reason to deny that Marshall acted in good faith
and with fidelity to the Constitution when he read Congress's powers to
authorize a national bank. The controversial nature of these and other
readings of the Constitution is, by itself, not sufficient to deny their
authors' fidelity to the Constitution. Nor is the fact that better readings

---

40. Chapters 3 and 4.
41. Chapter 8.
42. *See* Abraham Lincoln, "Message to Congress in Special Session, July 4, 1861," in *Abraham Lincoln: His Speeches and Writings,* ed. Roy P. Basler (New York: World Publishing Co., 1946): 594, 600–01.

may have been available. For if the Constitution itself establishes machinery for pursuing ends like justice, union, and the general welfare, then the Constitution itself authorizes the controversies that pursuing these ends entails. What the Constitution does not authorize is the substitution of some authority other than its own, like the preferences of self-willed and doctrinaire judges. Frank identified these judges as the ones who hide their personal responsibility by pretending mechanically to express the clear will of some other authority, like tradition or original intention.[43] Frank was right. These judges are not faithful to the Constitution as actually written and as it had to be written to be morally defensible. The philosophic approach is.

---

43. *See* Frank, *supra* note 14, at xxii–xxiii, 139–48.

EPILOGUE

A FUSION OF APPROACHES TO CONSTITUTIONAL INTERPRETATION

Ronald Dworkin has shown that fidelity in interpreting the Constitution as written calls for a fusion of constitutional law and moral philosophy.[1] We have taken up that call, arguing for a philosophic approach to constitutional interpretation. In doing so, we have systematically criticized competing approaches—textualism, consensualism, originalism/intentionalism, structuralism, doctrinalism, minimalism, and pragmatism—that aim and claim to avoid philosophic choices. We have shown that, contrary to these claims and pretensions, no responsible approach to constitutional meaning can avoid philosophic reflection and choice.

At the same time, we have disclaimed any wish to turn constitutional interpretation over to philosophers, to confound constitutional interpretation with moral philosophy, or to confound constitutional questions with questions of moral philosophy. The philosophic approach to constitutional meaning seeks to make the best of a legal document established by non-philosophers to meet their needs as they understood them and as their posterity continue to understand them. Looking for what the Constitution means is looking for the best it can mean *to these people and for the general aims of its establishment.* Constitutional interpretation as an activity is thus answerable to non-philosophers, and philosophers as such cannot accept those constraints because at some point those constraints may (inevitably will?) defeat the systematic and self-critical quest for truth or best account that defines the activity of philosophy as we understand it. We have therefore defended a certain attitude within and

---

[1] Ronald Dworkin, *Taking Rights Seriously* (Cambridge, MA: Harvard University Press, 1977): 149.

safely confined by a political practice, and we have defended that attitude (the philosophic attitude) as an imperative of that practice (constitutional interpretation).

Expressing the same thought in terms of the "approaches" to constitutional interpretation, we would say that fidelity in constitutional interpretation requires a fusion of philosophic and other approaches, properly understood. Within such a fusion, we would understand text, consensus, intentions, structures, and doctrines not as alternatives to but as sites of philosophic reflection and choice about the best understanding of our constitutional commitments.

In Chapter 4 we cautioned the reader to be wary of the "approach hypothesis." The approach hypothesis posits that you have to take an approach to something before you can know anything important about it. The presupposition behind the approach hypothesis is that each would-be knower of something is situated in some particular time and place and motivated by a mix of needs and prior beliefs that are more or less unique, and that what she (thinks she) knows about something is controlled by the factors that motivate her interest in that thing. We argued in Chapter 4 that if the approach hypothesis were true, the Constitution itself could provide no standard for selecting among contending approaches to constitutional meaning. And if we also assume that different people take interest in constitutional meaning for different and irreconcilable reasons—that is, to serve irreducibly different and fundamentally incompatible wants or values—then all interpretations ostensibly *of* the Constitution would be partisan impositions *on* the Constitution. Although the approach hypothesis may (somehow) prove to be true, it is not something that we should accept without argument. For if all knowledge of the Constitution along with everything else *must* be partisan, how can knowledge of knowledge be any different? What can save the approach hypothesis itself from the unavoidably situated and partial perspective of all human knowing? How can the approach hypothesis itself avoid being a self-serving imposition on nature?

In Chapter 4 we also cautioned against assuming that there was one correct approach to the exclusion of all others. Since then, however, we have tried to make the argument for one approach, the philosophic approach. Yet that approach claims to be an implication of the Constitution itself, not a separable approach to the Constitution. And the singularity of that approach seems compromised by its equivalence to some approaches and its connections to others or, rather, that approach seems to call for a fusion of approaches. With Dworkin we agree that the Constitution *as written* supports thinking for yourself in a spirit of self-critical striving for the truth about or best interpretation of the Constitution. The truth in question concerns (1) the true meaning or best interpretation of constitutional provisions and (2) the truth or best account about the world to which constitutional provisions must apply if the Constitution is to be an effective instrument of its ends.

The philosophic approach that we have defended is thus a kind of textualism, though not the kind of "plain words" textualism famously advocated by Justice Black. He thought that the point of establishing a written constitution was to minimize disagreement about constitutional meaning and application. While this seems the point of some constitutional provisions, we deny that is the point of all, including what may be the most important provisions. The Constitution *as written* demands a philosophic debate because it is only through such debate that we can approximate knowledge of its ends (justice, liberty, and the like) as real goods and because substituting lesser goods (like particular conceptions of liberty and justice) conflicts with what the Constitution actually says and undermines its moral authority in the process. For, as Dworkin might put it (recall the father in his thought experiment in Chapter 2), what virtue could there be in an ignorant and self-willed father who, convinced of his infallibility, in effect would instruct his children to be no better than himself? As a kind of textualism, the philosophic approach is concerned with maintaining and elaborating the structural norms implicit in the governmental structures and processes that the text provides. The chief difference between a philosophic structuralism, on the one hand, and the structuralism that sees itself as either eliminating or restricting moral responsibilities on the part of judges, on the other, is that the former can understand structures and processes not as ends in themselves, but as instrumental to improved knowledge of the ends and means of constitutional government.

The philosophic approach is also a kind of intentionalism or originalism, albeit not the kind advocated by Robert Bork and William Rehnquist. In keeping with their moral skepticism, they deny substance to ideas like justice itself and reduce the meaning of normative terms to their historical definitions and/or applications and examples. In contrast with their *concrete* intentionalism or originalism, *abstract* intentionalism or originalism takes the words of the constitutional text and the arguments of the framers at their public-spirited word. Though Rehnquist and Bork criticize the opinion in *Dred Scott v. Sandford* (1857), their brand of intentionalism or originalism is the same as Chief Justice Taney's in that infamous decision (as shown in Chapter 2).

The philosophic approach can even be interpreted as a kind of consensualism, as long as that consensualism incorporates a healthy appreciation of the fallibility of even the widest and deepest consensus. As Dworkin suggested a generation ago in criticizing the constitutionalism of Alexander Bickel, if a social consensus about justice is all that "justice" can refer to, then we cannot coherently criticize a community consensus as unjust or unconstitutional.[2] If this were true, Hitler's total and final domination of world opinion would have transformed the Holocaust into a step toward a just and decent order. In a society that actively cultivates the personal virtues and capacities for advancing diverse views, an evolving social consensus can be viewed as a closer and closer approximation of the truth or best understanding. But a society that appreciated its fallibility would not likely appeal to consensus as a reason for silencing its critics. In such a society, a consensus against homosexuality and abortion would not abridge personal autonomy without strong reasons that homosexuals and women could appreciate as genuinely respecting their dignity and equality and as reasonable approximations of the common good. As noted in Chapter 5, the Supreme Court's decisions in *Planned Parenthood v. Casey* (1992) and *Lawrence v. Texas* (2003), which seem to illustrate a consensus approach to constitutional interpretation concerning abortion and homosexual intimate association, accord with a philosophic approach in this respect.

Finally, we have seen that the philosophic approach can accept pragmatism's instrumentalist view of the law without accepting certain pragmatists' view that fidelity to law is a myth. Yet a hallmark of the philosophic approach is an appreciation of one's fallibility and a resulting self-critical striving for the truth about or best understanding of justice and other constitutional ideals. The philosophic interpreter of the Constitution therefore must accept her own fallibility and respond by working to ensure a place for the pragmatist as her most radical critic and, precisely for that reason, her most valued friend.

---

[2] *Id.* at 144–47.

INDEX

History
  multidimensionality of, 112-14
  philosophic approach and, 115-16
  as source of constitutional meaning,
    75-76, 102
  See also Tradition
Holmes, Oliver W., Jr. (Justice), 16
Homosexual rights, 6-7, 76, 103, 147,
    160n17, 192
  *See also Bowers v. Hardwick; Lawrence v.
    Texas; Romer v. Evans*
Hughes, Charles Evans (Chief Justice),
    xv, 4, 130
Hutson, James H., 84n12

Intentions of framers and ratifiers
  See Originalism
Interpretation, nature of, 32-33, 35-36,
    41, 105-07
  See also Constitutional interpretation
Interpretive questions
  distinguished from substantive
    questions, 5-6
  influence of on constitutional
    meaning, 6-8
Interpretivism, clause-bound, 69n3,
    78n24, 94-95

Jackson, Robert H. (Justice), ix, 110, 153-54
Jefferson, Thomas, xv, 24, 50, 113-14, 123
Judicial activism, 26, 28-30, 54-55
Judicial deference, 29
Judicial minimalism
  defined, 140
  analogical reasoning and, 150-51
  as depending on a version of the
    philosophic approach to
    interpretation, 141, 143-44
  as imperative of deliberative democracy,
    140, 146, 152
  as a judicial strategy (not a method of
    interpretation), 140-141, 152-53
  motivation of, 140, 142
  See also Sunstein, Cass R
Judicial monopoly (in constitutional
    interpretation), xiv-xvi, 4, 119
Judicial precedent, as source of
    constitutional meaning
  See Doctrinalism

Judicial underenforcement of
    constitutional norms, 128
  See also Constitution outside
    the courts

Kaczorowski, Robert J., xvi
Kahn, Ronald, xvi, 148n32, 158n7
Kalman, Laura, 111
Kelbley, Charles, xvi
Kennedy, Anthony (Justice), 75, 76
Koppelman, Andrew, 178n24
Kramer, Larry D., 4n7

Lane, Robert E., 43n24
Large commercial republic, and
    The Federalist, 41-45
Lawrence v. Texas (2003)
  on "animus" against homosexuals, 192
  Bowers and, 76, 149
  philosophic approach and, 76, 192
  as protecting homosexuals' right to
    autonomy, 6-7, 76
  similar to *Casey*, 76
  Sunstein's analysis of, 147-48
Lessig, Lawrence, 100-01
Level of generality or abstraction, 102-04
Levinson, Daryl, 49n45
Levinson, Sanford, xvi, 13n1, 43n25,
    77n23
Liberty
  See Due Process Clauses of Fifth and
    Fourteenth Amendments
Lincoln, Abraham
  constitutional democracy and, 24, 125
  opposition to judicial monopoly in
    constitutional interpretation, xv
  as positive constitutionalist, 37, 186
  responsible government and, 53
"Living constitution," Rehnquist's criticism
    of, 15-17
  See Consensualism
Lochner v. New York (1905)
  interpretive approach of, 111n27
  judicial protection of economic liberties
    and, 129
  Rehnquist's criticism of, 17-18, 22-23
Locke, John, 115, 123
Lopez, United States v. (1995), 124
Loving v. Virginia (1967), 159, 162